Church, College, and Clergy

McGill-Queen's Studies in the History of Religion
G.A. Rawlyk, Editor

Volumes in this series have been supported by the Jackman
Foundation of Toronto.

1 Small Differences
Irish Catholics and Irish
Protestants, 1815–1922
An International Perspective
Donald Harman Akenson

2 Two Worlds
The Protestant Culture of
Nineteenth-Century Ontario
William Westfall

3 An Evangelical Mind
Nathanael Burwash and the
Methodist Tradition in
Canada, 1839–1918
Marguerite Van Die

4 The Dévotes
Women and Chruch in
Seventeenth-Century France
Elizabeth Rapley

5 The Evangelical Century
College and Creed in English
Canada from the Great Revival
to the Great Depression
Michael Gauvreau

6 The German Peasants' War and
Anabaptist Community of
Goods
James M. Stayer

7 A World Mission
Canadian Protestantism and the
Quest for a New International
Order, 1918–1939
Robert Wright

8 Serving the Present Age
Revivalism, Progressivism,
and the Methodist Tradition
in Canada
Phyllis D. Airhart

9 A Sensitive Independence
Canadian Methodist Women
Missionaries in Canada and
the Orient, 1881–1925
Rosemary R. Gagan

10 God's Peoples
Covenant and Land in South
Africa, Israel, and Ulster
Donald Harman Akenson

11 Creed and Culture
The Place of English-Speaking
Catholics in Canadian Society,
1750–1930
Terrence Murphy and Gerald
Stortz, editors

12 Piety and Nationalism
Lay Voluntary Associations and
the Creation of an Irish-Catholic
Community in Toronto, 1850–1895
Brian P. Clarke

13 Amazing Grace
Studies in Evangelicalism in
the United States, Canada,
Britain, Australia, and Beyond
George Rawlyk and
Mark A. Noll, editors

14 Children of Peace
W. John McIntyre

15 A Solitary Pillar
Montreal's Anglican Church and
the Quiet Revolution
Joan Marshall

16 Padres in No Man's Land
Canadian Chaplains and
the Great War
Duff Crerar

17 Christian Ethics and Political
Economy in North America
A Critical Analysis of u.s. and
Canadian Approaches
P. Travis Kroeker

18 Pilgrims in Lotus Land
Conservative Protestantism in
British Columbia, 1917–1981
Robert K. Burkinshaw

19 Through Sunshine and Shadow
The Woman's Christian Temperance
Union, Evangelicalism, and Reform
in Ontario, 1874–1930
Sharon Cook

20 Church, College, and Clergy
A History of Theological Education
at Knox College, Toronto,
1844–1994
Brian J. Fraser

Church, College, and Clergy

A History of Theological Education at Knox College, Toronto 1844–1994

BRIAN J. FRASER

McGill-Queen's University Press
Montreal & Kingston • London • Buffalo

© McGill-Queen's University Press 1995
ISBN 0-7735-1351-5

Legal deposit second quarter 1995
Bibliothèque nationale du Québec

Printed in Canada on acid-free paper

McGill-Queen's University Press is grateful to the Canada Council for
support of its publishing program.

Canadian Cataloguing in Publication Data

Fraser, Brian J. (Brian John), 1947–
    Church, college, and clergy: a history of theological education at Knox
    College, Toronto, 1844–1994
    (McGill-Queen's studies in the history of religion; 20)
    Includes bibliographical references and index.
    ISBN 0-7735-1351-5
    1. Knox College (Toronto, Ont.) – History.   2. Presbyterian theological
    seminaries – Ontario – Toronto – History.   I. Title. II. Series.
    LE3.T56617F73 1995   207'.713541   C95-900245-6

This book was typeset by Typo Litho Composition Inc.
in 10.5/13 New-Baskerville.

Contents

Preface and Acknowledgments / vii

Illustrations / ix and following page 90

Introduction: Preserving and Propagating the Great
Evangelical Truths / 3

1 Founding Visions, 1844–1850 / 18

2 Conflicting Strategies, 1850–1870 / 43

3 Broadening Perspectives, 1870–1890 / 67

4 Creating a Progressive College, 1890–1905 / 91

5 Promoting the United Church of Canada,
1905–1925 / 115

6 Reconstructing the Continuing Church,
1925–1945 / 140

7 Diverging Views, 1945–1977 / 165

Epilogue: Continuing Challenges, 1977–1994 / 197

Notes / 207

Index / 257

Preface and Acknowledgments

For 150 years, most clergy who have served in the Presbyterian Church in Canada have been educated at Knox College in Toronto. Opened in November 1844 with fourteen students meeting in the rented house of Professor Henry Esson on James Street, the college grew rapidly in the early years as the expanding Free Church denomination it served spread through the united Canadas. Consolidations with other branches of Canadian Presbyterianism added to the faculty and student body and Knox's influence spread across the nation through congregations and colleges that its graduates staffed and around the world through foreign mission endeavours in which its graduates served.

When the Board of the college invited me to write a history of theological education at Knox some twelve years ago, I was honoured and not a little intimidated. At that time, the waters of the history of theological education in Canada had not been charted. Only a few brave souls, such as George Rawlyk and Kevin Quinn, had ventured into the deeps and returned to tell about it. In the past decade, however, a growing number of Canadian and American church historians have turned their attention to the history of the preparation of leaders for the denominational cultures that make up the Christian church in North America. I trust this effort will contribute to this enterprise to understand the development and exercise of ecclesial leadership in North America.

The sources upon which I have drawn include the Knox College Archives, housed with the Archives of the Presbyterian Church in Canada at Knox, and papers relating to the college and its faculty in the United Church Archives. The materials upon which I have focused are the views of the faculty expressed in lectures and published in books, pamphlets, and articles that had wide circulation within the church. References to these sources and the secondary literature that has informed my interpretation of the history of theological education at Knox College can be found in the notes.

Several institutions and people deserve thanks for their contributions to this volume. Knox College, St. Andrew's Hall, Vancouver School of Theology, and the Association of Theological Schools in the United States and Canada have all provided financial support for the publication of this book. Stuart Macdonald, Debbie Huber-McBride, Paddy and Larry Eastwood, Bruce McAndless-Davis, Linda Smith, and Dave Seymour have acted as research assistants at various stages of the process. The staffs at the Archives of the Presbyterian Church in Canada and the United Church of Canada, at the Knox College Library, and at the Vancouver School of Theology Library have been hospitable and helpful. John Moir, Bob Handy, Phyllis Airhart, John Duncan, and David Griffin, have been tough, but fair, critics of parts or all of the manuscript. Tirthankar Bose eliminated confusion after confusion through his expert copy editing. Principals J. Charles Hay, who initiated the project, and Arthur Van Seters, who saw it to completion, have been most patient and supportive. George Rawlyk, Donald Akenson, and the staff of McGill-Queen's University Press provided encouragement and support throughout the project. Without the simultaneous tolerance and intolerance of Joan, this volume would still be incomplete. It is dedicated with much respect and affection to the two men I consider my most influential mentors in theological education and scholarly endeavour, Allan L. Farris and N. Keith Clifford.

The first classes were held on 8 November 1844 in an "upper room" in this house on James Street in Toronto rented by Henry Esson, the first full-time professor at the college.

For the academic sessions of 1845–1846, classes were held in another house rented by Henry Esson on Adelaide Street.

Henry Esson was professor of literature and science (1844), then professor of literature and philosophy (1845–1853).

From 1846 until 1855, the college was housed in three adjoining houses on Front Street. The buildings eventually became the Swan Hotel.

Robert Burns was professor of theology (1845–1847) and later professor of church history and evidences (1856–1864).

Elmsley Villa, the residence of Lord Elgin, a former governor general of British North America, was purchased in 1855 and provided more spacious quarters for the rapidly growing college until 1875.

Michael Willis lectured in theology at the college during the 1845–1846 session, served as professor of theology (1847–1870), and was the first principal of Knox College (1857–1870).

George Paxton Young was professor of philosophy and biblical exegesis (1854–1864), then superintentent of preparatory training and professor of mental and moral philosophy (1868–1871). His most powerful impact on the Presbyterian clergy, however, came during his years as professor of mental and moral philosophy at University College, University of Toronto (1871–1889), during which time the university was given greater and greater responsibility for preparatory education for Presbyterian clergy. The United Church of Canada/Victoria University Archives, Toronto, 76.001/P7396.

Pictured seated at the table in the middle surrounded by the graduating class of 1872 were, from left to right, David Inglis, professor of theology (1871–1872) and William Caven, professor of exegetical theology and apologetics (1866–1869), then professor of exegetical theology and biblical criticism (1869–1896), then professor of New Testament literature and exegesis and biblical criticism (1896–1904). Caven served as principal of Knox College from 1873 to 1904.

The first buildings to be built specifically to house Knox College were located at 1 Spadina Crescent and completed in 1875. The college remained at that location until 1915.

Church, College, and Clergy

Introduction

Preserving and Propagating the Great Evangelical Truths, 1844–1994

The Rev. Dr. Robert Burns was not easily discouraged. On 19 April 1844, he arrived in Kingston, Ontario, to plead the cause of the Free Church of Scotland, the evangelical wing of Scottish Presbyterianism that had broken away from the Church of Scotland a year earlier. When he was denied access to the Church of Scotland pulpit, arrangements were quickly made for Burns to speak in the Wellington Street Wesleyan Methodist Church and large crowds came to hear him. In the audience were seven theological students attending Queen's, the Church of Scotland college in Kingston, six of whom indicated to Burns their sympathies with the Free Church cause following his address. Seven months later, five of the six found themselves in Toronto among the first class of students at the Free Church's new theological institution, soon to be named Knox College.[1]

Robert Burns was no stranger to Canadian Presbyterians. Between 1825 and 1840, he served as Secretary of the Glasgow Colonial Society, an evangelical mission organization within the Church of Scotland. He had been personally responsible for recruiting several of the ministers who served the Canadian church.[2] He was a prolific and prominent pamphleteer for the evangelical cause within the Church of Scotland and a natural choice to champion the new Free Church in Canada. The colonial body shared the same convictions and passions that motivated the founders of the new branch of Presbyterianism in Scotland.

The Free Church in Scotland was formed in 1843 when Evangelicals found it no longer possible to remain in fellowship with the Moderates in the Church of Scotland. The Moderates were the party of ecclesiastical and political establishment, standing "for a rational, impersonal and unenthusiastic religion, outwardly orthodox in Calvinist theology yet tolerant of intellectual deviation, and overwhelmingly polite and conformist in social tone."[3] At the core of the convictions of the Evangelicals was a passion for personal conversion and a determination to create in Scotland what their leading thinker and church politician, Thomas Chalmers, called the godly commonwealth. Initially, it looked as if the passionate enthusiasm of the evangelical revolt against the Moderates that led to the formation of the Free Church would sweep the country and attract the allegiance of the majority of Scottish Presbyterians. Every minister in Aberdeen went to the Free Church, as did the vast majority of the clergy and congregations in the Highlands. In Glasgow and Edinburgh, almost half left the established church. Outside of the cities in the Lowlands and the Borders, however, the majority stayed with the Church of Scotland. In the religious census of 1851, the numbers attending the Church of Scotland and the Free Church were almost the same. Later in the nineteenth century, the Church of Scotland would enjoy a revival of support, but during the decade following the Disruption the Free Church went from strength to strength.[4]

FREE CHURCH CULTURE IN CANADA

Church historian David W. Bebbington described four special marks of the evangelicalism represented by the Free Church wing of Scottish Christianity: "*conversionism*, the belief that lives need to be changed; *activism*, the expression of the gospel in effort; *biblicism*, a particular regard for the Bible; and what may be called *crucicentrism*, a stress on the sacrifice of Christ on the cross."[5] The specific issues at stake in the Scottish controversy had their origins in eighteenth-century politics, both civil and ecclesiastical.[6] Though often considered primarily a dispute over the relation of church and state, differences about matters considered central to the integrity of the Christian faith were of equal, if not greater, importance. It is only in the context of these broader issues of the interpretation of the faith that the establishment of the Free

Church in Canada made sense, since the civil and political situation in the Canadas was considerably different from that in Scotland.[7] Church historian Richard Vaudry has concluded that the culture of the Free Church in Canada "constituted a world-view which manifested itself in a remarkable missionary zeal and vitality, a commitment to theological orthodoxy, and a concern for the ordering of society according to Biblical precepts."[8]

The original protest of the Canadian Free Church founders presented in Kingston in July 1844 articulated the theological principles they thought at stake. The protest was drafted and presented by John Bayne of Galt, who had been recruited for the Canadian church by Robert Burns.[9] The key section listed the "great and fundamental truths which respect the supremacy of Christ in his Church": the spiritual independence of the church, its exclusive responsibility to Christ as its head, the rights and privileges of the people, and the proper relationship between the church and the state, in which the church is free from state control but receives state support. In order to properly serve "the honour of Christ's crown and the interests of His kingdom" the church had "the obvious duty of lifting up a full and unambiguous testimony for the truth" in order to strengthen "the hands of those who are witnessing for Christ and suffering for his sake." The Church of Scotland, in the view of the dissenters, was "enslaved" by "encroachments of the civil power" because it held "unsound views" on the great principles of the faith, thus endangering the purity of the Church.

The responsibility to preserve and propagate the true ecclesial culture with all the determination and vigour God provided was stressed over and over again. Purity of piety, doctrine, and morals was of primary importance for the founders of the Free Church in both Scotland and Canada. The new denomination was short of clergy and realized that it could not rely exclusively on the Free Church of Scotland or the Presbyterian Church of Ireland for an adequate number of ministers to fill its charges. It would have to recruit its own young men and educate them in its own institutions. When the signers of the protest gathered in the same Wellington Street Wesleyan Methodist Church that had welcomed Robert Burns to constitute the new Free Church Synod of the Presbyterian Church of Canada, they were already thinking of a theological college to educate their clergy to advance the cause of Christ as they understood it.

THE NEED FOR A COLLEGE

Free Church leaders maintained the Scottish Presbyterian conviction that their clergy needed a thorough education to exercise the professional leadership expected of them in both church and society. Such an education consisted of a knowledge of classical languages and cultures, advanced study in mathematics, the natural sciences, and philosophy, and the specialized studies in Scripture and theology. The learned profession of ordained ministry was expected to apply the accumulated knowledge and wisdom of the past to the cure of souls and to the preservation and propagation of the central social values and ruling ideas of a Christian society. Although the creation of the Free Church in Canada was part of a sustained effort to reform the political and economic privilege of the established Anglican and Presbyterian churches in the colonies and the learned professions of law, theology, and medicine that supported such privilege, the business and commercial interests that dominated among the leadership of the new denomination continued to believe that education and character were essential if the clergy were to provide the right kind of social and religious direction in the era of responsible government.[10] Free Church support of the establishment of the provincial system of grammar schools and a provincial university in Upper Canada aimed to provide education that was free of denominational privilege for the whole colonial population.[11] Debates would arise within the Free Church over whether the emphasis in the education of its clergy should be on piety or learning, but no one would question the need for a thorough professional education.

A "Theological Institution" was established by the Free Church Synod at its second meeting in October 1844, and opened on 8 November 1844, in "a small upper room" in a rented house on James Street in Toronto, with Henry Esson from Montreal and Andrew King, on deputation from the Free Church of Scotland, as its first professors.[12] The new college acquired the services of two of the most energetic of the original trustees of Queen's, Alexander Gale of Hamilton, a nephew of Esson's, and William Rintoul of Streetsville, another of Burns' recruits.[13] Rintoul was appointed convener, and Gale a member, of the Free Church Synod's Committee on Education in 1844. In January, 1845, Rintoul reported that ten students at various points in their preparation for the ministry at the college had been examined by the committee. He commended their "zeal for learning, and diligent application to it," and assured his readers that they could entertain high hopes for the leadership the students would offer to the infant church.[14] Rintoul would be appointed to the faculty in 1848, joining Gale, who since 1846 had combined faculty duties in the college's preparatory department with being Head Master of the Toronto Academy, the grammar school connected with the college.

Robert Burns himself became minister of Knox Presbyterian Church, Toronto, and Professor of Divinity at the college in 1845. In a letter sent to the students just prior to his arrival, he described the new college as "an instrument of mighty efficacy for advancing the interests of evangelical truth," and expressed his hopes for the kind of ministry that would be educated there:

My earnest prayer for you from day to day shall be, that your studies may all be conducted in the spirit of humble diligence, and entire dependence on God; and that each and all of you may ever be constrained by the love of Christ as your animating principle; and that the commanding view you shall take of the Christian ministry, may be that of a divinely appointed means of converting men to God, and saving souls from death. Oh! how miserably low and degraded are those views of the Christian ministry which elevate it no higher than a species of moral police; a kind of decent instrumentality for keeping the people in order, and smoothing the rugged surface of society! ... It is not in the want of a professional Christianity, that your country withers and is blasted. She needs a larger supply of men of power – men of unction – men of spiritual life and holy energy.[15]

Numbers grew rapidly. By the spring of 1845, the number of students had increased to fourteen. By 1847, there were forty-four students at Knox College and a year later fifty-two. The entrepreneurial spirit of Free Church evangelicalism appealed to a growing number of Canadians in the late 1840s and the 1850s, as what was to become Ontario filled with immigrants, expanded its economic and cultural institutions, and began looking west for new opportunities.

The fact that Knox College was located in Toronto, the metropolitan centre of the most entrepreneurial section of British North America in the last half of the nineteenth century, had a significant impact on the kind of Presbyterian culture developed and taught in the college. Canadian historian John Moir described the Canadian Free Church ethos as "the aggressive Presbyterianism of urbanized, industrialized, expansionist central Canada."[16] Church historian Richard Vaudry saw the emergence of the Free Church as "a form of religious revival," accompanied by a crusading spirit that gave the denomination "a renewed sense of mission, a unifying set of principles, and a greater determination to transform society."[17] Church historian and Knox librarian Neil Gregor Smith characterized Free Church leaders as "idealists in a hurry," primarily concerned with theological consistency founded on the principles of the spiritual independence of the church and the headship of Christ.[18] The founders of Knox College were determined that the college would play a central role in developing and sustaining this ecclesial culture. The spirit of the Free Church remained the dominant influence throughout the several unions of Presbyterian groups in Canada that eventually produced the Presbyterian Church in Canada in 1875. While much of that spirit entered the United Church of Canada in 1925, enough remained with the continuing Presbyterians to sustain them through reconstruction and restore a confident witness to the Gospel following the Second World War.

Though the literature on the history of theological education in Canada is growing, no one has defined precisely what constitutes a theological college.[19] In the United States, Robert W. Lynn has developed a useful working definition. The three essential characteristics are: a) a three year academic programme centred on studies in bible, church history, systematics, and practical theology; b) a resident faculty of three or more; and c) an institution independent of universities or other colleges and designed for the post-baccalaureate training of clergy.[20] Knox College was the first institution in Canada to meet all these criteria. It was established as a separate college in 1844. By 1856, Knox had three full-time professors: George Paxton Young in mental and moral philosophy and exegetics, Michael Willis in systematic theology, and Robert Burns in church history and Christian evidences.[21] By 1865, the four-fold curriculum spread over three years was in place at Knox and students were encouraged to take a full arts course in some approved university prior to entering theological studies.[22] By 1881, Knox had received degree-granting powers of its own from the Ontario legislature.

By tracing the development of the practice of theological educa-tion at Knox, we will see how one Canadian denomination edu-cated the leadership to whom it entrusted the preservation and propagation of its culture at the largest of its colleges between 1844 and 1994. The church was a denominational culture within which and for which the college worked. The purpose of the college was the passing on of the denomination's identity, and especially its be-lief system, to the clergy who were given a special degree of respon-sibility for safeguarding its integrity. Those who occupied the professors' chairs at Knox were the primary agents of the denomi-nation in handing on its culture from generation to generation, both through the curriculum and through the central role they played in the courts and agencies of the denomination. The sphere of influence thus comes full circle as faculty members shape and re-shape the nature of the denomination's culture. The professors' chairs provided pious learning for pastors who would occupy pul-pits across Canada and around the world.

When considered in light of the foundational documents that ar-ticulated the culture of Canadian Presbyterianism, such as the vari-ous bases of union, statements of faith, ordination services, and directories for church government and public worship, the conclu-sion is warranted that the views of the Knox faculty between 1844 and 1994 both shaped and reflected the views held by the majority of Canadian Presbyterians on the subjects of the church, its clergy, and their education. For the first twenty-two years of its existence, Knox was the only college of the Free Church and its successor, the Canada Presbyterian Church. Three of the first four teachers at Presbyterian College, Montreal, following its founding in 1866 were Knox graduates, as was the first professor at Manitoba College in Winnipeg, founded in 1871. Following the union of 1875, the Free Church ethos dominated the new denomination and shaped its culture. The older colleges in Kingston and Halifax and the new colleges established at Saskatoon, Edmonton, and Vancouver all represented the same theological perspectives as Knox until the in-terdenominational union of 1925. Though beset by controversy during the denomination's reconstruction following union, Knox retained its position of theological leadership in the Presbyterian Church in Canada and shaped the dominant theological identity of the continuing church.

Passing on the theological identity or piety of Canadian Presbyte-rianism was the focus of the college's work. The skills and knowledge offered by the various theological disciplines were seen to be at the service of the piety of the church for the sake of its mission in the world. The college sought to reinforce the basic faith, or "yearning to conform with the sources of one's being," that had been nurtured and tested in the congregations and presbyteries that sent candidates for the ministry to Knox. Further, the college sought to broaden and deepen the candidates' understanding, their "sense of what properly goes with what," by a thorough study of the crucial disciplines of theological study and periods in the church's history that shaped its identity and calling.[23] Both attachment to and knowledge of the church's heritage were essential dimensions of the clerical vocation in the Presbyterian Church in Canada.

APPROACHES TO THE CHURCH, ITS CLERGY, AND THEIR EDUCATION

In treating the Canadian Free Church and its successors, the Canada Presbyterian Church and the Presbyterian Church in Canada, as a denominational culture, I intend to draw on the understanding developed by historian William Westfall,[24] but augment it with perspectives found among organizational theorists and cultural historians. Westfall understands culture as "a set of ideas, beliefs, and attitudes through which an individual, society, or group interprets existence," and a pattern of understanding that "helps to hold society together by providing ways of ordering and explaining the phenomenon of existence; it answers questions of meaning and reduces the disruptive power of events that can threaten the social system itself." Christianity, according to Westfall, provided the ideas and concepts that made up the culture of nineteenth-century Ontario, supplying the creeds and stories that answered the questions the culture was asking about the deepest mysteries of life.

Business theorist Edgar H. Schein defines organizational culture as "a pattern of basic assumptions ... developed by a given group as it learns to cope with its problems of external adaptation and internal integration." The pattern works well enough to be considered valid and can be taught to other members of the group as "the correct way to perceive, think, and feel."[25] Schein's approach focuses on the responsibility of a specific group in a specific institution for the formation, preservation, and reform of culture and the role culture plays in relation to both the external relations and the internal life of the organization. The purpose of any given culture, anthropologist Clifford Geertz argues, is to provide a "web of meaning" by which a group interprets its life to itself and to others. The two fundamental components are worldview and ethos. Worldview is the group's understanding of the nature of reality and their notions of the world, self, and society. Ethos means its "tone, character and quality of life, its moral and aesthetic style and mood."[26] It is important to remember, however, that a culture affects its members in different ways in different times and circumstances. No culture that encompasses as broad a spectrum as a religious denomination is static or uniform. It develops over time and differs from one context to another.[27]

These developments and differences are not always the result of some historical determinism but often the product of conscious human endeavour driven by individual character and choice. This is strikingly demonstrated in the history of Canadian Presbyterianism, which has been deeply influenced by the professors who taught at Knox College, its premier institution of cultural formation and reformation. Their interpretations of the heritage of Presbyterianism have been the primary force in forming the denomination's worldview and ethos.

There is a growing literature on the history of clerical leadership in North America that provides frameworks for understanding the ways in which Presbyterians in Canada understood the role of the ministers they asked Knox College to educate. Historian Ronald Osborn has described four images for the clergy that have been predominant in the perceptions of both church and society in the United States: a) the Master who is the leading interpreter of the culture; b) the Persuader who must compete with other interpretations of reality; c) the Builder who focuses on organizational development and strategies for expansion; and d) the Manager/Therapist who tends to institutional survival or serves a particular clientele.[28]

Knox College was established during a period of competitive pluralism and prepared clergy for a combination of Osborn's first three roles. From the beginning, its intent was to educate students to be persuasive promoters of a particular interpretation of Christianity. By the time they graduated, they were to have mastered that interpretation and be ready to build a church that would propagate it. Over time, the interpretations changed and the attention paid to the skills of persuasion varied, but the intent of mastering and persuasively presenting Presbyterianism and building and managing a church to spread it remained constant. In 1925, the Knox College reconstructed by the continuing Presbyterians took a very different approach to modern society than did the faculty and students who went into the United Church of Canada. Among continuing Presbyterians, the focus was on the minister as preacher and teacher, with continuing emphasis on mastery of the heritage and persuasive presentation. There was a conscious rejection of the models of builder and manager/therapist in the post-union college.

Equally important for understanding perceptions about what denominations expect of their clergy is a genre of theological literature that appeared in the nineteenth century, namely, manuals of pastoral or practical theology.[29] They offered detailed advice on the practice of ministry. Allan Pollok, professor of church history and practical theology at Presbyterian College, Halifax, from 1873 to 1904 and principal from 1894 to 1904, published his *Studies in Practical Theology* in 1907, but they were based on lectures he had been delivering at the college for much of his teaching career. He derived his definition of practical theology from American church historian Philip Schaff:

[It is] the science and art of the various functions of the Christian ministry for the preservation and propagation of the Christian religion at home and abroad. It is the consummation of all sacred learning. It forms the connecting link between the professor's chair and the pastor's pulpit. It utilizes and popularizes the results of biblical, historical, and systematic theology for the benefit of the Christian community. It is the end which we ought to keep in view in our scientific labours. It is the 'goal' towards which we are constantly travelling in all our studies.

Pollok indicated that the branches into which Schaff divided practical theology accurately reflected the roles he expected the clergy to play in the church and community: a) ecclesiology dealt with the minister as ruler; b) liturgics with the minister in worship; c) homiletics with the minister as preacher; d) catechetics with the minister as teacher; e) poimenics with the minister as pastor; and f) evangelism with the minister as evangelist or missionary.[30]

Still other sources provide additional information on the role of clergy. A survey of obituaries in the *Acts and Proceedings* of the General Assembly of The Presbyterian Church in Canada between 1875 and 1985 reveals that Presbyterians expected their clergy to be pastors, preachers and teachers, presbyters, and citizens, in that order of importance. The first two roles were mentioned almost twice as often as the latter two, indicating that the work of the clergy within the congregation was more important than in the broader church or community, but all four functions appeared often enough to warrant the conclusion that they constituted the core elements in the practice of ministry for Canadian Presbyterians.[31] Faithful, devoted, dedicated, and sympathetic were all adjectives commonly used for the pastor throughout the periods and across the regions surveyed. Frequently noted in relation to preparation for preaching and teaching were diligence and care, extensive and accurate knowledge of the Scriptures, wide reading, able exposition, intellectual and scholarly attainments, and depth as a theologian. As to the quality of the preaching and teaching, the following descriptions recurred: evangelical, earnest, faithful, powerful, and fearless. The activities of the clergy in the courts and committees of the church were often noted. Loyal attendance and acceptance of duties was valued and skill in debate frequently mentioned. Both sympathy and efficiency in participating in the business of the court were honoured. The esteem in which a minister was held by the community outside the church frequently drew comment. As to civic activities, memberships on school boards and in temperance or social reform organizations were common in the earlier years, while service clubs and various forms of chaplaincy dominated in later years.

As to qualities of character, the description of the minister as a Christian gentleman (remember, there were no obituaries of ordained women clergy) continued throughout the period, though it was more common earlier. It included the attributes of being manly, rugged, strong, and firm in one's convictions. At the same time, it encompassed the qualities of humility, simplicity, friendliness, tenderness, gentleness, geniality, and generosity. The ethos represented by these qualities was rooted in the culture of Victorian middle-class evangelicalism. While challenged and adapted in many ways during the history of the college, the basic tone and character of the expectations revealed in the obituaries remained the same.

Knox was established by an enterprising new denomination in an environment of increasing religious pluralism to educate Presbyterian persuaders and builders. Its faculty and students were active promoters of home and foreign mission work and moral and social reform causes. Above all, however, the college endeavoured to educate effective pastoral leaders for congregations across Canada and around the world. In that role, the clergy were primarily responsible, through pastoral care, preaching and teaching, and the regular conduct of worship and celebration of the sacraments, for the nurture of the religious experience of the members of their congregations and its expression in their day-to-day lives in the community. The very ordinariness of this dimension of the clergy's work has led historians to ignore it, yet the faculty at Knox consistently declared their intent to prepare people for precisely this calling.[32] In an ecclesial culture that valued the truth claims of the Christian tradition and the articulation and application of its beliefs over ritual or emotional experience, the college curriculum emphasized the formation of students as preachers and teachers of the great evangelical truths for the pastoral benefit of their congregations. Throughout the entire history of the college, the four-fold program of Biblical studies, systematics, church history, and practical theology that had emerged in Germany and been imported into the United States in the early nineteenth century remained at the core of the curriculum.[33] There was a cord rather than a thread of continuity that ran through the development of the theological culture of Canadian Presbyterianism seen in the theological education provided by Knox College. What the professors called "the great evangelical truths" or "the great Christian verities" included the doctrines of creation, fall, redemption, atonement in Christ, justification by faith, sanctification through the work of the Holy Spirit, and eternal life. Christian orthodoxy for Canadian Presbyterians consisted of these great evangelical truths and the clergy were entrusted with a special degree of responsibility for their preservation and propagation. The ways in which these affirmations were expounded and interpreted by different generations of faculty at Knox changed four times between 1844 and 1994. The changes, from conservative orthodoxy, to progressive orthodoxy, to neo-orthodoxy, to divergent views of orthodoxy, reflected different ways of interpreting the central truths of the gospel to the culture in which the church found itself.

In the middle decades of the nineteenth century, Free Church Presbyterians were especially anxious to defend the intellectual integrity of the Presbyterian system of doctrine as revealed by God in the Scriptures and systematized most fully in the Westminster Standards, a series of documents dealing with doctrine, worship, and polity adopted as standards by the Church of Scotland in 1647. The faculty at Knox were convinced that the best means of preserving Presbyterianism was to inculcate in their students the essential tenets of a confessional orthodoxy based on the interpretation of Calvinism found in the work of Scottish theologians George Hill and William Cunningham and American theologians Charles and Archibald Alexander Hodge. The key to the church's identity for these theologians was its doctrinal stance, what it believed and said. Knowledge of God came primarily through a reasoned understanding of Scripture and the Westminster standards.

In the later years of the nineteenth century, the confessional orthodoxy of the founders of the college was replaced by a different approach to preserving and propagating the Christian faith that emerged within the Free Church community, especially in its Scottish wing through the work of A.B. Davidson, A.B. Bruce, T.M. Lindsay, Robert Rainy, and Marcus Dods. Instead of repeating the theological and moral propositions developed by earlier generations and applying them to contemporary conditions, these theologians were convinced that God had more to teach their generation about the redemption accomplished in Christ and revealed in the scriptures. New methods of study, especially in the area of biblical interpretation and history, were based on the conviction that progress in understanding had been made in the past and was possible in the future. The creeds and confessions of the past should be revised according to the progress made in the church's understanding as it sought to present the evangelical truths in a convincing way to each new generation. The key element to the church's identity for progressive orthodox theologians was its ethical stance, what it did. Knowledge of God came through a loving and reasoned attachment to the person of Christ that led people to follow his example.

Among the new faculty that were appointed to Knox following church union in 1925, yet another approach to the theological heritage of Presbyterianism emerged in the form of neo-orthodoxy. In the view of its proponents, influenced by Scottish theologians James Denney and P.T. Forsyth and German theologian Karl Barth, both confessional orthodoxy and progressive orthodoxy failed to understand the true nature of the gospel and the church. Confessional orthodoxy reduced the gospel to a system of thought and progressive orthodoxy reduced it to a system of morals. The church needed to recover the full heritage of the Protestant Reformation and recognize the transcendent, unique, and mysterious nature of Christ's encounter with humanity as the centre of the church's life and witness. Knowledge of God grew out of this transforming encounter with the person of Christ, in whom God's self-revelation was complete and by whom God redeemed the world.[34]

Different members of the faculty took neo-othodoxy in different directions in their teaching and writing during the 1950s and the 1960s. All attempted to draw the denomination out of the parochial defensiveness and infighting that had developed in the years following church union as the Presbyterian Church in Canada struggled to rediscover the sources of its identity and witness. Dramatic changes in the denomination's self-perception and in its social context during the late 1960s and the 1970s led to a further erosion of the confidence that the church had earlier placed in neo-orthodoxy, but no coherent alternative theological perspective emerged to replace it. The new generation of professors appointed in the 1970s came in the midst of this fraying of Presbyterian culture in Canada. They represented themselves a wider variety of denominational cultures and interpretations of othodoxy than had previously been present within the college's faculty. In addition, they came to the college at a time when closer ties with the university and the other Toronto theological colleges led to a greater emphasis being placed upon the distinct disciplines they taught than the overall ecclesiastical culture they handed on to their students.

Most of the faculty at Knox College were prolific writers, but not of the kind normally associated with the professorial office today. Church historians John Webster Grant and Gerald Cragg have noted the lack of original or seminal theology written by teachers in the Canadian church colleges.[35] What has gone unnoticed, for the most part, is the amount of writing these teachers did for the purpose of interpreting, popularizing, and applying the theological insights of Scottish, British, European, and American theologians for their students, the church, and the broader community. It is in published sermons, addresses, and lectures, devotional literature, magazine and newspaper articles and columns, pamphlets, and denominational educational materials that most of their writing is found. The focus of their work was the practical theology described by Allan Pollok as the link between the professor's lectern and the church's practice. Its primary audience was ecclesial rather than academic. Nevertheless, it represented an important and revealing form of theological research and scholarship that linked the professors' chairs to the pastors' pulpits.

Each chapter in this history deals with a distinct period in the college's life. They are: Founding Visions (1844–1850); Conflicting Strategies (1850–1870), Broadening Perspectives (1870–1890); Creating a Progressive College (1890–1905); Promoting The United Church of Canada (1905–1925); Reconstructing the Continuing Church (1925–1945); and Diverging Views (1945–1977). In each chapter, the attitudes of the Knox faculty towards the church, its clergy, and their theological education will be examined to determine the links between the pastors' pulpits and the professors' chairs. As well, the relations between the church courts and agencies and the college will be traced to determine the levels of trust and support that existed.

The untimely death of Principal Allan Farris in 1977 after only one year in office marks the end of this detailed account of the history of theological education at Knox College, Toronto. The era in the college's life represented by the generation of faculty who came to Knox in the late 1970s is not over yet and cannot be recounted with the same detail or objectivity possible for earlier periods, but the continuing challenges that confront the college and the church are noted in an Epilogue dealing with the last seventeen years.

This is not a comprehensive study of Knox College. There are several important aspects of the life of a theological college that readers will not find fully developed.[36] The personal lives and relations of the faculty, detailed accounts of student life and activities, the financial and administrative history of the college, and the life of the residential community, figure only insofar as they have a direct impact on the central theme of the book, the design and offering of theological education at Knox. Much is left in the archives of Knox College and in papers yet to be collected to attract the attention of future historians who will contribute to a fuller understanding of the college's influence on the life and mission of the Presbyterian Church in Canada.

1 Founding Visions, 1844–1850

John Anderson was anything but impressed the first time he met Robert Burns. He had immigrated from Scotland as a young man and settled in Bytown (later Ottawa) as an apprentice cabinet-maker. The resolution of his own spiritual crisis, characterized by feelings of extreme ignorance, painful anxiety, and restlessness of soul,[1] coincided with the creation of the Free Church and he became a founding member of Knox Free Church, Ottawa, under the ministry of Thomas Wardrope. Wardrope encouraged him to consider studying for the ministry and sent him to Toronto to talk with Burns in 1848. As Anderson remembered the interview, Burns seemed "determined to extinguish every ray of courage lingering in my anxious mind." He grilled Anderson on his sincerity, his piety, his knowledge of Latin, and his grasp of scripture and doctrine. In all areas, he declared him sadly wanting. To Anderson's dismay, Burns was part of the Professor's Court the following day that considered his application to Knox College and opposed his admission. The other professors disagreed, however, and Anderson was accepted into the Toronto Academy in preparation from the study of theology the following year. Within the week, Burns invited him to tea and assured him that he had passed his testing and "was just the right man for the college."[2]

The incident revealed several aspects of the early efforts of the college to prepare young men to become clergy in the Free Church in Canada. Both the prospective students and the professors were concerned with the sincerity of the call. Students agonized over it, often with clergy, elders, and close friends, before presenting themselves to the college, and professors tested it, often in blunt and harsh ways. What was at stake was the integrity of the new denomination and its effectiveness in the Canadian context. Many students who sought admission to the college lacked the preparatory education necessary for theological study. The Synod realized that it had to offer such education in Toronto, but simultaneously it promoted the establishment of a government-funded non-sectarian school system at all levels.

There was unanimity of purpose among Free Church Presbyterians about theological education. Michael Willis, appointed in 1847 to succeed Burns in the chair of divinity when parish duties and controversy forced Burns to resign from the college, conveyed to the students the high expectations the church had of them as "expositors of the Word of God, and missionaries of the cross of Christ:"

Let it encourage you, that the prayers of many a pious member of the body of Christ ascend in your behalf to God, for his blessing on the appliances that are used here to form a gospel ministry. Let it also quicken your diligence and application, let it deepen your sense of responsibility, and induce habits of seriousness, to know that our Seminary is so much the hope of a Church, placed by Providence in a position most favourable for ministering to the great spiritual necessities of this land, for wielding a most salutary influence on the religious and moral state of its people, at the same time, feeling every day the inadequacy of all its efforts, in consequence of the deficiency in the number of its spiritual labourers, to the wide field opening before it, and now more than ever convinced that, whatever reinforcement it may occasionally receive from the parent land, its dependence must be mainly, yea, for continuous exertion on any large scale, almost exclusively, on its indigenous supply. Disappoint not, then, the desires and prayers of those among us who seek the good of Zion, and tremble for the ark of God.[3]

The energetic efforts and debates that reflected the founding visions of Knox College all sought to prepare an indigenous clergy to serve the evangelical passion of the Free Church in Canada.

LAYING THE FOUNDATIONS

Knox's first six years were experimental, exhilarating, frustrating, and controversial, but they laid a solid foundation upon which the future of the college would be built. During that short period, one generation of faculty came and went, and a new one began. A consensus on the principle tenets of Presbyterianism for which the college stood and the best way of preparing clergy to propagate that culture emerged. Education of various kinds was offered by the college in response to the changing needs of the church and civic communities. Controversy within the faculty and between the faculty and the church arose but, in most cases, was well on the way to resolution by the end of the period. The original student body of 14 grew to 51 by 1850. The college moved from the rented house on James Street to larger quarters in three adjoining row houses on Front Street in 1846. Its sponsoring denomination, the Free Church in Canada, grew rapidly, especially in the region around Toronto. From the twenty-three congregations and twenty-three ministers that separated in July 1844, the synod grew to 111 congregations and 65 ministers by 1850. Some of the leading merchants and businessmen in Toronto played important roles in seeing the college through its early financial difficulties. The needs and opportunities of a new church, a growing city, and an expanding province led to varied and energetic student activities, especially as missionaries in areas in which new work was being opened and as advocates for moral and social reform. In all of these efforts, the people who designed and constructed the foundations of the college sought to provide the best means they could to prepare leaders for their church.

It was William Rintoul, by then minister at Streetsville and the new clerk of the Free Church Synod, who took the leading role in drawing up the plans for a college. It was not the first time he had helped establish a college for the education of Canadian clergy. He had been a central figure in the long process of establishing Queen's University in the 1830s. In the process, tensions arose between Rintoul, who wanted a college controlled by the synod, and William Morris, a prominent businessman and politician based in Kingston, who envisaged a university on the Scottish model, closely linked to the church, but independent of formal ecclesiastical control. The charter of Queen's University was issued on 16 October

1841 with the structure that Morris favoured.[4] More differences between Rintoul and Morris emerged over the criteria for the selection of the faculty. Rintoul was more concerned than Morris about
the spiritual attainments of potential teachers. He wanted "men of
deep piety, thorough scholarship, enlarged understanding and acceptable manners" who were experienced in church and civil affairs.[5] In the creation of the Free Church's theological institution,
Rintoul got his way. By the time the second Synod of the Presbyterian Church of Canada was constituted at Toronto in October 1844,
fifty-three congregations had been organized into four presbyteries
and thirty-two ministers were on the roll. The vast majority of congregations and ministers were located west of Kingston, with the
Presbytery of Hamilton and Toronto by far the largest.[6] The Synod
agreed to appoint Andrew King, a deputy from the Free Church of
Scotland serving as minister of Knox Church, Toronto, as professor
of divinity for the 1844–1845 session, and Henry Esson of Montreal
to the permanent position of professor of literature and science.
The professors were stationed in Toronto and the Synod assumed
responsibility for their maintenance and the boarding of the students. The Synod, "sympathizing with the spiritual destitution of
Canada East, and recognizing the duty of exercising a watchful care
over the young men that may be led through grace to devote themselves to the work of the ministry there," authorized the Presbytery
of Montreal to arrange for preparatory studies in that city while a final decision was made on the site of the Synod's college. There was
obviously support for a college in Montreal, but the Synod was convinced it could not support two colleges and the majority of the Free
Church population looked to Toronto as their metropolitan centre.
It was not until 1867 that the Presbytery of Montreal was able to
convince the Synod to establish a second college.[7]

The Synod established a Committee on Education with William
Rintoul as convener. Alexander Gale, John Bayne, George Cheyne,
and James Harris were the other ministers appointed and they
formed a sub-committee "for assisting the professors with their
counsel, in any matter regarding the education of the students."[8]
The Synod also dealt with a letter from Robert Burns suggesting
that he succeed King as pastor of Knox Church, Toronto, and professor of theology at the college on a more permanent basis. The
Synod agreed to the appointment, but made it clear that they
would prefer to separate the office of professor from pastor as soon

as possible and that they had not yet determined whether the final site of the college would be in Toronto or Montreal.[9]

Fourteen students began classes on 8 November 1844. The 5 students who had transferred from Queen's were Angus McColl, John McKinnon, Robert Wallace, Patrick Gray, and Lachlan McPherson. The others who joined them were John Scott, John Black, John Ross, William R. Sutherland, William S. Ball, W.J. McKenzie, David Barr, Andrew Hudson, and David Dickson. Of the 11 whose countries of birth have been identified, 7 were Scottish, 2 American, 1 Irish, and 1 Canadian.[10] Seven of the fourteen were students in theology. The others were at various stages in their preparatory studies.[11] The Committee on Education realized from the beginning that it would have to make provision for all departments of clerical education. The standard requirements for ordination to the Presbyterian ministry by the middle of the nineteenth century were grammar school, which consisted of arithmetic, mathematics, English grammar, civil history, Latin and Greek; an arts program that covered classics, philosophy, and science; and a three-year program in theology consisting of biblical history and exegesis, systematic theology, church history, and practical theology.[12] The founding fathers of the college showed no desire to compromise these standards. They opened the college two years before Egerton Ryerson drafted the Common School Act of 1846 that led to the creation of an effective system of public schools in Canada West. Not until the late 1860s was an adequate system of secondary schools created.[13] Only in 1849, with strong Free Church support, was the non-denominational University of Toronto created under government control with no teaching posts in divinity and not until four years later was University College formed for the teaching of arts.[14]

All of these developments were part of a broader shift in Canadian culture from the view that social stability depended on an intimate and formal connection between the church and the state to a view that social progress depended on "the instructed conscience" of citizens created through a school system that was Christian, universal, free, and compulsory.[15] This shift lay at the heart of the social vision of evangelicals in the Canadas in the 1840s. The exclusive vision of a state church was not acceptable in a pluralistic society. Pointing to the significance of this shift, Canadian intellectual historian Michael Gauvreau wrote that for the founding fathers of the Free Church and their evangelical allies in the 1840s:

there must be some vital, spiritual principle at the root of each stable society that was needed to resist corruption and decay. They found an alternative to a state church in the evangelical creed's emphasis upon "conscience." By the mysterious faculty of the conscience, the individual will encounter that of God. In the converted believer, the conscience would serve as a moral rudder, ensuring that the individual would act "responsibly" in both personal and social conduct.[16]

The system of public education that the government established between the 1840s and the 1870s in Canada West and Ontario was intended to be one of the primary means to create this common conscience. During the years it took for the new systems of education to develop, the Free Church college had to provide all the programs it thought essential to preparation for ministry.

THE FOUNDING FACULTY

The teaching staff at Knox during its early years was pieced together from deputies from the Free Church of Scotland, professors teaching at different levels, and lecturers who combined pastoral duties with their classes. For the first two years, Henry Esson provided classes in the grammar school subjects.[17] Esson was not able to continue to meet the demands for this level of education and in 1846 the synod established the Toronto Academy with Alexander Gale as the first principal. Gale was Esson's nephew and had come to Canada in 1827 after graduating with an MA from Marischal College at the University of Aberdeen in 1819 and failing to find a post in Scotland. He formed a congregation and a school in Amherstburg before moving to the Lachine Free School sponsored by the Royal Institution for the Advancement of Learning in 1831. The Synod appointed him missionary in the area as well. In 1833 he moved to Hamilton, where he served until appointed to the Academy. While in Hamilton, he tutored several students preparing for ministry. He was one of the original trustees of Queen's University and the Free Church appointed him to its first Committee on Education. As editor of the Synod's official paper, the *Ecclesiastical and Missionary Record*, for its first two years of publication, Gale knew the church well and used the pages of the paper to keep the progress and needs of the Academy as well as the college before the church's members. He was joined on the staff by Thomas

Wightman, another Free Church minister, and Thomas Henning, a student in theology who had taught at the High School of Quebec.

The purposes of the Academy were "first, giving the elements of a liberal education in common with a thorough training in Bible truth, and secondly making it an auxiliary to the College, both in the way of preparing Students for it, and of assisting to educate those admitted to the College, whose early education had been defective." The model they sought to emulate was the Scottish high school as adapted by the Free Church missions leader, Alexander Duff, at his school in Calcutta. Its advertisements in the *Record* offered three branches of instruction: first, elementary education in English, reading, spelling, writing, arithmetic, geography, and Latin grammar; secondly, classical and commercial education in more advanced English reading, recitation, grammar and composition, theoretical and practical geometry, trigonometry, and algebra, ancient and modern geography and history, and Latin and Greek language and literature; and finally, advanced education in mathematics and classics, French and other modern languages, drawing, and other accomplishments.[18] In 1847, the college committee recommended that the Academy have its own body of directors from the Toronto area and build up its own endowment. Two hundred and sixty-seven students were reported to have attended the school in its first two years. As the public school system grew, the need for the Academy declined and it ceased to function in the mid-1850s.[19]

From its beginning, Knox had a preparatory or literary department to provide courses at the arts level. The model in this area was New College in Edinburgh, with its departments of literature and science in addition to theology.[20] As Gale noted in November 1844, New College exemplified in its faculty and program "the combination of high Christian attainments and character, with eminence in talents and learning, in those who in this Institution are intrusted with the sacred duties of education."[21] Primary responsibility for teaching at the arts level fell to Henry Esson as professor of literature and science, a title changed to Professor of literature and philosophy in 1845. That same year, the college committee informed the Synod that it would prefer to leave literary and philosophical education to a provincial university founded on "enlarged and liberal" principles, and concentrate its attention solely on a theological seminary. Until this was achieved, provision had to be made for professors and tutors in all branches of education.[22] In announcing the opening of the second session, the college committee indicated that Esson would teach classes in Latin, Greek, logic, and moral philosophy, assisted in the latter two courses by the Rev. John Bayne of Galt. Rintoul would offer Hebrew and Burns history. Various assistants in Toronto would teach the physical sciences and mathematics.[23]

Esson had studied at Marischal College, Aberdeen, graduating with an MA in 1811. He came to Canada in 1817 as assistant to the Rev. James Somerville of the Scotch Presbyterian Church in Montreal. Esson's early career in Montreal was marked by tragedy and conflict. His wife and two sons died and, in the midst of a controversy with Edward Black, Somerville's successor, he was charged and cleared of sexual misconduct.[24] In addition to his pastoral duties, he opened the Montreal Academical Institution in 1822, served on the management committee of the Ecole Normale de Montreal in 1836, and helped found the High School of Montreal in 1844. He played a major role in resisting the efforts to make McGill University an exclusively Church of England institution. He edited the *Canadian Miscellany*, a short-lived religious magazine published between April and August of 1828.[25] When Esson left Montreal, he was praised for his work as a minister of the gospel, his classical and literary abilities, and the valuable service he rendered "to education, morals, and civil and religious liberty in this city."[26]

The teaching of theology proper was conducted primarily by the Rev. Andrew King during the 1844–1845 session. King was minister of St. Stephen's Church, Glasgow, and agreed to spend four months as professor of theology at the new college and minister of Knox Church, Toronto. His return to Scotland in 1845 was short-lived, for he accepted an invitation to teach theology at the new Presbyterian college in Halifax. In 1845, Robert Burns returned to Toronto to take up both of the positions that King vacated. In his first term at Knox, Burns taught ecclesiastical history, systematic theology, and pastoral theology. Other subjects in the theological curriculum were taught by lecturers from nearby churches. William Rintoul taught advanced Hebrew and biblical interpretation, while Alexander Gale, still at Hamilton, taught evidences of natural and revealed religion.[27]

Burns studied at the University of Edinburgh and in 1811 was inducted into Laigh Kirk in Paisley, a charge in which he would remain until his move to Canada. He was an active pamphleteer and controversialist in Scottish ecclesiastical and civic affairs, supporting reform politics and the evangelical wing of the church. His interest in urban poverty was heightened by the plight of the Paisley weavers during the depressions that followed the Napoleonic wars. He was a frequent contributor to the *Edinburgh Christian Instructor,* the leading journal of the evangelical party founded by Andrew Thompson in 1810, and served as editor from 1838 until 1840. He shared with Thompson and Thomas Chalmers the qualities of uncompromising conviction and passionate intensity in controversy. In 1828, the University of Glasgow conferred upon him a DD for his literary and philanthropic work. Burns received invitations from groups in both Montreal and Toronto to consider calls. The possibility of the teaching position at the Free Church's new college made the Toronto offer more attractive.[28]

Burns used his extensive connections in Scotland to provide the core collection of the college library. Before coming to Canada, he published a circular signed by William Cunningham, Robert Candlish, Thomas Guthrie, and John Pym, all prominent leaders at New College, Edinburgh, appealing for books and money for the Canadian college. Burns arrived with over 2000 volumes. Together with the 100 volumes already collected in Canada, they lined the walls of a room in Burns' house that served as the library until the college moved to the Front Street premises.[29] In the early years, students did the cataloguing and supervised circulation.

In addition to Burns and Rintoul, Ralph Robb of Hamilton and John Bayne of Galt combined teaching duties in the preparatory and theological departments with their pastoral duties. Alexander Gale did double duty at the Academy and the college. The Colonial Committee of the Free Church in Scotland continued to send out lecturers in theology, Michael Willis of Renfield Street Church in Glasgow during the 1845–1846 session and Robert McCorkle of St. Ninians the following year, but they were only temporary appointments.

The college committee took steps as soon as they could to address the concerns about temporary and part-time staffing. Burns resigned from the college in 1847 to concentrate on the congregation.[30] He continued to lecture occasionally and played a significant role in the management of the college and the Academy.[31] The Synod sent John Bayne to Scotland to search for a full-time professor of divinity and ensure the support of the Colonial Committee of the Free Church of Scotland for the appointment. He succeeded in convincing Michael Willis to return to Canada and accept the position at the college. Willis was inducted in December 1847, the same month William Rintoul was appointed professor of Hebrew and biblical criticism on a full-time basis.[32]

Michael Willis was born in Greenock, Scotland, into the family of William Willis, a leading theologian within the Old Light Burgher branch of the Secessionists. He graduated from the University of Glasgow and the Divinity Hall of his denomination, being ordained in 1821. In 1839 he was called to Renfield Street Church in Glasgow, having played a leading role in the reunion of the Old Light Burghers with the Church of Scotland that same year. In 1843 he and the congregation joined the Free Church. His passionate advocacy of the abolition of slavery began in Scotland and continued during his years in Canada. He told those gathered for the opening of the college in 1848 that theological education should be based on "the great prominent revelations of Christianity" found in the Scriptures and "the eternal moralities of the decalogue." He warned the students that they were preparing for ministry in the midst of "a torrent of wild and licentious criticism, as well as philosophy, which threatened to sap the foundations of Christianity, and even overturn the first principles of all truth." Careful and thorough training in the methods and results of devout biblical exegesis, philosophical and theological thinking, historical awareness, and pastoral practice were essential to effective leadership in the church.[33] Ministers must "be prepared to counteract prejudices – to defend the common version of the scriptures and Protestantism itself." Calvinism, in Willis' mind, was the best expression of this truth and the true source of civil and religious freedom in the modern world.[34]

Just prior to the opening of the winter session in October 1848, the Colonial Committee in Scotland provided the resources to add further staff in the preparatory department by granting three years of funding for a professor of English, classical literature, and mental science. William Lyall, born in Paisley in 1811 and educated at Glasgow and Edinburgh, was appointed. He only remained at Knox for two years, then moved to the new Free Church college in Halifax.[35]

Lyall was not the only faculty member to depart in 1850. William Rintoul accepted a call to Scotch Presbyterian Church, Montreal, in 1850, when the finances of the college forced the elimination of his position. He died a year later of cholera while on a missionary tour of the lower St. Lawrence River. Lyall was not replaced for the same reason. Alexander Gale's teaching responsibilities with the college came to an end when the Academy was set up as a separate institution in 1850, in part to prevent it from being a financial strain on the college funds. By 1850, only Henry Esson and Michael Willis were left as full-time faculty, and Esson had applied for the new chair of civil history and English literature at the University of Toronto. With an enrolment of 51 students in the session of 1850–1851, the college committee could not allow the situation to persist, but the level of financial support expected from the church was not forthcoming. The pattern of the college wanting to do more than the church was willing to fund was set in these early years and persisted throughout Knox's history.

All the men who assumed responsibility for the different departments of education at Knox met the criterion Rintoul had articulated in his dispute with William Morris during the founding of Queen's. They were men of proven piety and respected learning with extensive experience in civic and ecclesiastical affairs. They were passionate advocates of free and public education as a primary means of shaping an evangelical conscience that would guide the church in the paths of missionary fervour and the nation in the paths of righteousness. The confessional orthodox worldview they passed on to their students had been shaped in the midst of the evangelical-moderate debates in Scotland in the late eighteenth century and forged in the controversies surrounding the Disruption in the first half of the nineteenth century. It honoured reason, morality, and revelation as compatible and complementary, but insisted that revelation provided the ultimate criteria of truth in the case of apparent contradiction.[36]

CONFESSIONAL ORTHODOXY IN THE FREE CHURCH IN CANADA

As course outlines and examinations throughout the founding era of the college indicate, the five points of Calvinism defined at the Synod of Dort (1618–1619) formed the core doctrines around which the faculty designed the curriculum. The five propositions said that human beings, by nature, were totally depraved and could not contribute to their salvation in any way; that only some were elected unconditionally to receive salvation; that Christ's atonement was limited to the salvation of the elect; that transforming grace was irresistible; and that the saints persevered, for once given, grace was not taken away.[37] These doctrines did not prevent the Free Church founders from exhibiting a warm evangelical piety and a fervent desire to spread the Gospel and grow in grace.

Michael Willis indicated the proper place of doctrine in his confessional orthodoxy when he told his students:

My dear friends, we must not rest in simple historical belief, a mental entertainment of the message concerning Christ, though that is very precious and valuable, and nothing good can be got without it. We must not rest in a mere intellectual assent; we must commit our souls to Christ, we must come to Him, we must rest upon Him, we must welcome him to perform in us all that belongs to His office as Saviour, not only as having died for us, but as now teaching us by His word and Spirit, that he may reign over us and make us wholly His. That is the faith which gives life.[38]

Revelation rather than reason was the final arbiter of human knowledge, though the proper method of understanding revelation was the use of the Baconian method of inductive reasoning to analyze the data of revelation provided in the bible. Evangelical theologians, such as Thomas Chalmers and James McCosh, insisted that the purpose of mental and moral philosophy, as the culmination of the Scottish educational system, was not a rational account of the laws of personal and social development but rather a statement of the biblical principles of divine governance that ensured such development in ecclesiastical and civic life. This was the worldview that provided the basis for the education and expression of the Christian conscience sought by the founders of Knox College.[39]

The concerns that dominated the thinking of the college committee in preparing students for ministry were suggested by the topics they chose for the competitions established for bursaries and the presentations they required of the students. Twenty bursaries of £5 to £10 were announced in October 1845. One dealt with the reading and parsing of an English author and a chapter of the bible.

Three called for the translation and analysis of passages from the
Gospel of John, Romans, and the Aeneid. Two required the repeti-
tion and explanation of the Shorter Catechism, one in Gaelic. Others asked for essays on the proper qualifications and best methods
for the study of theology, the responsibility of humanity for using its
intellectual powers in matters of religion, the doctrine of revelation,
Bacon's method of induction, the advantages of the study of logic,
the inspiration of the bible, one of Butler's sermons, and faith as it
unites the soul to the Saviour. Still others called for outlines of ancient history, church history, the Papacy, and the Synod of Dort.
Two more were awarded for critical exercises on 1 Peter 3:19 (Jesus
preaching to the spirits of the dead in hell) and Matthew 16:18 (the
declaration that Jesus would build his church on Peter).[40] In November 1845, the college committee heard student presentations
on the value of a knowledge of civil history for a student in theology, the doctrine of causation, Hebrews 6:4–6 (the sin of apostasy),
and the fallacy of selfish systems of morals. In addition, they heard a
sermon on 1 Corinthians 6:20 (God's purchase of human salvation
by the blood of Jesus Christ).[41] In these exercises, the emphasis was
on the great doctrines of evangelical faith, the primary forces seen
to be resisting them, and the subordinate role of reason to revelation in their defence. The approaches to these concerns that the
early faculty took were made explicit for the whole church in the
outlines of courses offered by Esson, Burns, and Rintoul in the winter session of 1845–1846 printed in the church's official magazine,
the *Ecclesiastical and Missionary Record.*

Esson's lectures dealt with the philosophy of the human mind
and began with a consideration of the love of truth. The author and
source of truth was God; the subject and perceiver of truth was humanity; and its fruit and consummation was wisdom. Such wisdom
recognized the limits of the human faculties and the narrow
spheres in which they are effective. Humility in the presence of God
was the beginning of wisdom. Esson proceeded to provide a map of
human knowledge as a whole, dealing with the physical, political,
moral, and divine departments and arguing that the mental and
metaphysical sciences that made up the philosophy of the mind
were "the handmaids of Divine Revelation." Esson proceeded to
apply his theory of intellectual powers to moral principles and conduct. Personal, domestic, social, moral, and religious duties were
related to their proper objects in God, humanity, civil societies,

families, and self. All these considerations were subject to the authority of the Divine word. "It will be a paramount object at this stage," promised Esson, "to demonstrate how insufficient are all that man's knowledge and powers can effect in the enlightenment of the understanding, and the regulation of the will, without light and grace from on high." The course concluded with lectures on the moral constitution of humanity, using Butler, Abercrombie, and Chalmers as guides.[42] Human knowledge was clearly inferior to and found its proper role under divine guidance from the scriptures.

Burns outlined the lectures he would offer in theology. He began with 12 lectures on mental science, discussing its nature and relation to theology. The Baconian system of philosophy was applied to theological studies and the various systems of morals were tried by the standards of Christian truth. The 25 lectures on systematic theology covered:

the search of religious truth; the spirit with which theology should be studied; preparatory studies; the range of theology; connection betwixt systematic theology and the study of ecclesiastical history; ancient and modern theories regarding the being and perfections of God, as contrasted with the system of the Bible; imperfections of natural theology. General character and claims of revelation; internal evidences and outline of proofs at large; objections grounded on mysteries and supposed opposition to reason examined and refuted. Doctrine of the Trinity; divinity of Christ; incarnation; mediatorial scheme; modern views of the atonement, its nature, extent, and issues; justification by imputed righteousness through faith; divinity, personality, and work of the Holy Spirit; on goods works and the place they hold in the Christian system.

Further lectures dealt with the Westminster Confession of Faith and its scriptural proofs in the original Hebrew and Greek. The leading topics in church history were considered in the light of the crucial issues in theology. Lectures on preaching and pastoral care included "miscellaneous disquisitions on points of literature and history, bordering on theology."[43] As with Esson, Burns consistently subordinated reason to revelation in his approach.

Rintoul presented an outline of his lectures in biblical science and exegesis. He dealt with the importance of the study of Hebrew, the nature of biblical science and the prerequisites for its study, the structure and contents of the bible, the rhetoric of the original languages, the manuscripts available and "the means of approximating to the purity of the text, as written by the original penmen," the authenticity and genuineness of the scriptures, their inspiration, ancient and English translations and the merits of the authorized version, the interpretation of the scriptures, a classification and exploration of the difficulties in the scriptures, the ways in which progress in biblical science and the advancement of the gospel lessens these difficulties, and the "transcendant importance of a thorough knowledge of the holy Scriptures to the Christian Minister – the subordination of the critical to the devotional study of the Scriptures." Two classes, a junior and a senior, were offered in Hebrew and Greek.[44]

The underlying assumptions in Rintoul's approach to biblical studies matched those of Esson, Burns, and the others in their respective departments. Revelation as interpreted by the Westminster standards, not only in the area of doctrine, but also in church government and worship, occupied the core of the curriculum at all levels of study.

CONFLICTING VISIONS

While there was unanimity among the founding faculty on the content to be conveyed, a conflict arose between Burns and Esson over the preparatory program at Knox. At issue was Esson's orthodoxy and the proper curriculum of preparatory education for candidates for the ministry of preserving and propagating confessional orthodoxy. Both men were accomplished pamphleteers and journalists and used their skills to the utmost in the controversy. The first signs of tension were accusations in 1847 by Burns that Esson was departing from Baconian orthodoxy and teaching the heresy of Idealism. Esson vehemently denied the charges and threatened to charge Burns with slander in the church courts.[45]

The controversy escalated into a pamphlet war when Burns issued a printed circular in March 1848, a year after leaving the college to focus full-time on his congregational responsibilities.[46] It advocated the tightening of admissions standards and the hiring of an additional professor to take over the field of the philosophy of the mind from Esson. Burns considered the current curriculum deficient in those disciplines that would help the clergy communicate the faith, especially English composition, elocution, and philosophy.

He called for greater attention to "a plain common-sense view of the powers and capacities of the human mind, with rules for their improvement," in order to develop the students' persuasive abilities.

The Synod's college committee agreed with Burns when it recommended that a class be established and a tutor sought in general mental training, logic, and rhetoric, as they related to "the communication as well as the acquisition of truth." Esson dissented and asked that the matter be referred to a special committee of the Synod.[47] He was convinced that Burns' recommendations constituted a serious departure from the educational system at the college that would weaken the ministry of the Free Church in Canada. His detailed critique was published prior to the Synod meeting of 1848 as a *Statement Relative to the Educational System of Knox's College, Toronto; with Suggestions for its Extension and Improvement.* Esson accused Burns of attempting to perpetuate the older scholastic methods of the University of Glasgow which simply prepared a student to "inculcate a particular system of dogmas." Esson, on the other hand, was seeking to emulate the approach of his own university, Aberdeen, where the students were encouraged to develop their own reasoning abilities and judgement through careful and consistent direction from their professors and frequent and strict examinations.[48]

Esson rested his case on what he considered to be the purpose of the ministry and the special qualifications needed by those accepting its responsibilities:

As the great end of the Gospel ministry is to contend earnestly for the Faith once delivered to the Saints, to bear witness to the Truth, of which the Church of the living God is the Pillar and Ground, maintaining its scriptural soundness, integrity, and uncorruptedness, the first and most indispensable preparation for the work of the Lord, – next to the anointing of the spirit, – the actual conversion of the soul, – and the inward call to the ministry, – is, without all question, that kind and measure of knowledge, learning and science, which may fit its subject for the right understanding and faithful interpretation of the original and authentic text of scripture, the only genuine exponent of the mind of the spirit, the only perfect transcript of the divine will, and therefore the only infallible standard of Faith and Manners.[49]

He argued that Knox did not offer a preparatory course of this quality and must begin to do so. The role of a teacher, Esson concluded, was not to "inculcate a particular system of dogmas, but to prepare his pupils for exercising their own judgement, to exhibit to them an outline of the different sciences, and to suggest subjects for their further examination."[50]

The Synod sustained its decision to support Burns' position, largely because it lacked the resources to implement Esson's plan. Esson turned his attention to the development of the new University of Toronto, where provincial funding held out the promise of providing the full arts program he considered essential, not only for the preparation of theological students, but also for the education of the consciences of Canada's future leaders.

The Free Church Synod was enthusiastic in its support of a nonsectarian provincial university. Hopes were high in the late 1840s that the government would soon remove the Anglican monopoly on the University of King's College. In 1848, the Synod expressed its earnest desire to see that institution:

freed from its present sectarian management so as to deserve the confidence of the community at large and be available for the general benefit of the youth of this country, and at the same time so constituted as that some sufficient security be provided for the parties occupying chairs therein and placed in the responsible position of instructors of youth, shall be sound in the Christian faith, and that their instructions shall be pervaded by sound religious principles.[51]

Legislation to secularize King's College and create the University of Toronto finally passed in 1849.[52]

Following the secularization of King's, Burns overtured the Synod to eliminate the preparatory department and concentrate the church's resources on the academy and the theological department. The Synod remained suspicious of the new University of Toronto, however, because it had retained most of the staff of King's. John McCaul taught classics and James Beaven metaphysics and ethics. Both were Anglican clergymen. Henry Holmes Croft taught chemistry and Robert Murray, a Church of Scotland minister, mathematics.[53] Some on the Synod's college committee thought the new university was "defective in the religious element" and were determined to maintain at Knox "adequate means for all the leading branches of a liberal education – the whole being fully leavened with religion." They also worried that the new university would follow the medieval model of the English universities and preferred the model of Alexander Duff's college in India where the educational program was more suitable to the evangelical vision of the social and religious needs of a developing country.[54] John Bayne proposed that the Synod continue to monitor the development of the University of Toronto to ascertain whether changes would warrant the elimination of the preparatory department. Bayne's motion won over Burns' by a vote of 28 to 5.[55] Five years after the founding of the college, the Synod remained convinced of the wisdom of Rintoul's vision of a church-controlled college to ensure the propagation of the great evangelical truths that formed the foundation for civic and ecclesiastical righteousness.

CREATING STRUCTURES OF TRUST, SUPPORT, AND ACCOUNTABILITY

The work of finding a faculty and agreeing on a curriculum that would prepare men to preserve and propagate the great evangelical truths through the rapidly-expanding Free Church in Canada was only part of the story of the founding of Knox College. Financial support and accountable governing structures were essential to the viability of the college. The first six years of financing and governing the college developed in the same experimental fashion as the staffing and curriculum. A small college committee grew to a large one, the increase due mainly to the need for representatives in each presbytery to ensure communication, raise funds, and recruit candidates. Prominent business leaders in the Free Church, notably John McMurrich of Knox Church, Toronto, and John Redpath of Cote Street Church, Montreal, played key roles in the management and funding of the college. Careful plans were laid and executed to inform the church of the needs of the college and make sure that information reached every potential donor. The college authorities firmly believed that the work they were doing was crucial to the defence and propagation of the great evangelical truths in Canada and, therefore, worthy of generous support. At the same time, they recognized the importance of clear structures of accountability to maintain the confidence of the church.

The college committee appointed in 1844 was small, five ministers and four elders, and drawn exclusively from the Toronto and Hamilton presbyteries. They were commissioned to set professors' salaries, find accommodations for the staff and students, and oversee the educational program. The salary for Henry Esson, the first professor, was £200, exclusive of the rent for the house on James Street where staff and students lived and held classes. Andrew King's salary was paid by the Colonial Committee of the Scottish Free Church and Knox Church, Toronto. He boarded at the Esson house, along with several of the students. The Synod had asked the committee to distribute a letter seeking funds. On behalf of the committee, William Rintoul wrote:

We, dear brethren, strongly feel that our students, to become able and faithful ministers of the New Testament, must have the spirit of God enlightening, elevating, and purifying their souls, while they are in the way of acquiring useful gifts; that our professors must be under the same heavenly influence, in order to their being effective teachers of divine truth; and that our churches must be visited with a more plentiful effusion of the holy spirit, in order to their furnishing us with more candidates for the ministry, and in order to their sustaining the ministry.[56]

Rintoul asked for prayers and collections from each congregation in the new denomination. The letter was sent to the ministers, but also printed in full in the *Record*, suggesting that the college committee was well aware of the problem of communicating with congregations through their clergy. Treasurers were designated in each of the presbyteries, with John McMurrich of Knox Church, Toronto, being appointed the general treasurer.[57] This pattern of annual appeals to congregations and individuals, normally on the first Sunday in December, continued throughout the early years.

The *Record* also noted that ten Glasgow merchants had subscribed £1000 each towards the establishment of the Scottish Free Church's New College in Edinburgh. No such liberality was forthcoming from the colonial Free Church, however, though Isaac Buchanan tried his best to set an example with a donation of £500.[58] Most of the money came in small amounts. Knox Church, Toronto, for example, established a "Female Association" in 1846 under the leadership of Elizabeth Burns and Elizabeth Esson to raise money for missions and bursaries.[59] In 1847, anticipating a tripling in costs from £400 to £1200 in the new term, the college committee divided the synod into 15 districts and named several people within each to solicit funds. Henry Esson's efforts to organize college fund raising at Knox Church, Toronto, was given as an example.

Esson's report on his fund raising activities at Knox divided the congregation into seven classes based on occupation. It presented an interesting picture of the demographic mix within the congregation, as well as the levels of giving to the college. Twenty-eight professional men and merchants gave a total of £56; 35 clerks gave £26; 16 master mechanics gave £15; 39 journeymen and apprentices gave £14; and 26 females, married and unmarried, gave £12. Esson hoped to have children collecting funds for the college as well. In total, he hoped to raise at least £200 in the year.

At the end of the fiscal year in May 1848, the college had collected £1008. The grant from the Colonial Committee of the Free Church of Scotland enabled them to meet expenses, but the college committee expressed disappointment at failing to reach its goal.[60] Nevertheless, it had established a base of interest and support within a large number of congregations that continued well into the future. A similar pattern of support developed for the bursary funds.

Concerted efforts were made to keep the work and needs of the college before the church. Few issues of the *Record* were published between 1844 and 1850 that did not contain extensive information about the college and its service to the church. In the midst of the push to increase the givings in 1847–1848, the college reminded the church that it was not simply a school for ministry, but "a missionary institution ... a school for evangelists as well as a school for pastors."[61] Alexander Gale made a similar point five years later in the annual appeal letter. The college, he wrote, claimed the support of the church "on the highest Christian grounds:"

It is a thoroughly Evangelistic and Missionary Institution, and has, since its very commencement, rendered efficient and valuable service in that character. The community in which our lot is cast, exhibits a large, and yearly increasing amount of religious destitution. It has a claim, unquestionably, preferable to all other similar claims on our missionary efforts. How then can we better fulfil one of the primary and most honourable duties of the Church and of the individual Christian, than by extending a liberal support to this Institution. Many a Canadian wilderness have the students and young ministers of Knox's College already made to blossom and rejoice. What Christian would permit it to languish or fall, for want of pecuniary resources?[62]

Knox's students would all be missionaries in their own fields and, indeed, many of them served as missionary catechists in the six months of the year they were not in school. During the session of 1848–1849, for example, 17 stations in the Toronto area were supplied by the students and professors of the college.[63]

Without endowments or major benefactors, the financial health of the college was precarious throughout the founding years. At the end of the fiscal year 1848–1849, the college owed the professors a total of £300 in back salary. Throughout the year, the committee admitted to the Synod, the professors had suffered "very painful inconvenience and discomfort," at one point having to borrow from a bank using their own collateral to meet immediate needs.[64]

In 1848, the college committee sought to clarify the expectations surrounding its work, especially with respect to governance. The college asked the Synod to set up a committee to draw up a constitution for the college, "including arrangements as to the Government, discipline, and curriculum of study, and as to the standard of attainments to be required of applicants for admission." The proposal was to be sent to presbyteries for advice and to be reviewed by the professors at Knox and at New College, Edinburgh.[65] The early college committees were dominated by clergy, with a ratio of fifteen to five in 1846 and twenty-one to twelve in 1847. Throughout the first six years, the governing body was convened by a clergyman, sometimes a member of the Synod and sometimes one of the professors. While the general committee remained large, smaller sub-committees began to assume responsibility for specific aspects of the college's work after 1847. The most important division of powers occurred in 1848, when a professors' court assumed responsibility for the studies and discipline of the students and a management committee for the finances and other administrative concerns, but both remained under the oversight of the general committee. The Synod in 1849 approved the outline of governance and curriculum in principle and asked the college committee to consult further the presbyteries before presenting a final draft.

The number of students increased rapidly. The original 14 (7 in preparatory course and 7 in theology proper) grew to 40 by 1846 (16 in the preparatory course and 24 in theology proper) and reached 51 in 1850 (28 in the preparatory course and 23 in theology proper).[66] Most, with the encouragement of college authorities, stayed in the boarding houses attached to the college. Their studies were demanding and they worked under strict supervision. For the session of 1850–1851, classes ran Monday to Saturday, from 10:00 AM until 5:00 PM during the weekdays and from 9:00 AM until 1:00 PM on Saturday. W.J. McKenzie recalled the activities that made up college life in the late 1840s:

[There were] Saturday evening meetings of students for Christian fellowship and prayer, and mutual instruction; the monthly meetings of the Students' Missionary Society, in the Divinity Hall, to report on the progress of Missions at home and abroad, the progress of their own missionary to the French Romanists, their own progress in distributing tracts and conducting prayer meetings in the city, and to hear an essay from one of themselves on some kindred theme; the Debating society; the Dining hall, where about fifty sat down to table; the short chit-chat after dinner; the musical recreations, conducted by Robert Scott; the brisk morning and evening walks to brace up the system, for new mental toils; the long, silent evening studies, protracted sometimes to midnight and to "early morn"; the morning and evening devotions of the whole college; the reading of essays and trial discourses before the assembled professors and students in the Hall; the criticisms of the Professors and fellow students; the exciting, tearing, wearing examinations,[67]

Students were expected to prepare during the summer for examinations at the beginning of the session as well.

The faculty took two columns in the *Record* of June 1847 to remind their students of the readings required for each of these examinations.[68] The whole college committee were involved in the examinations and sought:

first, to satisfy themselves, as to the personal religion of the applicant, and the motives by which he had been prompted to the proposed dedication of himself to the Gospel ministry – secondly, to form a judgment as to his gifts and talents being such to justify his entering on a course of study, with a view to the sacred office – thirdly, to ascertain his actual state of mental culture, and his progress in Education.[69]

McKenzie concluded that it was "the general and growing conviction of the more intelligent portion of the Church" that Knox College was "capable of sending forth men whose literary and theological attainments will bear a fair general comparison with those of any other ministry within the British Empire."[70]

Enthusiasm for missions was something both students and faculty shared. The college's Missionary Society was formed in 1845. The purpose of the society was:

the diffusion amongst ourselves of a livelier interest, and a holier zeal in regard to the success of God's work in the earth; and also the furtherance of that work by means of united and persevering prayer. For the attainment of these ends we resolved to meet, that we might together more fully learn *where*, and *how*, and *through whose instrumentality* the cause of our Redeemer was advancing; knowing well that increasing information on these points is, generally speaking, necessary, in order to the sustaining and expanding of a healthful missionary spirit. It is only when influenced by such a spirit that we feel it sweet to gather round the throne, and beseech the Father to have respect unto his covenant. But a growing earnestness in prayer on behalf of the great work cannot in ordinary circumstances long remain dissociated from active effort for its promotion.[71]

Faculty members were regular in their attendance and frequently gave addresses on the importance of missions. Henry Esson told the members that the great aim of every missionary effort was "the conversion of souls to God." The systematic study of missions helped students understand "the great principles upon which [missions] may most successfully be conducted."[72] By 1847, the society had raised enough money to co-sponsor one of the college's first graduates, John Black, as a full-time worker under the Synod's French Canadian Missionary Society to the French Canadian settlements in Western Canada. Closer to home, the society coordinated the winter and summer appointments of the students as catechist missionaries and arranged for students to lead prayer meetings and distribute tracts and bibles in various parts of the city.[73]

The demands of the educational program combined with the enthusiasm for missions led to some tensions between the college and the presbyteries. From the opening of the college, students were in demand to supply in vacant congregations or new mission stations. During the term of 1848–1849, for example, nineteen students preached a total of 141 times in Oakville, Niagara, King, Vaughan, Chinguacousy, East Toronto, Humber and Weston, Darlington, Trafalgar, Hamilton, Brock, and Reach.[74] During the six months of the summer, most students served as catechists under the authority of the various presbyteries. James Ferguson reported that the senior students in theology had conducted fifteen services every Sunday during the summer break, with total average attendance of 3950; 637 families had been visited; fourteen sabbath schools conducted for a total of 480 children; six bible classes had been attended by 160 people; and eight prayer meetings had been led with 284 people participating.[75] In 1847, the Synod declared that the college committee had no power over the appointment of students as catechists, but could only certify whether they thought the student fit for such service. The college, however, was concerned with the time these practices took away from the studies of the students.

William Rintoul advised the students that all their studies and pursuits should be directed to the service of Christ and that devotional exercises were "an indispensable preparative" for the studies and pursuits of the day. He argued that the full occupation of their time in preparing for the sabbath and other public services, visiting, and teaching, as was the practice among the ordained clergy, was not proper for students. They should be spending one or two days a week throughout the summer in "their own proper studies." He did not miss the opportunity to encourage the students to appeal to the congregations in their presbyteries for additional support for the work of the college.[76]

The presbyteries, on the other hand, faced a growing need for men to supply congregations. In a lengthy editorial on the issue in the March 1849 *Record*, the legitimacy of using students as missionaries and preachers, even though the practice did not find support in "the ancient laws and usages" of Presbyterianism, was defended because of the desperate needs of the rapidly-growing church. The danger, the author acknowledged, was that zeal for such work on the part of both the presbyteries and the students would interfere with their studies. The writer encouraged the continuance of the practice, not least since it formed an important part of the students' education and provided financial assistance for the pursuit of their studies. At the same time, he insisted that the college and the presbyteries work closely together to ensure the proper use of the students' time in these appointments.[77] The tensions over these practices continued. The college gained the cooperation of neither the presbyteries nor the students.

In presenting the outline of a constitution to the 1849 synod, the college committee said that early years had been instructive "of the difficulties to be surmounted, and of the evils to be eschewed or obviated" in the administration of the college and its programs.[78] Of pressing importance was finding the funds and people to provide a full-time faculty. Hopes of being able to focus on theological studies and leave preparatory studies to the new provincial university ran high, but college authorities were cautious about the university being able to satisfy all their needs in the manner they expected. The cost of running the college had risen from £150 to over £1200 in the six years. Contributions from the church had almost kept pace, but not quite. Gale, King, Burns, McCorkle, and Rintoul had come and gone. Willis had come and gone and returned. Esson was interested in a move to the University of Toronto and a growing body within the church were determined to have Knox concentrate on theological studies. The Free Church founders had laid the foundations for a "School of the Prophets" in Toronto and were convinced that Knox College had to combine evangelical conviction and intellectual integrity. Differences of opinion surfaced early as to how that might best be done, both in the college and the denomination as a whole. The next twenty years of Knox's history were marked by controversy as well, some continuing over the differences in founding visions and some emerging anew as the denomination faced the pressures of growth and the challenges posed by developments in its social and political environment.

2 Conflicting Strategies, 1850–1870

Scottish Free Church missionary and educationist Alexander Duff, whose ideas had played a significant role in the establishment of Knox College, visited Toronto in 1853. He urged the members of the Students' Missionary Society of Knox College to see themselves as the church militant:

because the whole world is in opposition to the Head of the Church, and the commission of the Head of the Church is, go ye and act out the part of the church militant, and never cease giving vent to your belligerent propensities, not against one another, but against the common foe, until that foe is exterminated from the earth.[1]

Duff had been among the first generation of students who had studied under Thomas Chalmers at St. Andrews in the 1820s. His faith had been formed by Chalmers' comprehensive evangelical vision of the redemption of the nation as well as the individual. Duff's approach to evangelism in the church militant focused on Christian education, especially for the nation's potential leaders. A sanctified intellect was essential to "the empire of truth and order, godliness and sobriety." In substance, this education focused on "the record and interpretation of God's visible handiwork" in nature and human affairs in a way that demonstrated the compatibility of all true knowledge with biblical revelation.[2]

By the time Duff arrived in Toronto, Knox College had established itself as one of the key agencies in the Free Church's efforts to translate Duff's vision of an evangelical nation into reality in Canada. The faculty at the college, however, proposed conflicting strategies for accomplishing this mission. At issue was the wisdom of uniting with other branches of Presbyterians to create a more effective church. Discussions concerning church union, first with the United Presbyterians in the Canadas, then with Presbyterians throughout British North America, commanded considerable attention between 1850 and 1870.

The possibility of union with the United Presbyterians in Canada was raised shortly after the Free Church came into existence. It enjoyed the enthusiastic support of prominent business leaders within the various branches of Presbyterianism, and eventually of the majority of clergy.[3] It posed serious questions, however, about the degree of purity in doctrine and practice that was to be maintained in the ecclesial culture of the Free Church and about ways to assess it. The debate divided the faculty of Knox College in the 1850s, reflecting the conflicting strategies for advancing the church militant and funding the college. The debates over church union also reflected a struggle within the denomination to deal with pressures to broaden its ecclesial culture to permit varying interpretations of the Westminster Standards to co-exist within the church.[4]

CONFLICTING STRATEGIES FOR THE CHURCH MILITANT

Union negotiations between the Free Church and the United Presbyterians in Canada were based on the assumption that the two branches of Presbyterianism were in substantial harmony on the important principles. That was true for every principle but one.[5] The question of church and state brought the best minds in the church into conflict. Just how was Christ's Headship over the nations to be understood and how important was it to specify the applications of this principle in the standards of the church? Further, what were the criteria to be used in determining truth in these matters and what bodies were competent to judge in the case of disputes? In retrospect, the decisions reached in these controversies served to broaden the boundaries of what the Canada Presbyterian Church, as the united body was named, accepted in its

beliefs and practices and to clarify the process by which its ecclesial culture was formed. The faculty members at Knox were key
protagonists in the debates and lined up on different sides. Burns
and Willis, veterans of the voluntary controversy in Scotland,[6] insisted that the principles of a pure establishment were essential to
the cause of Christ in Canada, while Esson, Gale, and Rintoul, who
came to Canada before the Scottish controversy broke out, were
far more sympathetic to voluntarist views, especially in the Canadian context.[7]

Willis had written widely on the subject prior to leaving Scotland.[8] He argued that the civil magistrate did not have the power to
dictate what people believed or how they worshipped, but did have
the responsibility to "publically and nationally do homage to God
and the Lord and Mediator Jesus Christ" by calling for national
"days of thanksgiving and humiliation," by providing funds for the
maintenance of religious ordinances, by legislating the observance
of the sabbath as a day of rest and reflection, and by providing for
general and religious education.[9] Another application particularly
dear to Willis was the elimination of slavery, "that God-defying system which reduces man to the level of a brute; intercepts the light
of Heaven's saving truth from a portion of God's rational offspring;
and annihilates and dissolves relationships which the law of Christ,
and of nature, has made inviolate."[10]

Burns expressed his views in a heated debate lasting from May
1846 until May 1848 in the pages of the Toronto Banner with William Barrie, minister of the United Presbyterian congregation in
Guelph. The voluntarist, argued Burns, denied that nations had an
allegiance to God. They excluded "from the range of revelation, as
its guide and director, the most extensively influential of all agencies hitherto known among men." For Burns, the key principle was
that nations, like individuals, were capable of moral action and responsible for such. He used Sabbath observance as an example of
the kind of practice he expected from the civil magistrate. While
not commanding any specific religious duties, the state "may and
ought to legislate and secure by authority one day in seven to be
kept free from the business and amusements of ordinary days."[11]

Opposition to voluntaryism on the basis of the principle of a national establishment of religion led the Free Church in Canada to
break off early union talks with the United Presbyterians in 1848
and to expel Andrew Ferrier from its ministry in 1850.[12] From

1850 until 1854, the question of how the Free Church was going to understand chapter 23 of the Westminster Confession of Faith concerning the civil magistrate was thoroughly discussed at presbytery and synod levels. The result was a Declaratory Act in 1854, drawn up by a committee that included Burns and Willis, which was to be attached to every edition of the Confession of Faith published by the church:

The Synod, in declaring their adherence, as they now again do, to the Confession of Faith, as approved by the General Assembly of the Church of Scotland, in the year 1647, hereby declare that they do not understand the passages relating to the duty of the civil magistrate, as teaching or sanctioning an Erastian control of the Church by the civil magistrate or the persecution of individuals for conscience sake; principles which the Synod heartily disclaim as inconsistent with the liberty wherewith Christ has made his people free – opposed to the spirit and terms of the said Confession, and repudiated by the Church in her purest and best times.[13]

Elsewhere in the proceedings, the Synod clarified its understanding of this declaratory act by naming the conditions on which it would continue union discussions with the United Presbyterians. It was willing to allow the issue of state endowments to be "a matter of forbearance," but insisted that the Free Church views on the duty of the civil magistrate and the responsibility of nations to God be clearly stated in the basis of union because the practical results of these principles were "of such a character as to render the maintaining of these principles in all their integrity necessary to the best interests of the Church of Christ."[14] These official statements and decisions seemed to close the door on the possibility of union.

At the congregational level, however, there was a growing sentiment in favour of union. It was based on the assumption that union in the Canadas would not violate any scriptural principle and was necessary to confront "the boldness and arrogance" of the common enemies of evangelical Presbyterianism, specifically, "Popery, Infidelity, and Irreligion."[15] An important factor in this growing climate of support for union was the number of Knox graduates who had studied under Gale, Esson, and Rintoul, all of whom espoused voluntarist views in their teaching. Indeed, Esson and Rintoul had recorded their dissents to the decision to expel Ferrier from the church.[16]

In 1849, Esson wrote a series of lengthy letters in the *Record* on the issue. He argued that the voluntarist had the best position on the relation of church and state for Canada, especially in light of the impossibility of the Free Church principle of state support without interference ever being realized in practice. Compacts and covenants, Esson argued, implied a "reciprocity of obligation between the contracting parties." This element was absent from the Free Church principle, leading the vast majority of politicians to see it as "visionary and chimerical." Esson agreed that the state had an obligation "to seek the glory of God and the happiness of its subjects, which surely involves as its primary and all-pervading element the chief end of man, that is, his moral and religious responsibilities."[17] This was best accomplished, however, by providing public support to policies and institutions that eliminated "sectarian distinctions and divisions" and built a common culture in the new nation, while each distinctive group supported its own churches and colleges for educating its clergy. Especially important were public schools and a non-sectarian provincial university, that brought the youth of the province together "on perfectly equal terms in the generous pursuits of liberal knowledge and science, ... where an assimilating and harmonizing influence may be brought to bear on their minds and hearts, thereby rendering these institutions the cement of national unity, and the source of an equal, common, and liberal-minded patriotism."[18] A pragmatic assessment of the possibilities of ever seeing the Free Church principle realized, combined with questions about its scriptural warrant and the desire to see common institutions that would serve the best interests of the new country, led Esson, Gale, and Rintoul to conclude that there were no significant barriers to a union with the United Presbyterians.

Those sympathetic to union and a broader interpretation of the relations between church and state gained the upper hand in the Synod by 1855 and a Basis of Union was presented in 1857. Further negotiations led to the inclusion of a clause in the preamble to the Basis of Union that granted members of the new church freedom to interpret "the practical applications" of the section on the headship of Christ over the nations and the duty of the civil magistrate as they saw fit. Disputes over this issue would be dealt with according to "the recognized principles of Presbyterian Church order," in other words, by the community through the courts of the church.[19] Willis and a number of other members of the Synod were not satisfied with this compromise. They recorded their dissent, arguing that Article IV of the basis did not provide evidence that "substantial harmony on the important subjects which it embraced" had been reached. Specifically, it contained:

no declaration on the subject of the leading applications of the doctrine of Christ's Headship over the nations, such as its application to the question of Sabbath laws, or of the use of the Bible in Common Schools, or of the suppression of open blasphemy, and no definition of the extent or limits of the Province within which the Civil Magistrate is to confess and serve Christ as King – subjects on which unscriptural views are often entertained and acted upon by those who profess to hold the doctrine of Christ's Headship over the nations.[20]

A commission of the Synod answered the dissent. They argued that it was "neither expedient nor necessary to burden the Basis with any such definition" and that the differences of opinion that existed or might arise with respect to the applications of the principle would not be "inconsistent with ecclesiastical harmony" nor "invalidate the integrity of the testimony borne by the United Church to the truths which the Article sets forth."[21]

The new Canada Presbyterian Church remained firmly attached to the essentials of confessional orthodoxy as laid out in the Westminster Standards. The Basis, however, took care to define the ways in which those standards were to be interpreted in the Canadian context. Scripture was declared to be "the inspired word of God" and "the supreme and infallible rule of faith and life." In respect to the Confession's position on the civil magistrate, the Basis stated that the Canada Presbyterian Church gave "fullest forbearance" to differences of opinion on the question of state endowments for the church. Further, the church accepted no interpretation of the standards that denied "liberty of conscience and right of private judgement," based upon the freedom of people to search the Scriptures for themselves, and do what they believe the Scriptures to teach, provided that that interpretation does not violate "the peace and good order of society." Finally, the Confession was not to be read in a way that allowed the state to interfere with "the spiritual independence of the Church." The system of government was to be according to the Westminster form, "in so far as it declares a plurality of elders for each congregation, the official equality of Presbyters and the unity of the Church, in a due subordination of a smaller part to a larger, and of a larger to the whole." The entire Basis was to be read in the light of the first clause on the authority of the scriptures.[22] Final decisions on what was warranted and unwarranted by scripture in faith and life were made by the courts that governed the church, with the higher courts having clear authority over the lower.

Willis found himself involved in one of the first tests of this understanding of the standards and their interpretation. At issue were state endowments for churches, the matter upon which the united church had agreed to give its members full forbearance. That freedom of conscience did not prevent the church itself, through its courts, from taking a position on this matter, and the position that it took was one that Willis could not accept. In the revision of the University Act that created University College in 1853, denominational colleges were granted a small share in the endowment. Egerton Ryerson organized efforts to gain a larger share. Ryerson was particularly incensed at the creation of chairs in modern languages, English, history, agriculture, and meteorology at University College, a move enthusiastically supported by the Free Church Synod. The government appointed two commissions to review the matter, one in 1860 and the other in 1862. The second presented a report that would have significantly increased funding to the denominational colleges at the expense of the provincial university.[23] The Cartier-Macdonald government fell before the recommendations could be implemented, but the threat of this action brought forth a strong response from the Synod of the new Canada Presbyterian Church.

The Free Church synod had petitioned against increased grants to denominational colleges in 1860 and 1861. The *Record* doubted the wisdom and patriotism of those seeking a larger share of the endowments: "We cannot regard them as lovers of sound, liberal education, who would rob our country of its *one* first-rate University, and leave us with a few second or third rate schools, struggling with poverty, and weakened by sectarian jealousies. To our Wesleyan friends, in their present attempt, we say 'Hands off.'"[24] The first Synod of the Canada Presbyterian Church appointed a committee to lobby against any public funding for denominational colleges in 1862. Willis dissented from the actions of the Free Church in 1860 and 1861, and he and Robert Burns moved that no action be taken by the Canada Presbyterian Church in 1862. Their amendment was defeated by a vote of 46 to 4. It was clear that Willis was at odds with his denomination on this matter. Willis was in full agreement with the recommendations of the 1862 university commission to redistribute the endowment, in part because of his views on the government's responsibility to support religious education and in part because of the ongoing financial difficulties at Knox. Willis felt compelled to resign, but was eventually persuaded to stay.[25]

In addition to revealing tensions within the faculty and between Willis and Burns and the church, the incident illustrated the means chosen by the church to define and refine its ecclesial culture. Within the limits set by the Westminster Standards, differences of interpretation were expected. Further, new social conditions and needs called for different applications of the principles enshrined in the Standards. The courts of the church were to be the means by which these decisions were considered and made.

A NEW FACULTY FOR A BROADENING CHURCH

The college entered the 1850s with depleted resources. The permanent faculty had been reduced to two, Henry Esson in the preparatory program and Michael Willis in the theological program. Esson, as has been noted, was interested in moving to the new provincial university, but died in 1853 while waiting to hear of the appointment, leaving Willis as the sole permanent professor. The college committee worked hard throughout the next several years to find the funding that would enable them to add permanent faculty. Their efforts met with mixed results. Financing the new buildings was easier than attracting the support to expand the faculty.

John Bayne, who stood with Willis and Burns in their support of a pure establishment, was asked to succeed Esson in 1853. After he declined,[26] George Paxton Young was appointed. Young was born in 1818 and educated at the Royal High School in Edinburgh and the University of Edinburgh. He taught mathematics at the Dollar Academy, completed his theological studies at New College, Edinburgh, and was called to the Martyrs' Church, Paisley in 1847. He accepted a call to Chadwell Street Church in London in 1849, but left for Canada a year later. There he succeeded Ralph Robb at

Knox Church, Hamilton, the congregation of businessman and Free Church benefactor Isaac Buchanan.[27]

Young agreed with Esson and Willis that the college curriculum needed to be comprehensive and demanding, especially in the area of philosophy:

If there be persons who do not possess minds capable of reflection, or who are too idle to tax their reflective powers with vigorous and sustained effort – who are content to put up with dogmatism, and care nothing about ascertaining what can be known for certain – whom neither curiosity nor ambition prompt to trace the Nile of human thought and knowledge back to its sources – who are so blind to the bearing which the settlement in a particular way, of what are commonly called metaphysical questions, has upon religion and morality, as to be utterly indifferent how such questions are settled – it is only natural that *they* should turn away from philosophy, and cry out against it as useless. But we trust that among the students of Knox's College will be found, from one year to another, not a few of an opposite character of mind, and animated by very different feelings.[28]

The theological method and substance of Young's *Miscellaneous Discourses and Expositions of Scripture,* published in 1854, confirmed that he shared the confessional orthodoxy of the other founders of the college. It was "rich in evangelical sentiment, and pervaded by a spirit of earnest piety," stated the review in the *Record,* and did not "exalt the pretensions of human reason at the expense of revelation."[29]

Young was enthusiastic in his support of a broader union among evangelical churches. Mutual love among Christians, he suggested in a sermon on Christian love, edified the church and offered an effective witness to the world. Young urged his listeners "to put an end to wrangling and sinful debate in the deliberations of ecclesiastical bodies" and be "more ready to co-operate for the advancement of the common faith" in keeping with the principles of the Evangelical Alliance.[30]

In 1856, Robert Burns returned to the college as the third permanent professor, this time responsible for church history and Christian evidences. Burns' move to the college halted proceedings in the Presbytery of Toronto that had arisen from yet another controversy between him and the Knox congregation.[31]

Church history and evidences were appropriate fields for the broad and eclectic interests of Burns. His approach assumed that the driving force in all history was the providential will of God. History, then, provided corroborating evidence for the great evangelical truths revealed in the Scriptures. Church history recorded the "rapid progress and success" of the gospel and revealed the fulfilment of prophecy with "unquestionable relevancy." In addition, it furnished "a map of the human mind and the human character," and revealed the motivations of human action under varied and shifting influences. "God is the moral Governor of nations," Burns wrote, "and the Student of Church History waits on His mighty movements, in His gradual subjugation of all things to the setting up of that kingdom which shall last forever."[32]

Burns remained convinced that the emphasis at Knox should be on communication skills. He saw Knox as "a nursery for the pulpit," and thought the most pressing need of the college was to "keep abreast of the age, and the style and manner of its compositions and its appeals." Burns was convinced that students retained little of the education they received in biblical, classical, or modern languages. What was crucial in their preparation was education in the grammar and composition of "the vulgar tongue" of contemporary English. Not only must the mind be filled with ideas, he argued: "but it is necessary that these ideas be well arranged, clearly apprehended, accurately defined, and distinguished from their correlatives; put down from time to time on paper, improper words fitted to proper places, and then brought out to the people in such a mode of elocution as ordinarily educated persons are accustomed to use to one another when they mean to be understood."[33] The tensions between Burns' desire for greater attention to training in persuasive skills in theological education and the more academic approach of his two colleagues did not erupt into outright conflict, as they had in the Burns-Esson debate of 1848, but they did reflect two different emphases in the Free Church regarding the preparation of the clergy. There was consensus on the goal, to prepare well-informed and articulate preachers who would defend and propagate the great evangelical truths. The differences of opinion arose over the proper means of accomplishing that goal and over whether the emphasis in the studies required for ordination should be on piety and communication skills or on intellectual formation and powers of reasoning.

The United Presbyterians brought a theological college of their own into the Canada Presbyterian Church in 1861, but at the time of union it had no faculty, a minimal curriculum, and little established financial support. The Divinity Hall of the Missionary Synod of the Associate Secession Church was established in 1844 and opened the month before the Free Church college. The Rev. William Proudfoot of London was appointed professor, a position he held in addition to his pastoral duties, and the students boarded with him in the manse during their studies in literature, philosophy, and divinity. In 1846, the Rev. Alexander McKenzie, minister at Goderich, was appointed to teach Hebrew. The program was four years in length, ten weeks being spent with Proudfoot each year and a series of exercises and examinations being done under the supervision of the presbyteries throughout the rest of the year. In 1850, with the creation of the University of Toronto, the Divinity Hall moved to Toronto to take advantage of the courses in classics, literature, and philosophy offered there. Proudfoot died early in 1851 and was replaced by the Rev. John Taylor, called from Auchtermuchty in Scotland. Taylor added the pastorate of the second United Presbyterian congregation in Toronto, when it was established in 1853, to his teaching responsibilities. The Hall educated only 26 students between 1844 and 1861. It annual budget was less than $400 while in London, and $1400 while in Toronto. Taylor decided to return to Scotland when the union took place. The Divinity Hall was amalgamated with Knox College and Willis, Young, and Burns became the faculty for the united church.[34]

The Canada Presbyterian Church adopted the curriculum approved by the Free Church Synod in 1855. It organized the offerings of the college into three courses, the preliminary, the non-theological, and the theological. The preliminary program was for those who were considered not ready to begin the non-theological course. It consisted of arithmetic and mathematics, English grammar, civil history, and Greek and Latin. These courses were conducted by a tutor, who also served as the supervisor of the residence. The non-theological course took three years to complete. The first year consisted of studies in classics, mathematics, and English composition. The second covered classics, junior philosophy (logic and metaphysics), physical science (natural philosophy, chemistry, or natural history), history, and English literature. The final year dealt with senior philosophy (metaphysics and ethics), junior Hebrew, physical science (geology), history, and literature. Some of these courses were offered at Knox, but most were taken through University College at the University of Toronto.[35] The attaining of a degree was of little importance at this time. What mattered was the grounding in the humanities and the sciences that would prepare a minister to present the claims of the Gospel in as articulate and convincing a manner as possible. The theological course also took three years to complete. The first year consisted of classes in the evidences of natural and revealed religion, senior Hebrew, church history, and the exposition of scripture. The second covered systematic theology, church history, hermeneutics, biblical history, and pastoral theology. The final year dealt further with systematic theology, hermeneutics, biblical history, and pastoral theology.[36]

The college report in 1858 gave the church a more detailed description of how the various subjects in the theological curriculum were taught. Of particular interest was the indication of the sources used in each class. In systematics, Willis used the Westminster Confession of Faith, Augustine's *De Gratia*, and Calvin's *Institutes*, the latter two in Latin, together with George Hill's *Lectures in Divinity*. In hermeneutics, he used the two volumes of Thomas Hartwell Horne's *Introduction to the Critical Study and Knowledge of the Holy Scriptures*, originally published in London in 1825 and into its eighth edition by 1858. In evidences, the texts were Joseph Butler's *Analogy*, William Paley's *Evidences*, and compends of Beilby Porteous and Richard Whatley. Young used Charles Hodge's *Commentary on the Ephesians* in his exegetical classes, Thomas Reid's works in mental philosophy, and Francis Wayland's *Elements of Moral Science* in moral philosophy. Willis taught pastoral theology, combining lectures with readings of the Pastoral Epistles and Corinthians in Greek and Richard Baxter's *The Reformed Pastor*.[37] All of the sources listed by the professors confirmed the worldview of confessional orthodoxy, acknowledged the conscience as the internal witness to God's written law and moral authority, and recognized the need to cultivate and properly educate it.[38] Whatever differences and tensions may have existed among the faculty, there was consensus on the foundational principles of the Canada Presbyterian Church's theological system.

The creation of the Canada Presbyterian Church offered the opportunity to regularize the examination of students. In 1861, the

Free Church established a board for the examination of students that continued to function in the united church. It was made up of the college senate and a representative appointed by each presbytery. The board would examine students at the beginning of each session and presbyteries were directed to examine them at the beginning and the end of each session.[39] The system worked smoothly until the late 1860s, when tensions between the examiners and the presbyteries surfaced. The presbyteries of London and Huron presented overtures charging that the board deprived presbyteries "of their long established rights in regard to students in Theology." The Synod insisted that it continue to examine students itself through the board and created a second one to serve the Presbyterian College in Montreal. It clarified who was to examine the students for what purposes. The presbyteries were to ascertain suitability for ministry and the examiners to assign candidates their place in the curriculum.[40]

Financial problems continued to frustrate the Knox's attempts to mount the quality of program desired. The college reported in 1862 that the arrears in stipend owed to the professors alone were over $1700. In 1864, George Paxton Young resigned to accept Egerton Ryerson's offer to become Inspector of Grammar Schools. During his ten years at Knox, Young had experienced first-hand the inadequate preparation with which students came to higher education. His reports were filled with suggestions for improvement in the level of instruction, especially in classical literature and many of them found their way into Ryerson's School Act of 1871.[41] Young remained an ordained Presbyterian minister and continued to be connected closely with theological education. He was offered, but turned down, the principalship at the new college opened in Montreal in 1866, and returned to the Knox faculty in 1868. Robert Burns retired in 1864 after pleading unsuccessfully for help in the teaching of Christian evidences, help he was willing to pay out of his own pocket. Burns continued to offer the classes in church history, however, until his death in 1869.

The departures left the faculty complement at the college where it had been in 1850, with Willis as the only professor.[42] Given the financial situation at the college, the college recommended that only one new professor be appointed. On the floor of Synod, an amendment called for two additional positions, but was defeated by a large majority.[43] The Synod invited presbyteries to submit nominations for its consideration. In 1865, the Synod received two nominations, William Ormiston from the presbyteries of Ottawa and Brockville and William Caven from the presbyteries of Kingston and Toronto. Both were formerly connected with the United Presbyterians and educated in Canadian colleges. Ormiston graduated from Victoria College, Cobourg, taught mental and moral philosophy there in 1848–1849, had a short pastorate at Newtonville, was a professor at the Toronto Normal School and a grammar school inspector from 1849 to 1853, returned to the parish at Second United Presbyterian Church, Toronto, and went to Central Church in Hamilton in 1856.[44] Caven graduated from the United Presbyterian Divinity Hall the year after it moved to Toronto. In 1852, he went to First Church, St. Mary's, where he established a reputation of being "a preacher of first rank."[45] The reasons given by those presbyteries that did not make nominations were significant. Montreal was in the process of establishing their own college, and left the matter to the Synod; Hamilton, Huron, and Grey recommended that the college continue with lecturers; and Paris and Stratford simply thought it inexpedient to make an appointment at the time. In view of these differences of opinion, and no doubt with the financial situation very much in mind, the Synod decided to delay the appointment.

William Caven was elected unanimously to the chair of biblical exegetics in 1866.[46] He understood the ordained minister as, above all, a teacher of evangelical truth. He was not "a teacher of philosophy in the schools – not a governor of a province – not the steward of Caesar's palace," but rather "a steward in 'the house of God, which is the Church of the living God,' and this church is *'the pillar and ground of the truth.'* " The church, Caven argued, was found around the world in congregations of the faithful, "in which the word of God is preached, and the sacraments duly administered, according to Christ's ordinance, in all those things that of necessity are required to the same." Caven expressed sympathy for evangelical union among the various branches of the church, based upon the common profession of "the mediation and atoning death of the incarnate Son of God."

In 1868, a group of ministers and elders, concerned with the preparatory education of students who did not take the full university courses at McGill or University College, raised the money to reappoint George Paxton Young for two years while the Synod decided what to do in connection with the preparatory course. The Synod had decided in 1864 that "the Classes in Knox College shall be exclusively Theological." While eliminating the preparatory course as a formal program in the college, the senate realized that it would still have to make provision for some preliminary studies to supplement the education with which students came to Toronto.[47] These studies were assigned on a case by case basis and conducted by either the regular professors or lecturers from nearby churches, such as John Mark King from St. James Square.[48] The number of students who took these classes was small in the late 1860s, averaging only 8 each year. Most students completed their preparatory studies at University College or McGill. Young agreed to return in 1868 and immediately the number of students enrolled in preparatory classes jumped to 35. As a result, the Synod decided to revive the preparatory department in 1870, and Young accepted the appointment as professor of mental and moral philosophy and superintendent of preparatory training in 1870.[49]

As early as 1856, Young began to question the adequacy of the natural theology of Paley and Reid, with its reliance on analogies in nature as evidence for Christian revelation and reliance on the Baconian method. In the face of what he considered a growing pantheism, another defence of the faith was needed. By the late 1860s, the shape of that defence was beginning to emerge. Reality was orderly and rational, but the key to understanding it was the human mind rather than nature. Human beings enjoyed a freedom unknown in nature and developed true goodness through the "pursuit of knowledge, self-sacrifice for the good of others, and the habitual, constant performance of what a man regards as his duty." Moral reason or conscience guided the use of freedom. The effectiveness with which the religious and educational institutions of a nation developed that conscience determined the righteousness of a nation. These ideas reflected the influence of the idealism of Bishop Berkeley and developed in a similar fashion the those of British Idealist T.H. Green, though Young did not read Green until much later in his life.[50]

Young retained his interest in the reform of the province's grammar schools and the creation of a system of public education that would form the conscience of a Christian nation. He defended the introduction of uniform standards, centralization, and stringent examinations for teachers and inspectors before the Ontario Teachers' Association in 1869. He was elected president of the association in 1871. That same year, he was appointed to the Council of Public Instruction and to its examining committee for teachers and inspectors. A short correspondence with former prime minister Alexander Mackenzie in the 1880s indicated that Young saw his work in secondary education in intimate relation to the calibre of students that would go to university and become the leaders of Canadian society.[51]

One feature of these years that surprises the observer is how little reliance there was on American influences. Several reasons suggest themselves. The social, economic, ecclesiastical, and familial connections of the Canadian Presbyterian community were predominantly Scottish. In addition, there were concerns about American theology. Willis early declared his suspicion of the directions in which American theology seemed to be moving. In his *Discourse on National Establishments* in 1833, he expressed concern over the influence of the New England Theology. "Hopkinsianism," he warned, "a version of the Arminian heresy, as well as gross Arminianism itself, is reigning in some of their large and flourishing churches, and where it is not decidedly reigning, is often favoured by a large minority."[52] Included, in Willis' mind, was the Presbyterian Church in the United States of America, the largest Presbyterian church in the United States.

The Princeton theologians were more trusted on some issues. Young used Charles Hodge's biblical commentaries and Burns recommended Hodge's *Biblical Repertory and Princeton Review*.[53] But there was one issue upon which all American Presbyterian churches were suspect, and that was slavery. Willis and Burns were vocal and active abolitionists. The Buxton Mission in Kent County, serving a community of refugee black slaves and headed by Irish-born William King, attracted considerable interest and support from Knox's faculty and student body. In 1856, the Synod required presbyteries to reject American clergy applying for admission to the Presbyterian Church of Canada if their views on slavery were not abolitionist.[54] It was not until after the Civil War was over and the Caven era begun that American Presbyterian theologians, especially those who taught at Princeton, made a major impact on Knox College.

Willis' final years as principal were not easy. He was at odds with his denomination on the application of the principle of Christ's headship over the nations, an application he was convinced was costing Knox much-needed funding. He did not share his colleagues' enthusiasm for a broader alliance of evangelical churches if it meant compromising Calvinist orthodoxy and Free Church principles. He was often torn between his own need for an adequate stipend and the financial problems of the college. In 1864, for example, a request from Willis for an increase generated considerable debate on the floor of Synod. In the end, he received a $200 increase, but must have accepted it with mixed feelings when the synod decided it could not afford to appoint a second professor. In 1867, Willis again submitted his resignation, in part because of the continuing uncertainties about funding and staffing and in part because, having reached the age of 67, he wished to return to Britain to retire. The Synod pleaded with him to stay and Willis agreed.[55]

He finally retired from the college in 1870, then stayed in Canada for an additional year to serve as Moderator of the Canada Presbyterian Church. In his moderatorial address to the Assembly, he reminded the clergy, many of them his former students, "that your great business lies in the everyday work of proclaiming the gospel of Christ, and as faithful shepherd of the flock feeding his sheep, feeding his lambs. ... watch sedulously and affectionately for souls. ... regard yourselves as guardians of sacred truth, the precious inheritance of Scripture, and an inheritance of pure and Scriptural order which has been transmitted to us. Be faithful unto death ... when the chief Shepherd shall appear ye shall receive a crown of glory that shall not fade away."[56] He settled in London, England, but continued to travel widely and represented Canadian Presbyterians at the first meeting of the Pan-Presbyterian Alliance in 1877. He died while on a preaching tour of Scotland in 1879.[57]

When Willis retired in 1870, the faculty was only slightly stronger than it had been in 1850. There was one full-time professor of theology, assisted by a couple of lecturers, and a full-time professor of preparatory studies. Finances were still a problem. Voluntarism in relation to state funding for religious education had been adopted as the official stance of the Canada Presbyterian Church, leaving the mainstay of college financing the voluntary contributions of congregations. The college worked hard to establish credible structures of accountability and networks of support, but the dream of a balanced budget remained out of reach during the twenty years of Willis' leadership.

CLARIFYING STRUCTURES OF ACCOUNTABILITY

On 24 July 1858, the Act of Incorporation for Knox College was signed into law. All the ministers and members in full communion of the Presbyterian Church of Canada were named as the corporate body named Knox College. Property was held "in trust for the promotion of theological learning and education of youth for the holy ministry, under the authority and according to the principles of the Presbyterian Church of Canada."[58] The Synod was given the power "to declare ... the Theological Doctrines and Principles which shall be taught in the said college, or what are the books and documents in which the said principles and doctrines are contained; and such declaration so made and recorded shall be irrevocable in so far as the said college shall be concerned, and shall be held at all times thereafter to contain the Theological Doctrines and Principles to be taught in the said College."[59] The Synod was given the power to appoint and remove professors and tutors, establish bylaws for the governance of the college, amend the same, and constitute the governing bodies of the college. Two governing bodies were created, both appointed by and accountable to the Synod. The senate was made up of the professors together with five ordained ministers on the roll of the synod and three elders or members in full communion of the church. It was responsible for academic oversight and discipline, with powers to enforce the statutes, rules, and ordinances of the college established from time to time by the Synod. A board of trustees was given the whole management of the financial affairs of the college and its property. In light of the talks with the United Presbyterians, provisions were included for what would happen in the event of union with other branches of the church.[60]

The bylaws were approved by the Synod in 1860. The board of management consisted of 35 persons, all ordained ministers or elders, seven of whom constituted a quorum. The board was appointed by and subject to the direction of the synod. The principal and professors of the college, together with seven members of synod, formed the college senate and were entrusted with "the reception, academical superintendence and discipline of the Students, and all other persons within the said College." The position of principal was created and given "a general superintendence" of the studies of the students, but subject to the direction of the senate. Other professors were responsible "only to the Synod" for the exercise of their duties. All professors and tutors were required to sign the Formula in order to teach at the college. The school term would run from the first Wednesday in October to the first Wednesday in April, and all students had to sign the "Album of the College" and agree to submit to its discipline. The curriculum was to be determined by the Synod.[61]

The act of incorporation, the declaration of doctrine, and the by-laws clearly made the college an agency of the church for educating its clergy and defined the theological doctrines and principles the denomination wanted taught there. The church had powers to clarify the way it understood and applied them, but it was tied closely to their substance as expressive of the great evangelical truths it was called to preserve and propagate. The act represented the culmination of fourteen years of concerted effort on the part of a young and aggressive evangelical denomination to provide for the education of a Canadian clergy. The legal framework established by the act clearly named the ministers and members of the whole church as the body corporate that constituted Knox College and made those responsible for educating the clergy directly accountable to the highest court of the church.

COMPETING CLAIMS FOR SUPPORT

The acquisition and renovation of permanent buildings for the college were the major financial challenges for the college committee in the 1840s and the 1850s, but the raising of funds for the buildings, necessary as they were, did reduce the amounts available for the academic program of the college. For two years after its birth in 1844, the college operated out of the cramped quarters provided by the rented home of Henry Esson. In 1846, it moved to other rented quarters in three adjoining houses on Front Street. By 1854, the college had outgrown these premises and there was a growing sense that escalating costs of real estate in Toronto made a move to buy property for the college imperative. The Synod

formed a building committee in 1854, with John McMurrich as
convener. McMurrich was a prominent Toronto merchant in the
wholesale drygoods business who would continue to serve on the
governing board of Knox until his death in 1883.[62] The building
committee was appointed in the manner that had evolved for the
raising of ordinary funds for the college, with representatives from
each presbytery. Several prominent figures in business, politics, the
professions, and the press, agreed to serve on it, notably Isaac
Buchanan, John Redpath, and George Brown.[63] In 1854, McMurrich wrote to the congregations of the Synod. He reminded his
readers that the decade just finished had been a "season of anxious
exertion in securing the means of grace in many localities." Those
efforts had resulted in 90 settled congregations in the Synod and
the time had come to consider permanent quarters for the college,
"apart from the noise and bustle, constantly accumulating, at the
present location." He expressed confidence that the church would
agree:

that it is only befitting the great enlargement God has given to our Church
in this land, and our great appreciation of the benefits of Sacred Learning,
that the walls of our School of the Prophets should stand forth visible to
observers, a testimony not by gaudy and extravagant appurtenances, yet by
solid – and why not somewhat ornamental architecture – to our Church's
united interest in its rising Ministry, and a pledge of our purpose to provide, as God enables us, for the transmission of the principles we maintain,
and the privileges we enjoy, to an unborn generation.[64]

Elmsley Villa, the residence of Lord Elgin, governor-general of
British North America from 1847 to 1854, was purchased in 1855
for £5250. It occupied an acre of land on College Street, between
Yonge St. and St. Vincent St. (now Bay St.). The session of 1855–
1856 opened in the new buildings. The villa had space for the
classrooms, the library, the museum, and nearly 40 students who
lived in the college while studying. The following year, plans were
developed to expand the facilities to accommodate 70 students.
The purchase price and cost of renovations came to slightly more
that £6500, £1000 of which was paid on purchase. The college
building committee proposed to raise the rest over the next three
years,[65] but only half of the debt had been retired by 1858. However, Alexander Topp, minister of Knox Church, Toronto, and an

active participant in college governance for several years, devised a plan that reduced the debt substantially in 1862.[66]

The new college buildings offered spacious quarters in which a community of pious learning and formation among faculty, students, and interested supporters could develop. In a circular soliciting support for the building fund in 1856, the board pointed out the central place the college had in the growth of the denomination and the kind of life and learning that it was designed to house:

The College will be the home of our Church; and the many pleasing associations which must gather around it, in years to come, will contribute essentially to its prosperity and progress. These are not the times when it could be made a question, whether solid learning is necessary to qualify the Ministers of the Church for their professional duties. We live in an age of stir, of search, of movement. The human mind is whetted by every appliance; – and the combat between truth and error becomes closer every day. Moreover, "the harvest is plenteous," and well trained laborers must be sent forth into the fields, which are ripening to the harvest. Piety, heartfelt, sincere, and active, must be the foundation of all pastoral qualities; but grace does by no means supersede mental qualities and literary attainments. The age of miracles is over; but a wise and gracious Father has provided suitable substitutes, the faithful use of which He has blessed abundantly, from age to age.[67]

The most active student organization remained the Missionary Society. Monthly meetings were held and work supported in summer fields, winter supply, Gaelic worship services, and city missions. During the 1850s and the 1860s, there was a focus on work among French Canadians, reflecting the strong anti-Catholicism of Canadian Presbyterians at the time. By 1869, however, the society had decided to shift its emphasis to English-speaking work in new church development.[68] Though smaller and younger, the Knox's College Total Abstinence Society, founded in 1851, was equally fervent in its work. It sought to inform its members of the issues and arguments related to temperance reform and to contribute to "the benefit of the community at large, by bringing before the public many of the crying sins and appalling evils, which are daily resulting from the use of ardent spirits." The meetings during the term consisted of prayer, mutual encouragement, and papers on the spiritual, moral, and physical benefits of total abstinence. Resolutions in favour of prohibition legislation were passed and forwarded to George Brown for presentation to the legislature.[69] During the summer, members spoke throughout the province and tried to establish similar societies in churches.[70]

New buildings were not the only drain on funding for the academic program at Knox. In 1864, the Synod received an overture from the Presbytery of Montreal seeking to establish a theological college there. The initiative came from William Dawson, Principal of McGill University; John Redpath, sugar baron and leader in education and moral reform movements; William Taylor, secessionist minister in Montreal and a founder of the Evangelical Alliance and the French Canadian Missionary Society; and A.F. Kemp, minister of St. Gabriel Street Church. Over eleven percent of the 40,000 communicant members of the Canada Presbyterian Church lived in the Presbytery of Montreal, and under Dawson's leadership McGill was developing a strong faculty and program. After long debate, during which several participants argued that the creation of a second college was premature, especially in light of the financial difficulties at Knox, the Synod authorized the formation of the college and instructed the Presbytery to obtain a charter, modelled on that granted to Knox College. In 1865, the Presbytery reported to the Synod that the charter had been granted and that 26 students had indicated interest. Nevertheless, those opposed to the immediate opening of the college convinced the Synod to delay and ask the Presbytery to raise an endowment adequate for the support of at least one professor. Financial figures presented that year by Knox indicated the reason for the concern. Givings fell almost $2800 short of the needed $8300. Almost $1000 of the shortfall in apportioned amounts happened in the presbyteries bordering Montreal. By 1867, however, the Montreal promoters had over $20,000 pledged and the Synod approved the opening of the college, though not without a bitter debate over the method of financing and the impact the college would have on the fortunes of Knox. In the end, the new Synod of Montreal, composed of the presbyteries of Brockville, Ottawa, Kingston, and Montreal, was given the responsibility for supporting the new college.[71]

In 1864, the Synod approved a plan by which the Knox College Board was allowed to allocate amounts expected from the presbyteries and instructed the presbyteries to circulate a similar statement of allocations to each congregation within their bounds.[72] After the first year of operation, the Board observed that the recession in the country was affecting its ability to raise money and that several presbyteries were spending most of their resources to support missions within their bounds. Other factors, however, were contributing to the shortfalls, not least of which was the growing support for the college in Montreal. The presbyteries that would eventually join together in the Synod of Montreal and be designated to support the Montreal college raised only $1021 in 1864–1865, less than 50% of its allocation. The other presbyteries together contributed 66% of their allocations. Toronto was the only one that oversubscribed and Hamilton reached 87% of its target. "Congregation after congregation," the Knox Board complained, were "found returning the same sums as the previous years, or considerably smaller ones, while a very large number, amounting to a *fourth* of the whole, have made no contributions at all."[73] The general pattern that emerged by 1870, then, was one of strong support in the urban Ontario presbyteries, moderate support in the rural ones, and a shift of support in those in the Synod of Montreal to the Presbyterian College.

The college had little success in developing other sources of income. The boarding house operation supported itself, but contributed nothing to the educational operations. Willis found virtually no support for his desire to secure a portion of the province's endowment for education for Knox and the other denominational colleges. The possibility of establishing an endowment fund for the college seemed to hold the most promise. In 1866, a committee was appointed to consider the practicality of seeking an endowment and to develop a plan if they found it expedient. Convened by William Gregg, it included Alexander Topp, John Mark King, and John Laing of Toronto, William Ormiston and David Inglis of Hamilton, William MacLaren and Thomas Wardrop of Ottawa, and Donald H. MacVicar and William Taylor of Montreal, all ministers of the largest congregations in the largest urban centres in the church. Among the prominent laymen appointed was John McMurrich. The committee reported to the next synod that an endowment campaign would fail in the present circumstances.[74] In 1869, although still not convinced that the times were propitious for an endowment campaign, the board did say it needed at least $120,000. In 1870, interest was reported in the Toronto area to endow a chair in memory of Robert Burns, who had died the year before, but no concrete steps were taken.[75]

By 1870, Knox College had established itself as a key agency in the Presbyterian division of the church militant. The denomination experienced substantial growth, reflected in the corps of clergy needed to serve the expanding number of congregations and mission stations. In 1850, there were 65 ministers in the Free Church. In 1860, just prior to the union that created the Canada Presbyterian Church, that number had grown to 150. In 1870, just as new union talks began with other Presbyterian bodies in the new Dominion of Canada, the Canada Presbyterian Church fielded 292 clergy. Over half of them had graduated from Knox College. Membership in the church grew from 30,000 to over 50,000 through this period and contributions for all purposes went from just under $200,000 to over $500,000. In spite of the rhetoric of support for Knox that appeared in all the public documents of the denomination, not enough of those contributions were going to the college in 1870. In the years to follow, Knox College would receive an increased share of the prosperity of its constituency in the form of larger contributions, substantial endowments, and yet another new building. The denomination had accepted its place within the plurality of religious options that existed in the province, though it had lost none of its confidence that the confessional orthodoxy that shaped its culture was the truest interpretation of God's revelation in the scriptures. Just how that worldview was to be defended and propagated would pose the most pressing challenge for the next generation of faculty and college supporters.

3 Broadening Perspectives, 1870–1890

Robert Campbell had grandiose visions for Presbyterianism in Canada. He expressed them in an essay that won a contest sponsored by a group of Montreal businessmen who were promoting further Presbyterian union in the Quebec and Ontario at the time of Confederation. Campbell suggested that all the branches of Presbyterianism in the new Dominion of Canada be invited to consider union, since a larger church would be better equipped to meet the mission needs of the new country and broader opportunities would attract better men to the ministry.[1] Several of those who supported union also supported the confederation movement among the colonies in British North America, and their vision of a nation stretching from sea to sea included the presence of an aggressive Presbyterianism in the intellectual, moral, and social life of the new dominion. The union, which formed the Presbyterian Church in Canada, took place on 15 June 1875.[2]

The group of Free Church businessmen in Montreal who sponsored the essay contest, led by sugar magnate John Redpath, and a similar group in Toronto, led by *Globe* editor George Brown, were the driving force behind the union. They argued that differences of doctrine and practices and old animosities were softening as Canada turned its attention to the practical necessities of nation-building. They believed that interdenominational cooperation in moral and social reform movements had prepared the way for a broader union of Presbyterians. Laity in the Church of Scotland agreed, recognizing that their branch of Presbyterianism was slowly dying in Canada. Maritime support for the vision grew rapidly, fueled by a growing concern with a shortage of clergy. The number and types of colleges to be kept by the new church sparked heated debate, but the resolution of the controversy was left to the post-union church. While union negotiations were going on during the early 1870s, issues of doctrine did not create much of a stir. Only two hours was needed to reach agreement on doctrine at the first meetings in 1870 and the same spririt of forebearance led to a quick acceptance of the doctrinal basis of union and its supporting explanatory resolutions. As in 1861, liberty of conscience was granted on the matter of church-state relations.[3] The desire for reconciliation and tolerance was not shared, however, by all within the new church. Three months following the consummation of union the new denomination had its first heresy trial.

D.J. Macdonnell was the minister of St. Andrew's Presbyterian Church, the only Church of Scotland congregation in Toronto, and Robert Campbell's brother-in-law. In a sermon at St. Andrew's and in remarks at the opening of Knox College, to whose board he had just been appointed, Macdonnell raised questions concerning the consistency of the Westminster Confession's statements on eternal punishment with the testimony of Scripture. The Westminster Confession of Faith, he said, should be kept subordinate to the Word of God and not considered infallible. In the sermon in question, Macdonnell analyzed the various theories of sin and death, dismissed the Pelagian and Arminian interpretations, and concluded that the combination of Augustinian and Federal views found in the Westminster Confession seemed most reasonable. However, he claimed that all these views were "human interpretations of the Divine record" and not "Gospel truth." He noted that Romans 5 seemed to teach universal salvation and wondered whether a loving God could "look complacently upon not only the misery but the sin of the lost" for all eternity.[4] In the minds of some of Macdonnell's new colleagues in the Presbytery of Toronto, this attitude to the confession confirmed their worst fears about the doctrinal soundness of the Church of Scotland. Eleven members of the Presbytery, all formerly of the Canada Presbyterian Church, challenged Macdonnell's position.

The resulting heresy proceedings were a test of the strength of the confessional orthodoxy of the Canada Presbyterian Church in the new united church.[5] At the General Assembly in 1877, with William Caven playing a central role, Macdonnell signed a compromise statement that was accepted unanimously by the commissioners. He acknowledged that he subscribed to the teachings of the Westminster Confession of Faith on the "endless duration of the future punishment of the wicked," but was allowed to state that there were still doubts and difficulties that perplexed his mind.[6] The case revealed Presbyterians in Canada struggling to find the appropriate ways of maintaining their orthodoxy in an age of expansion, both in the church's engagement in mission at home and abroad and in its understanding of the faith. In the end, the standards were affirmed as traditionally understood, but the right of conscience to struggle with their inconsistencies was also upheld. It indicated that tolerance within the denomination was growing, though the Free Church majority were not yet willing to allow it to change the public stance of the church.[7]

Macdonnell himself would continue to press for the recognition that the confession was subordinate to Scripture and for the adoption of a briefer statement of the evangelical truths held essential by the church.[8] In 1878, the year after Macdonnell's statement, changes were made to the formula signed at the ordination and induction of ministers that acknowledged that Scripture takes precedence over the confession in interpreting the faith. Scripture alone was "infallible" as a rule of faith and life and candidates were no longer required to declare the confession as their "own faith."[9] This stance would be crucial in the long struggle just beginning to broaden perspectives in the Presbyterian Church in Canada.

The Macdonnell trial showed the growing tension between the older confessional approach to the Reformed tradition, according to which piety was formed within a comprehensive system of propositions that centred on divine justice and control as revealed in the scriptures, and a newer progressive approach that focused on the more relational dimensions of piety, based upon the attributes of divine life, light, and love found in the scriptures. Knox College, as the largest of the six theological colleges that came into the Presbyterian union and the *alma mater* of the majority of the ministers in the new church, played a central role in these debates. Its faculty personified the contending approaches and its student body entered into the struggle with surprising enthusiasm and effectiveness.

CONTENDING FOR THE FAITH

In his moderatorial sermon in 1885, William MacLaren, convener of the Foreign Missions Committee as well as professor of systematic theology at Knox, reminded the church of the importance of the great commission in Matthew for the expansion of both home and foreign missions:

A commission that is to turn the world upside down must need rest on a firm foundation. Christ himself is that foundation – the King and Head of the Church, and invested with all authority in heaven and on earth. By virtue of his mediatorial work, it is His prerogative to reign, and unto Him shall every knee bow and every tongue confess that He is Lord to the glory of God the Father. ... If we are asked for proof of the Divine presence and guidance in His Church, we have but to lift our eyes and look around. The success of missions to the heathen cannot be gainsaid. National power everywhere has passed into the hands of Christian rulers. The world is open for the reception of the gospel and we seem to be standing on the very threshold of its evangelization.[10]

The leadership for the campaign to evangelize the world would come from the theological colleges of the church. Presbyterians in Canada came to see themselves in the vanguard of evangelization in the last quarter of the nineteenth century. Throughout the 1870s, the faculty remained convinced that the most effective interpretation of the faith was found in the central tenets of confessional orthodoxy. During the 1880s, however, pressure built, especially from a more widely-travelled and better-read alumni, to accept a more progressive interpretation of the central truths of evangelical Protestantism at the college.

When George Paxton Young moved to teach philosophy at University College in 1871, William Caven was left as the only permanent professor at Knox. J.J.A. Proudfoot, minister at First Presbyterian Church in London, continued to lecture in homiletics and pastoral theology as he had since 1867, but was only at the college for one term each session. Caven had been appointed chair of the senate when Willis retired and became principal in 1873. The Assembly of 1871 received several nominations to replace Willis as professor of theology. A.A. Hodge, son of Princeton theologian Charles Hodge and then professor of systematic theology at Western Theological Seminary in Allegheny, Pennsylvania, received three, but the majority were for William Gregg of Cooke's Presbyterian Church, Toronto, and David Inglis of MacNab Presbyterian Church, Hamilton. Inglis was appointed by a vote of 58 to 50, but remained at Knox for only one year, accepting a call to a Dutch Reformed congregation in Brooklyn, New York. When the General Assembly of 1873 considered who should replace Inglis, they chose William MacLaren, then minister of Knox Church, Ottawa, the first Knox graduate to hold a chair in the college.[11] After losing the close vote for the chair of systematics to Inglis in 1871, Gregg was elected unanimously to the newly-created chair of apologetics in 1872.[12] Gregg was born in county Donegal in Ireland, studied with Thomas Chalmers in Edinburgh, and came to Canada in 1847. He ministered in Belleville before going to Cooke's. Caven, Gregg, MacLaren, and Proudfoot were the faculty of Knox when it took its place among the six colleges of the new Presbyterian Church in Canada in 1875. MacLaren and Gregg were staunch defenders of confessional orthodoxy, while Caven was cautiously open to a different approach.

William MacLaren outlined his views on the role of the clergy at the close of the college session in 1883. They were "to seek and save the lost, and then to train the saved for Christ" through the "faithful presentation of God's truth." The clergy had the primary responsibility for preserving "the central truths which cluster around the cross." To accomplish this, the clergy needed to maintain a wide reading in literature, science, and history, but above all, they needed "to study human nature, and the truth in its relation to the wants of the human soul." In everything, the clergy depended on the presence and power of the Holy Spirit. He concluded:

I almost envy you the privilege of dealing directly with the souls of men, and bringing to them God's way of life. I do not undervalue the work to which I and the other members of the Faculty have been called in training those who are to preach Christ to others, but it deprives us largely of the opportunity of dealing directly with living souls. We must preach through you and others. We will follow you with our sympathies and our prayers, and in your success will see our own. And whether you labour in the well-tilled fields of the older provinces, or sow and reap in the virgin soil of the North-West, or reap in those fields already white to harvest in India, China and Japan, when you return in the Great Day bearing your sheaves with you, we will rejoice in your joy, and in some measure share in your reward.[13]

MacLaren was very clear about the tendencies within the church that he feared would undermine its mission.

The greatest threat came from the New Theology being propounded in New England by Theodore Munger and Newman Smyth through the *Andover Review.*[14] MacLaren found the sources of their thought in Thomas Erskine, John McLeod Campbell, Frederick Denison Maurice, Frederick W. Robertson, and Horace Bushnell. He was particularly concerned with their attitude to the atonement, the inspiration of scripture, and the question of future probation.[15] In essence, he accused them of denying the supernatural dimension of Christianity. "If Christianity is anything," MacLaren wrote, "it is not merely a supernatural revelation from God, but a supernatural revelation that a supernatural work has been accomplished by a supernatural person for man's salvation, and is applied by a supernatural agency to the human heart."[16]

Equally threatening to MacLaren was the rejection by Munger and Smyth of the traditional method for constructing systems of doctrine. The proper method, explained MacLaren, was, "to apply the inductive method to the study of Scripture. ... The method followed is that pursued with success in modern times by the students of physical science. The scientist goes to nature and gathers his facts from it, and Protestants, at least, have been accustomed to hold that the divine should not excogitate a system out of his own mind, but go to the Word of God to learn the system which is there revealed."[17] The best exposition of the faith reached by this method was that of A.A. Hodge in his *Outlines of Theology,* originally published in 1860, revised in 1878, and used by MacLaren as his basic text in theology throughout his career.

MacLaren called Hodge's book "a singularly clear and able exposition of the system of revealed truth." Its system of theology was "in substance that of the Creeds and Confessions of the Reformed Churches. He would have been the first to disclaim originality for the system which he taught. It was, however, no servile acceptance of the ideas of others. He had grappled with the great problems raised by divine revelation, examined them anew in the light of Scripture, philosophy and human experience, and the results were none the less his own that they coincided with the conclusions of great and good men, who had gone before and lit up the way for him."[18] Hodge's Calvinism, MacLaren was convinced, was especially suited "to commend itself to earnest, thoughtful men who desire to grapple intelligently with the great questions raised by religion" and "wherever it has been generally embraced, it has tended to stimulate so powerfully the mental energies, and to develop the moral fibre of the community."[19]

William Gregg shared MacLaren's conservatism on these matters. Thomas Chalmers shaped Gregg's approach to theology and the education of the church's clergy more than any other influence. At the opening of the college session in 1892, he recalled the impression Chalmers had made on him. His sermons and lectures set forth "with great plainness and power, the doctrines of ruin by the fall, redemption by the blood of Christ, and regeneration and sanctification by the Holy Spirit, and the other fundamental doctrines of Christianity" by which "sinners were converted and saints edified." They sought "to bring home to the hearts and consciences of men the conviction of their sinfulness and exposure to the wrath of God, and then to unfold to them the fullness and the freeness of the great salvation." Preachers were called to plead with sinners to give immediate attention "to their spiritual and eternal interests" and the teachers of preachers should be men of piety and faith as well as of ability and learning.[20]

In 1873, Gregg assumed responsibility for the teaching of church history as well as apologetics. Gregg spelled out his views on Presbyterianism in the introduction to his *History of the Presbyterian Church in the Dominion of Canada*, published in 1885. The central doctrines accepted by all Presbyterians, according to Gregg, were: the trinity; the incarnation; the atonement and intercession of Christ as the one mediator between God and humanity; the original guilt and depravity of humanity; regeneration "not by water baptism, but by the gracious agency of the Holy Spirit;" justification, "not on the ground of personal obedience to the law of God, but on account of the righteousness of Christ which is received by faith;" and sanctification as "a work of God's free grace" by which the whole self was renewed in the image of God and "enabled more and more to die unto sin and live unto righteousness."

These doctrines of grace had their roots in the Augustinian and Calvinistic traditions and were "fully exhibited" in the Westminster Confession and Catechisms. The "tendency and effect" of maintaining these doctrines of grace was "to bring glory to God, and to produce, in the greatest measure, the fruits of humility, reverence, gratitude, love, and holy obedience; and, in justification of this belief, [Presbyterians] point to the fact that, in their own and other churches, those were the purest and best times in which these doctrines were most faithfully upheld." Doctrinal and moral faithfulness was not sufficient to accomplish the mission God had given the church. Scripture also provided the rule for worship and church government. Gregg acknowledged that there were differences of opinion and practice among Canadian Presbyterians on "matters of subordinate importance" but insisted that there was substantial agreement on "the great leading principles."[21]

William Caven believed that the clergy were interpreters of Scripture, theologians, and apologists. As interpreters, the clergy were called "to explain the oracles of God, and to exhibit, as far as possible, the full meaning and contexts of these inspired compositions." As theologians, they were public teachers with the responsibility to know "how best to arrange [their] thoughts and set them forth, in order to instruct and edify, to convince and persuade." As apologists, they had to conserve Christian truth in an age when it was being "vehemently assailed": "We must have men who can do for us what was done by the great Apologists of the past for the generations to which they belonged. But not this only, – not only do we seek from God men who shall stand and do battle as they did: the evil has become so wide-spread that hardly can we regard any Christian minister as well prepared to hold his position, unless he has made himself acquainted with the principal phases of antichristian thought, and with the true methods by which it may be combated."[22] The apologetic task drew its material from all of the theological disciplines and attempted to integrate them into a persuasive message that would touch both the heart and the mind.

In preparing people for this kind of ministry, Caven knew that the college could not avoid the pressing questions of the age concerning the structure and characteristics of the bible, the authority of the scriptures, and the doctrinal issues of God and humanity, sin and salvation, and life and death. "Something far higher than the gratification of scholarly tastes or philosophical curiosity," Caven wrote, "presses us forward in the study of these things. Our aim is intensely practical. We are seeking for life; we are seeking to know God."[23]

Caven's trust in the reliability of the Scriptures' testimony to the central facts and purpose of God's economy of salvation was firm. The Bible was written, he believed, by people who "were moved by the Holy Ghost" to provide knowledge of things that the most rigorous examination of nature or history will not reveal. It was written to show "that it is God who saves and that salvation comes through the knowledge of Him." The Scriptures revealed that the "entire method and process of human salvation" was the activity of the triune God. This truth was evident in specific statements in the Bible, in "its general tenor," and in the effects the Bible produced "wherever embraced by a genuine faith."[24]

If the mind of the church, as determined through the prayerful deliberations of its courts, could be convinced that Scripture taught something at variance with her subordinate standards, Caven argued as early as 1873, the standards should be revised. "All our Creeds," he wrote, "and all our teachings are amenable to Scripture:"

It is, therefore, a perfectly reasonable thing that the Church should be asked to shew that, in constructing her Confessions, she has rightly understood the Word of God, and neither gone beyond nor fallen short of its statements. The Church may not claim infallibility in the interpretation of Scripture, and meet with her anathema every one who questions her exegesis. Nay, apart from any challenge given, it may be right and proper that the Church's Formularies should, at times, be carefully revised, so as to have them not only in harmony with Scripture, but to secure that their presentation of the truth shall be well suited to the peculiar necessities of the period.[25]

In the debates on progress in theology and credal revision, Caven counselled caution.[26] He insisted that Presbyterians should never "waver in our attachment to the Doctrines of Grace, and in our love of those great Evangelical Principles which our Church has been so much honoured to uphold and propagate." He warned the church, however, against a conservatism that became obstructive and prevented the kind of progress in Biblical interpretation and theology that clarified and improved the church's understanding and presentation of God's revelation in the Scriptures.[27]

J.J.A. Proudfoot did not take an active part in these debates. He normally spent the fall term in Toronto teaching homiletics, church government, and pastoral theology, with homiletics commanding by far the majority of the time. Sacred rhetoric, as Proudfoot referred to his discipline, appealed to all the human faculties and must understand them all. "Rhetoric," he wrote, "does not furnish the facts nor the arguments, but it tells you that you must have them and it teaches how to arrange them for effect, when you have found them."[28]

The purpose of rhetoric was persuasion. It appealed to the intellect, the emotions, and the will in that particular order. The preacher had to satisfy the intellect before seeking to excite the emotions and the emotions had to be excited before the will could be influenced. This was a natural progression in human action that culminated in practical results. The master rhetoricians in Proudfoot's mind were George Campbell and Hugh Blair, both prominent preachers and educators in the Moderate party in the Church of Scotland during the latter part of the eighteenth century. They sought to follow a middle way between the dogmatism and emotionalism of the evangelicals and the rationalism of the deists. The Scottish rhetorical tradition of Campbell and Blair also emphasized the importance of an exemplary life for effective communication. Since persuasion depended largely on the attitude of the listener to the speaker, sincerity and moral integrity were essential characteristics for the preacher.[29]

By 1890, the ecclesiastical climate surrounding the college had begun to change. Knox graduates in unprecedented numbers spent a year or two pursuing further studies in Scotland and Germany. They returned convinced that the sane and cautious steps taken by Presbyterians in Scotland and England towards a revision of the creed and a more progressive orthodoxy that reinterpreted the great evangelical doctrines in modern modes of thought deserved a more prominent place in the Presbyterian Church in Canada and its largest college.[30] These advocates of change did not yet constitute a majority in the church, but they did wield considerable influence at the college, not least through the *Knox College Monthly*, the journal established by the students, who were later joined in sponsorship by the alumni association, in 1883.

STUDENT PRESSURE FOR A PROGRESSIVE ORTHODOXY

In the first issue of the *Knox College Monthly*, Malcolm McGregor, minister in Tillsonburg and member of the graduating class of 1881, praised the faculty without reservation: "He is certainly an ungrateful man who can think with anything but the feeling of deepest gratitude for the earnest, scholarly and lucid expositions of the various branches of religious truth to which we listened from the professors whom we learned not only to respect as scholars but to love as men. What an anxiety was manifested by these faithful servants of God that we should go out into the world with clear and decided views, giving no uncertain sound on the great cardinal doctrines of our holy religion."[31] At the opposite end of the spectrum of student opinion was C.W. Gordon, minister of St. Stephen's in Winnipeg, best-selling novelist under the pen name of Ralph Connor, and a graduate of 1887. As he looked back on his days at Knox, he recalled, "The trouble with many of our theological seminaries is that they shut out a man from contact with real life, and shut him up with professors who know mighty little about it, with the result that when they are through with their preparations these young preachers wouldn't recognize a "social problem" if they saw it walking straight at them. That was the trouble with men when I got out of university."[32] Both McGregor and Gordon would become aggressive advocates of a more progressive orthodoxy at Knox College and in the church as a whole. Their differences in perception of Knox had more to do with the content of the curriculum than their theological perspectives.

The Presbyterian Church in Canada sought to create a uniform system of recruitment, preparation, and examination for ministry soon after its formation in 1875. Under the leadership of William Caven, a report was presented and approved by the General Assembly in 1879. The first thing the report did was remind parents to encourage their children who "seemed marked out by the Head of the Church as proper persons to receive training for this office." It then dealt with the responsibilities of sessions and presbyteries to recruit, examine, and supervise candidates. It was recommended, though not required, that students take an arts degree at an approved university prior to entering theological studies. If a degree was not earned, a three-year prescribed course with appropriate examinations was required, unless special permission for an alternative course was granted by the General Assembly. Greek and Hebrew were required prior to entering theology. The course in theology extended over three sessions of six months each and had to include apologetics, systematic theology, exegetics, biblical criticism, church history, homiletics, and pastoral theology. Biblical and church history, systematics, and exegetics were to be studied in all three sessions, apologetics in at least two, and biblical criticism, homiletics, and pastoral theology in at least one. The colleges were required to report to the General Assembly annually.[33]

In a further effort to improve the standard of education for ministers in an age of improved higher education, Knox sought and received the power to grant degrees in divinity in 1881. The board was confident that the move would raise the standard of theological education. The regulations approved for the Bachelor of Divinity degree stated that only those with an arts degree from an approved university were eligible in the future, though former graduates of the Knox literary and theological courses and students currently in the program would be accepted.[34] Included in the extensive required reading lists for the degree were the manuals on practical theology by W.G.T. Shedd of Union Seminary, New York, and J.J. Van Oosterzee of the theological faculty at the University of Utrecht. The purpose of the whole degree, expressed well in the preface to Shedd's book, was "to promote, what is now the great need of the Church, a masculine and vigorous Rhetoric, wedded with an earnest and active Pastoral zeal."[35] At the same time, it was designed to help the ministry recover some of the distinction, power, and influence that Van Oosterzee claimed it had lost. The office had gained much in freedom during the nineteenth century, he acknowledged, but the challenge facing ministers was the proper use of that freedom: "If we are now passing through an essentially critical period in every domain of life, not a little as regards the immediate future will depend upon the question whether ministers of the Gospel show themselves to understand the signs of the times and to be acquainted with the demands of the times. More than ever is it necessary to cultivate no mere churchliness, but true devotion, and to travel in the evangelical-apostolic highway, to the avoiding on the one hand of all narrow by-paths, and on the other of all Modernistic abysmal depths."[36] A broad and thorough preparation of body, mind, and spirit was deemed necessary by the college authorities to meet the demands of the office in the late nineteenth century. Malcolm McGregor appreciated the sincere piety and intellectual depth of the faculty at Knox, while C.W. Gordon was frustrated that their application of the truths of the Gospel was not more progressive in its vision of social reform. He was not alone in his dissatisfaction, as the growing debate over belief and practice showed.

An important forum for that debate was the *Knox College Monthly*, which played a significant role in the affairs of the college, especially under the editorship of James A. Macdonald between 1885 and 1891. The *Monthly* began in 1882 under the editorship of James Ballantyne, who would return to the college as one of the new progressive generation of faculty in 1896. He promised to discuss questions affecting the welfare of the college and the interests of theological education, especially in the context of contemporary challenge to the church to prove the fundamental truths of Christianity and the pressing need for missionary expansion in the Canadian situation.[37] The journal earned the praise of such international scholars and educators as Francis L. Patton of Princeton, J. Munro Gibson and Donald Fraser of London, and William Rainy Harper, then of Yale.[38] Not only did it give the faculty a vehicle for disseminating their views on Presbyterianism, but it invited discussion and critiques of their positions. Under Macdonald, the *Monthly* built up a large readership across the country. The articles, for the most part, dealt with theology, missions, and the practice of ministry, reflecting the two reasons identified in 1885 by the editors for the church founding the college. The first was "that the college shall be a training school for future ministers," and the second was "that those who are appointed to the professorships shall be so posted in the scientific details of theology that they can refute errors which may menace the great convictions of the church."[39] The debates the *Monthly* sparked not only raised but also broadcast questions about whether the confessional orthodox consensus that held sway in 1870 was an adequate apologetic for the church in the 1880s.[40] For an increasing number of Canadian Presbyterians, the answer was no. They did not question the importance of the orthodox evangelical truths, but no longer thought that the confessional framework for interpreting and presenting them was effective.

What really lay at the core of the complaints of C.W. Gordon and many of his generation was exposure to the different kind of apologetic they encountered in Scotland in the late 1880s. Whether they came to know it first-hand in lectures or through the writings of its proponents, they found a new attitude that was more prevalent in Scotland than in Canada and promised to provide a more convincing defence of the faith in the intellectual and social context of late-nineteenth century Canada. It was, in A.C. Cheyne's words, a "less strait-jacketed, less censorious, more broadminded way of life."[41] The pages of the *Monthly* chronicled the dissemination of these views within the Canadian church in articles and reviews. James A. Macdonald also served as college librarian throughout his time as editor of the *Monthly*, and ensured that books and periodicals that espoused a more progressive orthodoxy were featured prominently on the shelves and in the reading room.

In the first issue of the *Monthly* for which Macdonald was responsible, he noted that a new professorial position was being considered and stated that the students "would like to see a young, vigorous, intellectual man appointed to this office, yet they certainly would desire a man in whom they as well as the whole Church would place unbounded confidence."[42] By January of 1886, several presbyteries had responded to the college's inquiries concerning an additional professor and a majority recommended a continuation of the lectureships. They argued that the finances of the college did not permit the change, that any new appointments should be postponed until the question of college union was resolved, and that the interests of the students were best served by the lectureship system. Macdonald himself had advocated more lecturers at the college, specifically experienced ministers with proven track records in generating missionary enthusiasm among their people or in organizing a bible class or Sunday school.[43] He was adamant, however, that "the great essential subjects in a theological curriculum" be in the hands of full-time professors who would give them "undivided and life-long attention." With over 50 students in the theological course, he felt that the college needed at least four full-time professors.[44]

Macdonald's five-month sabbatical in Scotland in the fall of 1888 confirmed his growing respect for the new apologetic that he found in the writings of the Free Church progressives and convinced him that someone holding these views was needed at Knox.[45] The first clear statement of his position appeared in a review notice of George Adam Smith's commentary on Isaiah in May 1889. S.H. Kellogg, minister at St. James Square Church in Toronto, where Caven and many of the students attended, dismissed the volume as "not only somewhat crude but decidedly heretical." Macdonald pointed out the praise Smith's book had received from leading British scholars like A.B. Davidson, Marcus Dods, W.G. Elmslie, and Robertson Nicol. He thought that "the hope of the

Free Church is in her so-called heresy": "Certain it is, that among those who are whispered about and suspected and called heretics are many of the most earnest and devoted Christian workers and the most noble and simple Christian characters; while some of the tremorless bulwarks of orthodoxy are dead up to the neck and their souls are as dry as dewless Gilboa."[46] Those whispered about, besides Smith, included A.B. Davidson, A.B. Bruce, Marcus Dods, James Stalker, and Henry Drummond. Macdonald was convinced that men such as these were the church's only true defence against "the Goliaths of German unbelief." They entered the field of theological battle and knew "how to sling "smooth stones." The result is that theological speculation is being wisely directed, and not only will the intellectual life of the students be quickened, but their faith will be strengthened and their spiritual life deepened."[47] The new apologetic, in both its academic and popular forms, was less dogmatic and more practical than the old. It deserved the designation it received from its contemporaries as the "Back-to-Christ" movement. Its driving concern was to proclaim the love of God and foster belief in Jesus Christ, using the teaching, person, and work of Christ as the criteria for revising the confessional formulations and the ecclesial practices of the churches.[48]

Macdonald likened the new apologetic to the evangelicalism that had guided the Free Church at the time of the Disruption. The successors of the founders of the Free Church, Macdonald claimed in 1890,

are not the men who, parrot-like, repeat their words, or imitate their tone and gesture. Their true successors are those who desire to know Truth at first hand, to stand loyal to Duty against all odds, to face present-day problems in present-day light, and above all, to know, be faithful to, and serve their Master Christ. That oneness of spirit makes Dods and Davidson and Bruce and Stalker and Smith and Drummond and Martin and an ever increasing number of kindred souls in the Free Church, the true spiritual children of Chalmers, Cunningham and Candlish, Guthrie, McCheyne and the Bonars. Craven-minded criers after Use and Wont may be children after the flesh, but the true seed are they who breathe the same free spirit and stand fast in the liberty wherewith Christ makes His people free.[49]

Macdonald's linking of the Free Church founders and the new apologists may have been too strained to qualify as careful historical analysis, but it was effective as sacred rhetoric designed to win the new views a hearing in the Canadian church. The focus on knowing Christ, being loyal in the face of strong challenges, and confronting the moral and social problems that faced the community was consistent with the spirit of the founding generation of the Free Church in both Scotland and Canada.[50] Impelled by that spirit, Macdonald and his growing body of supporters felt they had been given the teacher they had been seeking when Robert Yuile Thomson was appointed to the chair of Apologetics and Old Testament at Knox in 1890 .

The debates in the *Monthly* were not confined to theological perspectives and revealed much about other issues that concerned the college community during the 1880s. Teaching methods, the appropriateness of evaluations, the length of the term, the content of the curriculum, and the suitability of the preparatory course, all attracted attention. Running throughout these discussions was the question whether the college was primarily a centre for theological scholarship and research, similar to the emerging university, or primarily a professional school for pastors and preachers. The consensus of students and alumni was expressed by J.C. Smith in 1886: "A college established and equipped by the church, while it may be a school for expert specialists, ought to be above all, a training school for impressive ministers who can feel the truths, who know the times in which they live, who are abreast of the social agitations and who can sympathize with and guide popular movements."[51] Discussion and debate centred on the methods of education and the preparartory course.

There was general satisfaction with the four-fold curriculum of biblical studies, theology, church history, and practical theology, though the *Monthly* advocated more professors to allow a separation of Caven's responsibilities into chairs of Old and New Testaments, a similar move with Gregg's areas of apologetics and church history, and a full-time position in practical theology. The method of teaching these subjects, however, was much criticized. "The complaint," wrote Robert Haddow in 1889, "is that four hours of steady work, much of the time bending over a table, writing rapidly from dictation, and generally in a class-room well filled and imperfectly ventilated, is so exhausting as to make the last lecture poorly appreciated and to leave little energy for further study during the day."[52] Not only was the lecture system at the college bad pedagogy, another writer claimed, but it also produced "physical wrecks," turning out one or more candidates a year for the sanitoriums at Dansville and Clifton Springs.[53]

Another complaint was about the number of examinations. Not only was there a full set at the college, but many of them seemed to be repeated by the presbytery. The system of presbytery examinations, claimed an editorial in 1885, dated from before the time the colleges were established and was no longer necessary.[54] Queen's students, Macdonald reported in 1889, had entered "a righteous war" with the Presbytery of Kingston. "If a few presbytery examiners are slain," he wrote, "we will contribute to the building of their sepulchres." Toronto students had little cause for complaint, he noted. Normally the university and college diplomas were respected, though "occasionally a man with a hobby worries a candidate."[55]

A major tension between the church and the school was over the number of Sundays students might be available for conducting worship services, but it took a different form in the 1880s than it had earlier. The question was no longer how many Sundays during the term students could preach, but how long they would be available to stay on the mission field, especially in western Canada and northern Ontario. The Home Missions Committee tried to have the college open on 1 November each year to accommodate the needs of the mission field. Macdonald urged the strongest possible opposition, claiming that "the student has certain rights, the college has certain rights, and the claims of theological education are particularly strong just now." The interests of theological education, in his opinion, had been "too often subordinated to the necessities of practical work."[56] The Home Missions proposal, wrote R.D. Fraser of Bowmanville, later to be the editor of Presbyterian Sunday school publications in Canada, would seriously impair the standard of theological education at a time when a "thoroughly educated" ministry was essential. "The pulpit in Canada," he continued, "addresses a public of high general intelligence. The half-educated minister is discounted at sight. ... The Church will be held to a firm anchorage not less by sound learning than by fervent spirituality."[57] Both Macdonald and Fraser advocated the lengthening rather than the shortening of the college, adding April onto the spring term, since it was impossible to reach many of the mission fields during that month.[58]

The most persistent issue during the last half of the 1880s, and one that was not resolved until the end of the 1890s, was the advisability of continuing the preparatory or literary course at Knox as an alternative to the full university course. J.F. McCurdy, professor and head of the department of Oriental languages at University College, was one of the most insistent advocates of its abolition. He saw its continuance lowering the standard of scholarship at the college, "which is none too high, and which the Professors and Senate would gladly see perpetually rising with the advance of science and research in Biblical as well as secular fields." To do this, however, the college needed to free up the resources devoted to the preparatory course and insist that its students take a full university program to gain admission to theological studies.

McCurdy made his own views on the qualifications necessary for the ministry clear:

The Church needs, as she had never needed before, trained thinkers and scholars in the ranks of her leaders, just as the teaching and guiding of the people is becoming a more complex and difficult affair with the wider diffusion of education and of the spirit of inquiry. Especially does the teacher of God's Word in these days need to be a trained *exegete*. The study of the Bible should occupy a least half of the student's busy hours, as the basis of that broader and deeper study which is to be the task of his life.[59]

The continuance of the course was defended by John Laing, minister of Knox Presbyterian Church, Dundas, and a graduate of Knox in 1853. "The seal of Divine acceptance," he argued, "has been too manifestly set on the labors of devoted, though comparatively illiterate, men of God in all the churches" to allow the lack of a BA to prevent those with "natural gifts and graces" to be prevented from studying for the ministry.[60] The specifics of the debate were different, but the question was the same as that which had divided Burns and Esson during Laing's days as a student at Knox. What was the nature of the pious learning needed by clergy in the Presbyterian Church in Canada? What was the relative weight to be given piety and learning in their formation, and what kind of piety, and what kind of learning?

Student societies were more numerous and active than ever in the 1880s. Fifteen pages in the April 1887 edition of the *Monthly* was devoted to their activities for the year. The Alumni Association was better attended than ever before. It decided to cooperate with the Literary and Metaphysical Society in publishing the *Monthly* throughout the year, with Macdonald as the managing editor of the expanded enterprise. The other major initiative was the sponsoring of Jonathan Goforth as a foreign missionary to China. The Student Missionary Society had pledged $600 and the Alumni Association $800. Three other graduates of 1887 – W.P. McKenzie, C.A. Webster, and D. McGillivray – had indicated their intention to seek appointments in foreign missions. The missionary society continued to work closely with the Home Missions Committee to provide summer students, primarily for northern Ontario and western Canada. Students still met weekly for prayer. The Metaphysical and Literary Society met regularly each Friday night. During the business meeting, intense debate was common. Papers were read and criticized for both elocution and content. Formal debates followed in which the questions of the day were considered. From time to time, the society sponsored public meetings with prominent speakers. The weekly meetings were seen as an important part of the formation of the students in public speaking and participating in the courts of the church. The Glee Club and the Football Club also reported successful years.[61]

PUBLIC PRESENCE AND PROSPERITY

Between 1870 and 1890, under the leadership of William Caven, Knox College came to occupy a place of geographical and social prominence in Toronto unknown in previous years. New buildings were built on Spadina Crescent at the entrance to the new Toronto suburbs just opening up in the 1880s. The buildings cost $130,000 and were paid for within ten years of opening in 1875. Prominent ministers from throughout southwestern Ontario served on the board and senate, together with leading businessmen and politicians. Caven himself was a civic figure of note in Toronto and throughout Ontario. He served as a close advisor to Oliver Mowat as premier and George W. Ross as minister of education and later premier. Ross sat on the Knox board or senate from 1882 until his defeat as premier in 1905. The college amassed an endowment of almost $190,000 by 1890, $185,000 more than they had in 1870. In spite of such prominence and success in building and raising endowments, the financial affairs of the college remained a constant concern. Givings to the ordinary fund usually fell well short of expenses and the church failed to find an acceptable strategy for supporting all six colleges it had decided to leave open in 1875.

In early 1873, the college held a public meeting to suggest the construction of larger facilities on a site closer to the university. The response from Toronto Presbyterians was enthusiastic. A parcel of property just north of Spadina and College was acquired, construction plans devised, and fund raising begun. Caven and Gregg collected over $40,000 in subscriptions by the time the General Assembly met in June. The new college housed 72 students and was full from the beginning. Its lecture halls, library, and common rooms provided ample facilities "for study and social intercourse and meetings for mutual improvement."[62] Students studying for the ministry were expected to live at Knox and take advantage of the community life and activities as part of their formation.

Presbyterians were not the only ones to recognize the desirability of the site. In 1889, a group of neighbours offered to purchase the property from the college and turn it into a park. The *Monthly* reported that the city council had passed a resolution saying that the college should have "recreation grounds," and therefore move. Macdonald pointed to several distinguished schools in Great Britain and the United States that did not have such property, thanked the city fathers for their interest, and stated that the price was $300,000 and not a penny less.[63] Nothing more was heard from the neighbours.

When the Presbyterian Church in Canada began in 1875, all six colleges belonging to the uniting churches came into the union without any changes to their governance, powers, or position. Ten years later, many in the church were convinced that there were too many colleges and better theological education required a consolidation of resources. A Committee on the Consolidation of Colleges was struck by the Assembly in 1885 and reported in 1886. In its majority report, it recommended that the theological faculty at Queen's be united with Knox and that Knox become the theological faculty of Queen's. Further, Pine Hill in Halifax was to amalgamate with The Presbyterian College in Montreal, "or with any other Theological School in the Dominion that may be preferred by the said Synod." Manitoba College in Winnipeg and Morrin College in Quebec City were not included in the consolidation plans. The committee acknowledged that its discussions with the colleges and its deliberations had been "a peculiarly difficult and delicate task." Its recommendations were governed not by what its members thought ought to be, but by what they found possible. Even then, the recommendations had passed in committee only by a bare majority of the members present. A minority report, signed by five members, including the chair of the Knox board, William Mortimer Clark, stated that "the interests of the Church will be best preserved by the various Colleges being maintained by the Church in increased efficiency" and recommended that no action on consolidation be taken. After a lengthy debate, the minority report was adopted and the topic of college consolidation dropped.[64]

Government officials and university administrators were discussing similar schemes of consolidation and federation among the various institutions of higher education in Ontario during the 1880s. Toronto was rapidly becoming the major centre of higher education in the province and the Knox board stressed the importance of this fact in its repeated plea for additional funding. Caven played an influential role in the final resolution of the disputes surrounding the various schemes for university federation in Ontario in 1887.[65] Knox itself entered the federation that created the University of Toronto in 1887. As a result, the university recognized its teaching and granted it a seat on the Senate. These developments indicated the determination of the college authorities to support and benefit from the growth of the modern university in Ontario. As historians of higher education have noted, Canadian universities maintained the broader vision of a character-forming liberal education well into the twentieth century, while universities in the United States and Europe shifted their emphasis in the late-nineteenth century to the pursuit of scholarship and research.[66] In the minds of the leaders at Knox, a well-balanced liberal education was an essential foundation for theological study.

Knox retained its close connection and clear accountability to the church throughout this era. There were several debates over how that accountability should be structured and exercised. In the end, the assembly continued to appoint the professors, though no consistent process was developed until the 1890s. The presbytery rather than the college conducted the induction of a new professor. One significant change did take place, however. In 1887, on recommendation from the college senate, the separate Board of

Examiners was abolished and its duties passed over to the senate.[67] The church was not relinquishing its right to examine the students independently of their college courses and evaluations, but simply reassigning the responsibility for this role to the senate of the college, which included all of the faculty.

The growth of the Presbyterian Church in Canada and its various schemes for home and foreign missions meant that there was increased competition for funding from the church. The appeal made by the Knox board in 1880 touched on the concerns that troubled the college fund raisers throughout this era. There was a debt of over $10,000 in the operating account at Knox and the Home Missions Fund of the national church also had a large deficit. The college sought to explain its failure to eliminate the debt and made an appeal in view of the importance of its work:

That so little has been done [to reduce the debt] during the past year is due to the difficulty in finding persons willing and having leisure to canvass, to the great commercial depression which has prevailed, and to the strenuous special effort made to relieve the Home Missions Fund of serious embarrassment. It should not be forgotten, however, that the efficiency of the Theological Colleges is vitally connected with the edification and extension of the Church, as an educated and well-furnished ministry is now more indispensable than ever, and as our students are generally pioneers in the Home Mission field, while the desire evinced by several to carry the Gospel to the heathen has awakened much interest in Foreign Mission work, and has greatly encouraged and incited the Church to enter upon it. It is much to be desired that the more intelligent and wealthy members of the Church would evince a deeper interest in the Colleges, as they most specially are in a position to know the great cost and value of a liberal education, while others seem less capable of realizing this, and hence give reluctantly to the Colleges, while they respond liberally and generously to appeals in favour of Missions.[68]

In addition to the competition for church dollars from mission work, however, there was also competition among the colleges, especially among Presbyterian College, Montreal, Queen's, and Knox. Financing Knox College during this era, then, was a juggling act. Sources were unpredictable and debts were consolidating in new mortgages on the buildings more than once. The bulk of the givings came from larger churches in larger centres of population whose ministers were either on the board and senate or alumni or both. Additions to the faculty that were desperately needed had to be delayed because of lack of funds.

In 1881, in an attempt to provide a level playing field, the General Assembly established a common fund to receive donations for all the colleges. The distribution of income was set on the basis of the requirements of the colleges in 1881, with Knox receiving 53%, Queen's Theological Faculty 21%, and Presbyterian College, Montreal, 26%.[69]

When Knox began complaining about the common fund in 1882, the board pleaded loyalty to the decision of 1881 and expressed its desire to give the scheme a fair trial. Accordingly, it protested a second appeal specifically for contributions to Queen's as contrary to the intent of the common fund. It also noted that the figures indicated that many congregations gave nothing to the colleges, while others gave small amounts quite out of proportion to their givings to other schemes.[70] By 1884, the board was convinced that the common fund scheme was costing them money.[71] In 1885, the college recommended that the fund be abolished.[72] The board recommended that the colleges be given the freedom to approach each congregation on their own behalf. The recommendation to abolish the common fund and grant permission for each college to appeal separately was repeated in 1886. The fund was retained, but permission to appeal separately was granted. By 1888, contributions to the common fund had dropped and those to the individual colleges had grown. Knox again recommended the abolition of the fund and asked that each college be listed separately in the literature sent out to solicit support from congregations. This time their recommendations were adopted.[73]

The wrangling over an equitable scheme for raising and distributing money raised through a common fund, together with the constant shortfall of congregational givings, led the college to make determined efforts to build up its own endowment funds. Initial efforts in the early 1870s were not encouraging. The efforts to endow a chair in memory of Robert Burns failed miserably. As a result, the decision of the 1871 General Assembly of the Canada Presbyterian Church to endow each of its colleges with $250,000 was dismissed as wishful thinking.[74] It was not until the 1880s that Knox began to experience any degree of success in this form of funding. Between 1880 and 1890, the endowment fund of the college grew from just over $50,000 to $190,000. The most significant addition came from James MacLaren, the older brother of William. The MacLaren family fortune had been made in the Australian gold fields in the 1850s and the Ottawa valley lumber business in the 1860s. James was the founder and first president of the Bank of Ottawa, later to merge with the Bank of Nova Scotia. In 1883, he gave the college $50,000 to endow a chair, predictably, in systematic theology.[75]

Knox College in 1890 was a very different institution from what it had been in 1870. The faculty had doubled from two to four and the student body had grown from 70 to 100. The college had come closer to the university in both legal status and geographical location. A breadth of opinion unthought of in 1870 had developed, though the church had not yet faced the question of the degree of tolerance it would allow. The church's resources had been consolidated by a national union and its rapid growth in Canada's cities and in the west was beginning. In spite of these changes, however, one cord of continuity remained strong. Knox continued to be the church's major institution for preparing clergy with evangelical conviction and intellectual integrity for the mission of the church. An intensified debate over the nature of intellectual integrity and the scope of the church's mission would develop during the 1890s, a debate in which the faculty, students, and alumni of Knox would continue to play a central role.

Seated in the midst of the graduating class of 1883 were, from left to right, William MacLaren, professor of theology (1873–1908) and principal of Knox from 1904 to 1908; William Gregg, professor of church history and apologetics (1872–1896); William Caven; and J.J.A. Proudfoot, lecturer in homiletics (1866–1901).

The first editorial committee of the *Knox College Monthly*, begun as a student magazine in 1882. Over the following fourteen years the *Monthly* played a major role in the acceptance of progressive orthodoxy by the Presbyterian Church in Canada and provided a training ground for religious and secular journalists and popular writers, the most prominent of whom were James A. Macdonald, editor of the Toronto *Globe* from 1903 to 1915, and Charles W. Gordon, who wrote the Ralph Connor novels.

Knox College Graduating Class - 1898-99.

The beginnings of a new generation of faculty were evident in the faculty photographs included with those of the 1899 graduating class. The older generation consisted of Proudfoot, Caven, and MacLaren. Just arrived from Scotland was John E. McFadyen, who taught Old Testament (1898–1910). James Ballentyne, first editor of the *Knox College Monthly*, was professor of church history (1896–1921). Canadian journalist and cartoonist J.W. Bengough was teaching elocution at Knox that year.

The faculty pictured in the bottom row of the graduating composite of 1910 was made up almost entirely of progressives. The single exception is William MacLaren, though he had retired in 1908 and become principal emeritus. From left to right, T.B. Kilpatrick, professor of systematic theology (1905–1925); John D. Robertson, professor of apologetics, homiletics, and pastoral theology (1903–1919); James Ballantyne; William MacLaren; Alfred Gandier, principal and professor of practical theology and English Bible (1908–1925); John E. McFadyen; H.H.A. Kennedy, professor of New Testament (1905–1909); and Robert Law, professor of New Testament (1909–1918).

The college invited seven architectural firms to submit plans for the new Knox College at the heart of the campus of the University of Toronto. A Gothic structure designed by Chapman and McGiffen was chosen and opened in 1915. Chapman and McGiffin Architects, *Construction*, 2 February 1991.

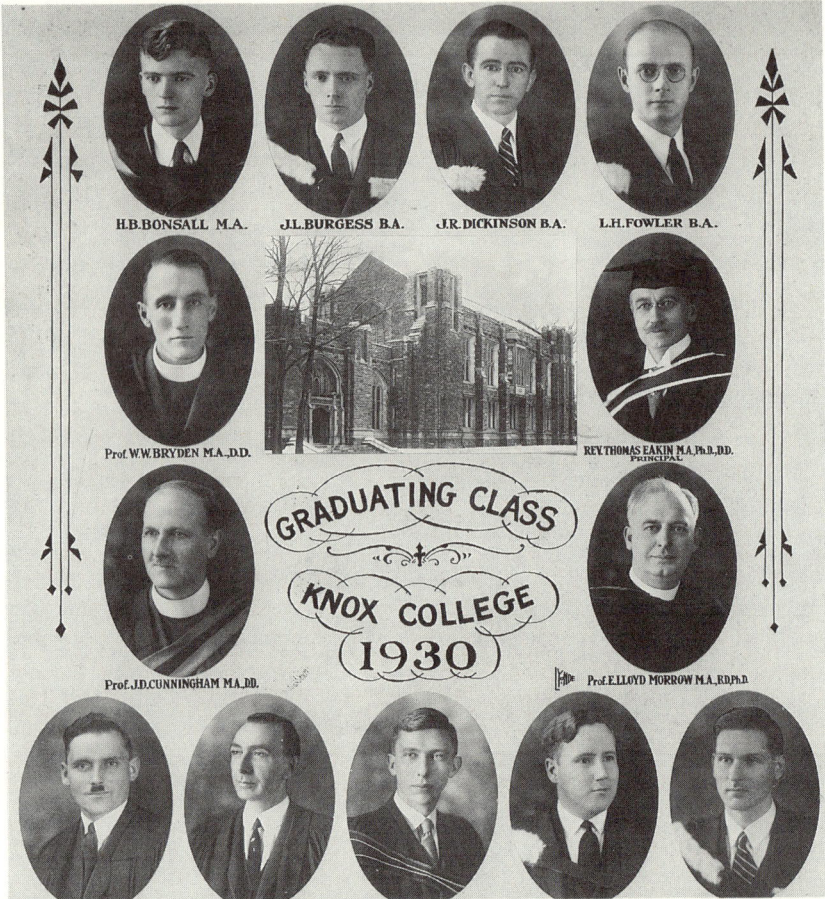

Knox College had four full-time faculty by 1930. As pictured from left to right in the two middle rows, they were Walter W. Bryden, professor of church history and the history and philosophy of religion (1927–1952) and principal (1945–1952); Thomas Eakin, professor of Old Testament and principal (1926–1944); J.D. Cunningham, professor of New Testament (1926–1944); and E. Lloyd Morrow, professor of systematic theology (1926–1936).

1961

J.G.S. BLYTH, B.SC. — J.B. DUNCAN, B.SC. — W. FAIRLEY — M.R. GELLATLY, B.A. — E. HERRON — K.G. KNIGHT

J.H. MC INTOSH, B.A. — W.H. MC LENNAN

REV. PROF. D.W. HAY, M.A. D.D. — REV. PROF. D.V. WADE, M.A., PH.D. — REV. PRIN. J.S. GLEN, PH.D. TH.D. — REV. PROF. D.K. ANDREWS, M.A. PH.D. — REV. PROF. A.L. FARRIS M.A. B.D. M.TH.

Graduating Class
knox College

I.G. MAC LEOD, B.A. — W.K. POTTINGER, B.A. — R.M. SHIELDS, B.A. — S.R. THOMPSON, B.A.

Of the faculty in 1961, pictured in the row below the picture of the college, all but David Hay had been formed by Walter Bryden and all, including David Hay, carried forward Bryden's legacy, though in diverging ways. Left to right were David W. Hay, professor of systematic theology (1944–1975); Donald V. Wade, professor of the history and philosophy of religion (1947–1967); J. Stanley Glen, professor of New Testament and pastoral theology (1945–1976) and principal (1952–1976); D. Keith Andrews, professor of Old Testament (1945–1967); and Allan F. Farris, professor of church history (1952–1977) and principal (1976–1977).

W.D. ALLEN C.D., B.A. | J.P. CHALMERS B.A. | R. DOCHERTY B.A. | D.L. ELDER CLARK B.A. | G. FORD B.A. | J.A. FULLERTON B.A. | J.T. HURD B.A. | A.D. JACQUES B.A.A. | C.H. LOUDON B.A. | M.S. McCUTCHEON B.Sc., B.Ed.

J.E.S. McINTYRE B.A. | S.F. MATHESON-REEVE B.A. | L.A. MILNE B.Sc., M.R.E. | B.Y.Y. NAVRATIL B.A. | J.E.C. PICKERING B.A. | R.N. SCHROEDER B.A. | W.L.S. SEAMAN B.P.E., M.A. | J.P.C. SMIT B.A.

A.R. SONG B.A. | P.J.S. STINSON B.A. | D.J.M. STRICKLAND M.A. | R.E. VANDENBERG B.A.

G.P. YANDO B.A. | J.P. YOUNG B.A.

1986 Graduating Class Knox College

PETER CATON GERALD CAMPBELL STUDIOS

PROFESSOR J.C. HAY M.A., B.D., Ph.D., D.D. | PROFESSOR W.J.S. FARRIS B.A., M.A., Ph.D. | PROFESSOR I.G. NICOL M.A., B.D., Ph.D. | PROFESSOR S.D. WALTERS B.A., B.D., Th.M., Ph.D. | PROFESSOR D.J.M. CORBETT B.A., LL.B., B.D., Ph.D. PRINCIPAL | PROFESSOR C.A. PATER B.A., B.D., Th.M., Ph.D. | PROFESSOR D.C. SMITH B.A., B.D., Ph.D. | PROFESSOR R. HUMPHRIES B.A., B.D., Th.M., Ph.D.

The faculty in 1986, pictured in the bottom row from left to right, were J. Charles Hay, professor of homiletics, evangelism, and church administration (1963–1976), principal (1977–1985), professor of New Testament (1976–1979), and professor of preaching and worship (1979–1986); W. James S. Farris, professor of Christian ethics and the history and philosophy of religion (1967–1992); Iain G. Nicol, professor of systematic theology (1975–present); Stanley D. Walters, professor of Old Testament (1975–1992); Donald J.M. Corbett, principal and professor of historical theology (1985–1990); Calvin A. Pater, professor of church history (1978-present); Donald C. Smith, registrar and director of field education (1976–1978), and professor of church and ministry (1978-present); and Raymond Humphries, professor of New Testament (1979-present).

4 Creating a Progressive College, 1890–1905

Robert N. Grant, a frequent contributor to the church press under the pen name Knoxonian, was not at all happy with the progressive changes being suggested for Knox College. Two distinctive features, orthodoxy in theology and aggressiveness in mission work, had characterized Knox in its first sixty years and Grant was convinced that the college had to hold fast to both. "Whatever the future may bring," Grant wrote in 1903, "old Knox has always stood for evangelical theology of a pronounced type. With comparatively few exceptions, the men of Knox have always been ready to do battle for a conservative theology as opposed to the latitudianarianism so popular in many quarters."[1] Principal William Caven offered a more nuanced and accurate description of the situation at Knox College. Changes had taken place, Caven admitted in a 1902 interview, but they had been in method and perspective rather than content. "Substantially," he observed, "the same doctrines are taught today that were taught when I was a student fifty years ago. The changes are partly due to the changed conditions, partly to more careful study of the Bible, and partly to changes in the philosophical basis of doctrinal statements."[2] Changes in the faculty and curriculum between 1890 and 1905 all contributed to the shift in perspective at Knox from confessional orthodoxy to progressive orthodoxy, while maintaining the commitment to aggressive mission work. The tensions these changes brought about focused on differing assessments of their value. Did they contribute to the preservation and propagation of the Gospel or to its demise?

The mission needs of the church continued to be the dominant focus for Canadian Presbyterians. New conditions in Canada and around the world played a major role in determining the practical aims of the church. New frontiers of mission in western Canada, the growing cities, and overseas mission fields tested the ability of The Presbyterian Church in Canada to organize and fund the institutional means to accomplish its mission. A more settled, educated, and prosperous membership, especially in central and eastern Canada, brought changes in the patterns of piety seen in church music, church architecture, modes of worship, and devotional literature. The Presbyterian Church in Canada grew dramatically in the scope of its activities and the institutional means to pursue them. Along with most other traditional mainline denominations in North America, it was transformed from a voluntary society loosely organized through a network of church courts into a corporate denomination with regional and national boards and staff people whose purpose it was to provide and coordinate the goods, services, and personnel needed for the organization's business.[3] The headquarters of the growing corporate structure were in Toronto. In the course of organizational growth and consolidation, a gradual but decided shift took place in the source of policy initiative and the balance of power in the church. Committees and agencies, including the colleges, became more independent of the courts of the church than had been the case in earlier years.

Changes in thought were assessed not in academic isolation but for the contribution they made to the power of the church in Canadian society. The gradual but comprehensive replacement of Scottish Common Sense teaching in the philosophy departments of Canada's universities by British Idealism in the 1870s meant that students for the ministry entered their theological education with a very different worldview from that of their older professors. The expanding religious press, especially when guided by the entrepreneurial hand of James A. Macdonald, made these progressive views and their theological implications a commonplace within the denomination.[4] The public discussions of the differences, in both press and church court, led to a broadening of the limits of tolerance within the Presbyterian Church of Canada rather than to the open warfare that broke out in Scotland and the United States. The tensions were real, nonetheless. A resistance movement to some of these changes began to emerge. It held strong reservations about even the moderate revisions being introduced into the Canadian Presbyterian culture. In some cases, alternative institutions were established to counter what was seen to be the liberal and latitudinarian tendencies of the majority in the church, and especially of Knox College.

APPOINTING A PROGRESSIVE FACULTY

Throughout the 1880s, the debate over the best interpretation of Presbyterianism took place between a faculty united in its support of confessional orthodoxy and a growing body of students and alumni who found the progressive orthodoxy of the Scottish liberals more convincing. In the final years of Caven's leadership, the progressives gradually came to dominate the faculty itself. Surprisingly, there was little open conflict between the two factions within the faculty. The new members of faculty appointed between 1890 and 1904 were all sympathetic to the newer apologetic, but they also had impeccable records of piety and devotion to the great evangelical truths and the mission of the church. Indeed, they were convinced that their progressive orthodoxy provided a better foundation for pious learning than the confessional orthodoxy of their elders.

Even as staunch a defender of the older confessional orthodoxy as William MacLaren had to admit that the teaching of the new generation at Knox College was tolerable in the light of their commitment to the essentials of evangelical Protestantism and the practical task that faced the Canadian church. Reminiscing in 1907, he described the college as "a fountain of living waters" where the teaching had been "distinctly evangelical." Both faculty and students, in MacLaren's opinion, had "held fast to the Reformed type of doctrine" which emphasized "divine sovereignty and human freedom, the impotency of fallen man and the all-sufficiency of divine grace." The great work of the Canadian church was practical and this, in MacLaren's mind, limited the scope of theological change among Presbyterians: "[The work of the church] is not to indulge in speculative theology, but to give the gospel and its institutions to a new land. And we venture to think that one of the safeguards which has helped to preserve our theology pure and wholesome has been the concentration of the thought and energy of the Church on its great practical work, the salvation of souls and the upbuilding of the Kingdom of Jesus Christ. No church which keeps these aims steadily before it is likely to wander far from the fundamental verities of the Christian system." MacLaren acknowledged that there had been "a measure of theological activity" within the denomination over the past sixty years, but he regarded it "as a help rather than as a hindrance to the practical aims of the Christian church."[5]

MacLaren understated the tensions in the theological transition that did take place in the final years of the Caven era. The key difference of opinion within both college and church concerned the relation of confession and scripture. Did the confessional orthodox interpretation of the Westminster standards, especially as found in the Princeton theology, continue to provide a comprehensive and persuasive case for the truth and power of Christianity, or did new methods of Biblical study and new philosophical frameworks point to the necessity to revise the confessional standards of Presbyterianism in the light of progress made in the church's understanding of revelation? Another way in which contemporaries described the difference was to set systematic theology, as represented by the Hodges of Princeton and Watts of Belfast, against Biblical theology, as represented by Smith, Bruce, and Lindsay of Glasgow. The older confessional orthodoxy was seen by the new generation as dry and arid in its emphasis on the intellect and propositional truth. New approaches to the study of Scripture uncovered the experience of faith that underlay the dogmas of faith. Criticism, one of the new generation of faculty assured the church in 1898, clarifies the form, but does not question the facts, of revelation.[6] Systematic theology as such was not rejected, but the old formulations needed revision in the light of progress in understanding drawn from new methods of studying the Scriptures and new frameworks for understanding humanity and its relation to God.

The rhetoric used in these debates, especially in the religious press that served Presbyterians in the 1890s, was neither tame nor polite. Throughout the transition from confessional to progressive orthodoxy, however, Caven played the role of senior statesman and diplomat. While cautiously open to new understanding, he vigorously defended the centrality of the essential orthodox affirmations of evangelical Protestantism in the curriculum, the pious learning essential to effective ministry, and the importance of both to the mission of the church at home and abroad. In the end, the practical needs of the church, diplomatic leadership on both sides of the debates, and the moderate stance of the progressives on key issues, such as the reality of the spiritual and the supernatural, the inspiration of Scripture, the objective nature of the atonement, and the centrality of the great evangelical truths, prevented the bitter and divisive battles that plagued Presbyterianism in the United States and Scotland.

The closest that Canadian Presbyterians came to the kind of heresy trials that resulted from theological tensions elsewhere in the Anglo-American world in the late nineteenth century was in the case of John Campbell in 1893–1894. Campbell was a student at Knox from 1865–1867 and lectured there in the fall of 1872. He served as minister of Charles Street Presbyterian Church, Toronto, from 1868–1872, during which time George Paxton Young was a member of the congregation. In 1873, he was appointed professor of church history and apologetics at The Presbyterian College, Montreal, and remained in that position until his death 31 years later.[7] Late in 1889, he published a blunt attack on confessional orthodoxy. The scholastic methods of the Hodges, Campbell charged, destroyed the totality of scripture and confused the student with partial truths. When confronted with texts that speak of God's love for all, "The young minister shuts the book, and chooses some other text, lest, on the one hand, he should with his limitations offend the common sense of his hearers, or, on the other, with his declaration of God's all embracing love and of Christ's common grace, give to some heresy hunter the foundation for a false charge of universalism."[8] Campbell's words proved prophetic when four years later he himself was charged with heresy.

An editorial cartoon in the *Montreal Daily Star* on 11 September 1893 portrayed Campbell in shirt sleeves with a pick axe called heresy destroying the foundations of the Presbyterian Kirk. The stones of doctrine of inspiration and doctrine of judgement lay scattered on the ground while the presbytery rushed to prevent further damage. In the end, Campbell and the church agreed that "the statements of the Old Testament writers as to the character of God were true as far as they went, but in a few cases were not the whole truth" and that "in the great majority of cases, the Father, when smiting in judgement, and in discipline or chastisement, acts in accordance with general laws or through secondary causes."[9]

This was a very different kind of compromise from that reached in the Macdonnell case, because it accepted the validity of differences of opinion and attitude in interpreting the scriptures and the Westminster Standards within the church, rather than simply the private right to doubt. Neither Macdonnell nor Campbell were radical latitudinarians or liberals. Both sought to subordinate the traditional interpretations of the Westminster Standards to the new insights arising from devout Biblical scholarship. Both were convinced that such progressive orthodoxy was essential to provide a more effective interpretation of the traditional affirmations of the evangelical faith and to further the mission of the church. By 1894, Canadian Presbyterians were more willing to accept broader perspectives on the nature and interpretation of the faith than they had been in 1877.

Throughout the 1890s, the college and the church continued to debate the best way to educate the clergy. The need for a larger faculty was acknowledged by all, but the resources to provide it remained elusive. Retirements, changes in the allocation of subjects, alterations in the kinds of programs offered by the college, and a slow but steady increase in financial support from the denomination, eventually enabled the college to add faculty and readjust the attention given to different subjects in the curriculum. The changes made followed the emphasis of progressive orthodoxy on Biblical theology and the practice of ministry.[10]

The kind of men sought for the faculty also reflected the influence of a more progressive and practical apologetic. While lobbying for the appointment of the young Scottish Old Testament scholar John Edgar McFadyen in Old Testament in 1898, Macdonald wrote that the professors at Knox should be scholarly, reverent, and inspirational. "The theological college," he insisted, "is maintained for the furnishing of properly-trained preachers, not for the making of a few first-class scholars. The practical end in view must guide the selection of the man for the chair. And in the making of a preacher the personality of the professor is the most important factor."[11] The emphasis on the personality and practical focus of the faculty did not imply a lessening of concern with the academic standards maintained at the college, but both college and church were clear that the purpose of pious learning was the preparation of practitioners of ministry in a church engaged in aggressive mission at home and abroad.

The first of the new generation of faculty at Knox College was Robert Yuile Thomson, appointed in 1890 to relieve William Gregg of apologetics and William Caven of Old Testament. He and the colleagues who joined him over the next decade taught the new progressive orthodoxy, convinced that it was true to the content of the scriptures but more appropriate to the changing conditions in which it must be understood, proclaimed, and applied. Progress in the evangelical cause, they argued, came through the development of the church's comprehension, presentation, and use of revealed truth. The changes came slowly, and always sought to improve the church's knowledge and communication of the salvation offered in Jesus Christ. Differences remained among different generations of Knox faculty concerning the extent of change advisable and the relative importance of Scripture and confession in the process, but they remained united in their determination to provide a firm and articulate defence and propagation of the traditional essentials of the evangelical faith in face of the intellectual and social turmoil of the last quarter of the nineteenth century.

Thomson was in his early thirties when appointed and had been educated at the University of Toronto, in Edinburgh, and in Germany. By 1904, five other appointments had been made, all men open to a more progressive orthodoxy. In 1896, George L. Robinson was appointed in Old Testament after Thomson's tragic death and James Ballantyne in apologetics and church history after William Gregg's retirement. John E. McFadyen replaced Robinson in Old Testament in 1898 after the latter accepted a position in Chicago. W. Halliday Douglas was called to the position in apologetics, homiletics, and pastoral theology in 1901, but died within a year of his apppointment. John D. Robertson replaced him in 1902. All combined a solid grounding in the evolutionary moral and religious worldview of Idealist philosophers, the historical methods of the believing practitioners of higher criticism, and the movements among university students, inspired by Dwight L. Moody and Henry Drummond, to spread the intellectual and social benefits of Protestantism throughout the world.

When William Gregg informed the college of his desire to retire in 1890, they convinced him simply to drop apologetics and retain church history. R.Y. Thomson, who had been appointed lecturer in Old Testament in 1889 to allow Caven to concentrate on New Testament, accepted the position of professor of apologetics and Old

Testament. Thomson's sympathy for the pious and carefully considered conclusions of higher criticism was apparent in a review of F.R. Beattie's attack on modern critical theories in *The Higher Criticism.*[12] Earnest and advanced Christian scholarship, Thomson countered in his review, served "evangelical truth and Biblical learning" when it affirmed the supernatural, accepted inspiration, and denied the theory of a natural evolution in the religion of the bible.

Thomson's approach to progressive orthodoxy was outlined in his inaugural lecture, "The Evolution in the Manifestation of the Supernatural." He traced three periods of God's self-manifestation to human intelligence. The evidences of natural and revealed religion, he suggested, were "really a setting forth of the different ways in which God has manifested himself." These stages could best be understood as an evolution insofar as "they bear witness to an agency, continuous, progressive, and gradually attaining fuller development, so as to reveal new features and deepen the definiteness of those already revealed." The first stage was nature, the second was humanity, and the third was the coming of Jesus Christ. "The revelation in Christ," Thomson stated, "completes those progressive manifestations of grace, which had been taking place ever since the need for reconciliation arose, and whose history the Scriptures contain. The abiding presence of the Holy Spirit in the Church, professedly secures the continuance of the completed supernatural manifestation. As the Old and New Testaments are organically connected in setting forth Christ, so Christianity has its root in Him." The promise of God to continue his progressive self-manifestation through the power of the Holy Spirit gave the church the confidence to defend Christianity against all rivals. "The defender of the faith," Thomson said of his future students, "has to hold forth the word of life, and clearly shining in its proper light, it will dispel all darkness."[13] The mental, moral, and spiritual evolutionism of Thomson reflected the British Idealist philosophical framework he would have learned from George Paxton Young during his studies in Toronto, a perspective that would have been reinforced in his biblical studies at New College, Edinburgh, with A.B. Davidson and Marcus Dods.[14]

The Rev. Dr. Henry Martyn Parsons, minister of Knox Church, Toronto had been commissioned by the Presbytery of Toronto to address those gathered for Thomson's installation. He must have grown more and more uncomfortable as he listened to Thomson's inaugural address and realized the sympathy the new professor had for modern critical methods, however orthodox his conclusions might be. Parsons had succeeded Alexander Topp in 1880 and by 1890 was actively involved in at least two organizations that advocated a premillennialist dispensationalism in biblical studies and proved to be seed-beds of fundamentalism in North America, the China Inland Mission and the Niagara Bible Conference.[15] Among the members of Knox during Parson's pastorate were William MacLaren, William Gregg, the McMurrich family, and William Mortimer Clark. Parsons himself served on the board and senate of the college throughout the 1880s. Parsons used the occasion to plead with Knox to establish lay programs for people "who have no capacity for philosophical analysis and no comprehension of metaphysical statements of revealed truth," yet wished to serve the church as missionaries, teachers, catechists, and volunteers.[16] He clearly wanted a more popular and conservative approach to "the real manna of the Word" than was emerging at Knox. Parsons never did convince Knox to implement his suggestions, but they came to fruition in the founding of the Toronto Bible Training School, the forerunner of Ontario Bible College, in 1894.[17] Parsons' premillenialist views did not represent those of the majority of Canadian Presbyterians, but many shared his concerns over the progressive changes being advocated in the *Knox College Monthly* and represented in Thomson's appointment.[18]

Thomson's tenure at Knox College was cut short by his death in 1895 at the age of 38. The same year, Gregg insisted that he retire from all teaching duties. At the meeting of the assembly, tensions over the faculty and curriculum at the college surfaced and delayed any new appointments. Discussions focused on the number of chairs the college could afford, the qualifications needed to fill the chairs, and how the teaching responsibilities should be allocated among the faculty. The college board recommended two chairs, one in Old Testament and the other in apologetics and church history, and nominated two non-Canadians. George L. Robinson, a Princeton graduate completing doctoral work in Leipzig, was nominated for Old Testament and Hope W. Hogg from Oxford for apologetics and church history.

When their nominations became known prior to the meeting of the Assembly, a storm of criticism appeared in letters and editorials in the weekly church press. The *Presbyterian Record* summarized the objections:

that it is a slight upon our own men, a confession of inferiority which circumstances do not warrant; that these men are both comparatively young
and untried; that they are strangers to the life and work of our Church;
that there are graduates of Knox who have proved themselves able men
and earnest devoted workers, and far better fitted to train men of their
own stamp, such as are wanted in the Church; that a practical knowledge
of the life and needs of our Church and sympathy with it, are as essential
as Arabic and Sanskrit; that we want "Occidentalists," rather than "Orien-
talists;" that men who are known in our Church, especially alumni of
Knox, would bind together the College and the Church and win for the
former the support upon which it depends and which it just now so much
needs; while to ignore her own sons and choose strangers would do much
to alienate the affection and support of the Alumni and the Church at
large.[19]

Overtures from the Presbyteries of London and Toronto brought
these concerns to the floor of the Assembly. The matter was referred back to the college with instructions to clarify the chairs
needed and continue the search to fill them.[20]

In 1896, the college brought Robinson's name in again for the
Old Testament chair, indicating that he had received nominations
from a large majority of the presbyteries. For apologetics and
church history, however, they presented the name of James Ballantyne, born in Stratford, Ontario in 1857, a graduate of Knox in
1883 who had also studied at Princeton, Edinburgh, and Leipzig,
and was currently minister of Knox Church in Ottawa. Both were
appointed.[21]

Ballantyne saw apologetics and church history closely related,
history providing the material for a persuasive interpretation of the
faith:

The historian must exhibit this subject as the history of the Church of
Christ – the history not of an isolated community with inferior and selfish
ends in view, but of the most wonderful organization the world has known,
maintaining itself as no other, and comprehending the vastest purposes
possible to the grasp of man. God has made a revelation of himself to man.
The object of this revelation is to meet man's need as a sinner by offering
him redemption. It is centred in the person and work of Jesus Christ, in
the facts of a divine-human life. For this culminating event of all history
there was a long preparation, and the record of the society founded by

Him is but the narration of the working out of the historical fact for which the world had been preparing.[22]

Ballantyne did not publish widely, but concentrated his efforts on teaching, advising, and administration in the college. He spent considerable time and energy assisting the principals of the college in the exercise of their duties. He was remembered as a teacher of balanced mind and steady effort, a churchman with great conciliatory skills, and a pastor and counsellor to students of great spiritual insight.[23]

The *Westminster* welcomed Robinson's appointment as a sign that Knox students would continue to be introduced to the best of modern scholarship and methods of biblical interpretation. Further, "what is of chiefest concern, the cherished faith of the Church in the great evangelical doctrines of her historic creed, will not be disturbed."[24] While at Knox, he worked closely with the rapidly growing Department of Orientals at University College, established at the insistence of Caven and Principal J.P. Sheraton of Wycliffe and headed by Presbyterian J.F. McCurdy. In his inaugural lecture, Robinson outlined an approach to higher criticism that was consistent with the "sane and tactful course" that McCurdy and his colleagues were developing at University College:[25]

I come to [the Old Testament] as a believer in its historicity, and also in its essential inspiration. At the same time, I believe also in criticism. I believe that criticism, if scientifically conducted and kept in its own sphere, is a very important aid to knowledge. A lantern to the farmer driving home from the country village through a deep wood, where the light of the stars is dim, is a good thing. Only, the lantern must not be held too near the eye, or it will simply dazzle and blind. So with criticism; it is a new light, and a useful light in illuminating the dark places of Scripture; still, it is only a lantern, and it is not intended to usurp the function of the Holy Spirit. The brightest and the clearest light comes from Him.[26]

Robinson remained only two years before taking an appointment to McCormick Seminary in Chicago. His resignation in early 1898 reopened the debate about the appropriate kind of person for the chair.

Macdonald continued his pattern of open and opinionated discussion of college affairs in the pages of the *Westminster.* He argued for the best person, regardless of nationality, and remained firm in his earlier conviction that the college should be the body that searched and recommended to the assembly. The candidate had to be "an enthusiast in Old Testament study, scholarly, prudent, spiritual." Macdonald did not hesitate to let his readers know that his choice was John Edgar McFadyen of Glasgow. When McFadyen withdrew his name just prior to the meeting of the General Assembly, believing that only a traditionalist would get the appointment, Macdonald assured him through the pages of the *Westminster* that he was mistaken: "It would be a calamity were the impression to go abroad that Knox College is the home of the outworn traditionalism. It is not so. Knox College wisely avoids both extremes, radical and conservative. ... Canada has been mercifully saved from both the blind-eyed conservatism and the pugnacious radicalism which have wrought such havoc in the United States and made American Presbyterianism a by-word and a hissing. We have no heresy-hunters, nor any hare-brained heretics. We want neither."[27] No agreement could be reached on an appointment by the assembly and the college received permission to make the appointment prior to the next assembly, should a suitable candidate be found.[28]

Caven, Clark, and MacLaren all went over to Scotland to convince John Edgar McFadyen, the top graduating theological student in the country, to reconsider. They succeeded in changing McFadyen's mind and he accepted the appointment. He had studied at Glasgow with Edward Caird, A.B. Bruce, George Adam Smith, T.M. Lindsay, and Henry Drummond. During his theological studies, he had spent a term in Marburg. McFadyen stood firmly in the tradition of believing higher critics represented by his mentors. Caven assured the church that, for McFadyen, "the message of the Book, and the making of that message clear and powerful to his students, is of more importance than merely critical views on questions of date and authorship."[29] Somewhat surprisingly, there is no evidence that MacLaren disagreed with the appointment, even though his own views on biblical criticism and confessional revision were decidedly more conservative than McFadyen's.

McFadyen's views on Biblical criticism were developed most fully in *Old Testament Criticism and the Christian Church*, a volume that he wrote in 1903 for theological students and interested ministers and laity. Higher criticism, he wrote, was only a means to increase the credibility of faith. Its aim was constructive. It sought to remove "many a stumbling block from the path of honest doubt" and create not simply more knowledge but "the increase of faith through the scientific presentation of knowledge."[30] McFadyen recalled his own "confusion and sorrow" when the newer views began to make their appeal to him, but was convinced that the assured results of the method made it "easier to hold fellowship with the men who wrote [the Bible], and through them, with the God who inspired it."[31] He began his first year classes in Old Testament with a study of the Psalms, introducing students to the faith and worship of Israel prior to unravelling its history. Of the nine books he published while teaching at Knox, three were collections of devotional columns he wrote for the religious and secular press, four were study manuals for congregational bible classes, and two were introductory texts for theological students.[32]

When James Ballantyne was appointed in 1896, he was assigned responsibility for both apologetics and church history. The college authorities, however, recognized that this was too heavy a burden for any one professor to carry very long. In 1900, the assembly granted the college power to make an appointment in apologetics. They offered the chair to David W. Forrest, a prominent United Presbyterian scholar in Scotland, but he declined.[33] With the retirement of J.J.A. Proudfoot in 1901, the college decided to combine apologetics with homiletics and pastoral theology. W. Halliday Douglas, minister of the Presbyterian congregation in Cambridge, England since 1893, was recommended and appointed. Douglas had been born in Edinburgh and educated there and in Glasgow. During his arts and theological education, he drank deeply from the wells of T.H. Green and Henry Drummond. While in Cambridge, he played a key role in the transfer of Westminster College, the theological college of the Presbyterian Church in England, from London to the ancient university town in 1898.

The most powerful interpretation of Christianity, Douglas believed, was the Christian life lived according to the example of Jesus both in its consecration to the common duties of the home and the higher calling of public service. Along with American social gospeller Washington Gladden, whose book, *The Christian Pastor and the Working Church*, Douglas used as a text in pastoral theology, he had a vision of Christianity permeating the whole of the social order through its influence on the individual will and its power to make good citizens. The church was an essential means of promoting "a disinterested, a truly public spirit in public life." The result would be a large, dedicated body of Christian reformers who worked in their various callings to remove "everything in the political state of the people which hinders or endangers their moral well-being."[34] His brother Charles recalled that Douglas' vision of public Christianity was shaped by the social criticism of Carlyle, the political philosophy of T.H. Green, and the evangelical preaching of Henry Drummond.[35] Douglas had little time to share this vision with the Canadian church. After only a year at Knox, he died of complications following an operation for appendicitis.

In a memorial tribute, McFadyen described for a British audience what he considered to be "the peculiar theological position of the Presbyterian Church in Canada:"

The urgent pressure of the practical problems has left little time for speculative and scholarly pursuits, and the general temper of the Church has been not unnaturally conservative, though by no means obstinately so. At the same time many, especially though not exclusively among the younger men, some of whom have studied in Britain, have felt the growing importance and even necessity of keeping the Church in touch with the movements of modern theological scholarship. Thus the general conservative leanings of the Church are tempered by a distinctly progressive and growingly influential element; and the occupant of the chair [of apologetics, homiletics, and pastoral theology] had to be, if possible, a man who could satisfy the hopes of both parties. He must be neither an obscurantist nor a radical; he had, on the one hand, to be able to reassure the conservative spirits, and on the other, he had to justify the hopes of those who believe that theology has a future as well as a past.

Douglas won the admiration of both sides, McFadyen concluded, by being "a powerful constructive and reconciling influence within the church."[36] McFadyen's remarks reflected more the agenda of the younger generation of faculty at Knox than the actual impact Douglas had been able to make. They described the shifts that were taking place in the final years of the Caven era both in the church and at the college.

Following Douglas' death, the assembly again gave the board power to make an appointment and John D. Robertson, another Scot, was chosen. Robertson graduated with first class honours in philosophy from Edinburgh in 1880, studied theology at the Divinity Hall of the United Presbyterians under John Cairns, and received a doctorate in philosophy from Edinburgh after studies in France and Germany in 1887. When offered the chair at Knox in

1903, he was minister at the United Free Church of Scotland in North Berwick. He had already written two books, *Conscience* and *The Work of the Holy Spirit in Christian Service.* Robertson's address at the opening of the college in 1903 focused on his impressions of the country and the college. He noted with enthusiastic approval the optimistic spirit of Canada and the determination of The Presbyterian Church in Canada to play a large role in establishing "sound and enduring" foundations for a righteous nation. At the college, he was pleased with the combination of apologetics, homiletics, and pastoral theology because it united theory with practice in an effort "to communicate the highest modern ideals of life and work and the true impulse to their attainment."[37]

If the story of the growth of the faculty at Knox College through the closing years of the nineteenth century seems convoluted, it is because the events reflect the turmoil over ideas of the church, its clergy, and their theological education that was shaking the Presbyterian Church in Canada. In these troubled times William Caven guided Knox College through the treacherous deeps of theological change. The passage was not without its storms, but it was made safely. When Caven died late in 1904, a new generation of faculty was well-established, a generation of progressive interpreters of Christian orthodoxy who combined the best in higher education that the theological world had to offer with a devotion to the church and its mission that centred on the person and work of Christ. MacLaren, who succeeded Caven as principal until his own death four years later, might have had serious misgivings about their theological formulations, but he had no hesitations about their piety nor their commitment to the evangelical progress of the church at home and abroad. As the Presbyterian Church in Canada entered the twentieth century, that unity of purpose and devotion meant that the broadening range of theological perspectives within the denomination would be tolerable to most and celebrated by many.

NEW STRATEGIES FOR SERVING THE CHURCH

Between 1890 and 1905, Knox College found itself at the centre of three lengthy debates concerning the relation of theological education to the emerging university and the expanding church. The first concerned the continuation of the preparatory course at Knox and other Presbyterian colleges. The second concerned the possible amalgamation of several of the colleges to achieve a better use of resources and keep pace with the larger American and Scottish colleges. The third involved suggestions that the faculty make itself available for lay education, continuing education of the clergy, and the education of women for professional church work. All the debates reflected the determination of the denomination to remain a central force for moral and spiritual values in the face of the changes taking place in Canadian society. The colleges, in their role of educating leaders for the church, were crucial components in the social uplift of the nation.

From its beginnings in 1844, Knox had provided classes for those who were not able to take a full arts course at university. At first, the primary reason was the inadequacy of the universities. As their faculties and resources improved, the rationale shifted to the importance of providing a path into ministry for pious and devout men who were unable to gain admission to the university. Robert N. Grant pointed to all the ministers without an arts degree who had served the church with honour and distinction, including several moderators of the General Assembly. The abolition of the preparatory department had been suggested as early as 1858, Grant noted, but the church had always rejected the suggestion and should continue to do so. The fundamental prerequisite for ministry, he argued, was "an experimental insight into truth – obtained through divine illumination," and insistence on a full arts course prior to theological study would bar too many people with such qualifications. The arts course, argued Donald MacVicar of The Presbyterian College, Montreal, brought future ministers into contact with people who would be the lawyers, doctors, merchants, and politicians of the country. "By rubbing against these," MacVicar advised, "a man learns patience, learns to give and take, and to recognize that others have minds and ideas of their own." An arts course provided a broad and thorough grounding in contemporary knowledge and culture and developed the mental and moral powers needed to communicate the Gospel in meaningful language. MacVicar used some concrete examples, mostly in the Scottish dialect, to illustrate the problems an arts course would remedy:

Much pulpit eloquence of the day could be defined in the words of an old elder in Guelph, who thus characterised the production of a stranger who took the service one Sabbath: "It was naething but a braw blether o' words, an' what-nots, and whurlie-whas, and things they ca' eemages." ... The feelings of many congregations might be voiced in the words of Duncan the deacon, who complained of his minister thus: "He aye tak's a new text, and aye begins differently, but he aye gives the same auld sermon."

Ministers had to present the truth to their people in a new way and the tools to accomplish it were best provided by a thorough liberal arts education.[38]

By 1897, Knox board chair William Mortimer Clark was convinced that the preparatory course should be abandoned. The ministry, he wrote to the *Westminster* in 1897, required "the highest culture" in its practitioners and the maintenance of the preparatory department put "a premium on superficiality." The church's policy was "in painful contrast" to that of the legal and medical professions and the university itself, so much so that prominent Presbyterians were refusing to donate to the college until the course was abolished.[39] In 1898 the General Assembly abolished the preparatory courses at Knox and replaced it with a modified university course of three years to include the following subjects: Latin, Greek, English, mathematics, and one of biology, chemistry or physics in the first year; Latin, Greek, English, logic, psychology, and ancient history in the second; and English, mental and moral philosophy, medieval or modern history, and Hebrew in the third. Presbyteries remained responsible for examining all students for ministry in their knowledge of the Bible, the Shorter Catechism, and the Westminster Confession.[40] The decision reinforced the trust that the church had in the emerging universities of Canada.

In July of 1903, following the General Assembly's rejection of a plan to dissolve all formal links between the non-theological faculties at Queen's and the church, John Charlton, a Liberal MP and a leading opponent of the secularization of Queen's, presented yet another plan for college consolidation. Charlton had convened the Committee on Consolidation of Colleges in 1886 whose report had been rejected.[41] The denomination still had too many colleges, he argued, with the result that resources were scattered, efficiency impaired, and students often sought their education at superior institutions in Great Britain or the United States. He calculated that the student/faculty ratio in Canada was six to one, with only two graduates for each faculty member. To correct this waste of money and effort, he proposed that Manitoba College continue to serve Western Canada and that the other four colleges be consolidated. Queen's University, he argued, should stay in church hands as a means of permeating all the professions with Christian principles and contributing to making Canada a model Christian nation.[42]

The plan sparked a lengthy exchange of letters in the *Presbyterian* that lasted well into September. A.S. Morton, then minister of a three-point charge in New Brunswick, made the argument for retaining the present system that won the support of the majority in the church. The ideal to be retained, according to Morton, was to maintain a theological college in relation to, or at the very least in proximity to, the major universities in the country. This strategy, Morton argued, was the only way to ensure that the church retained its influence on higher education in Canada and kept the best men in the country. It also acknowledged the historical links that each of the colleges had developed with their regions.[43]

Behind the consolidation debate was the question of financing theological education. Knox had been successful in abolishing the common fund in 1888, but was left with only two sources of revenue – contributions from congregations and income from investments.[44] Throughout the 1890s, the former remained inadequate and the latter declined, due to the recession that hit the country. The board complained annually to the General Assembly about the lack of support from the congregations. Over 300 congregations gave nothing and many more who contributed generously to the other schemes of the church gave "only the most trifling amounts" to the college.[45] The board estimated in 1897 that it would take an additional $100,000 in the endowment fund to make up for the loss of interest alone, without considering the drop in value of the securities held. Expenses in 1895–1896, for example, were $21,907 while income was only $15,330, leaving a deficit of $6,576. With the appointments of Robinson and Ballantyne, the deficit grew at one point during the following year to $15,000, but the collection of arrears in interest on some securities, several legacies, and a campaign among friends of the college eliminated it by year's end.[46] Still, uncertain sources and extraordinary measures were the staple components of Knox College financing.

The endowments did grow substantially during the final years of the Caven era, due largely to the efforts of the members of the

Knox College Endowment and Sustention Fund, established in 1896. One dollar bought an annual membership and $50 bought a life membership. The purpose of the organization was "to extend and deepen the interest felt in the College, throughout the Church, to secure its more adequate endowment, and increase the ordinary revenue, so as not only to meet present requirements, but provide for additions to the staff, and other improvements which may from time to time be found necessary."[47] By 1904, the endowments stood at $350,000. At the urging of George L. Robinson, the college established its first two travelling scholarships in 1898 of $300 each to enable recipients to engage in further study outside Canada. The express purpose was to develop Canadian scholars who would be qualified to take chairs in the country's colleges and universities.[48]

The buildings were aging and the space inadequate for the growing needs of the college, presenting another financial challenge. The fire that destroyed University College in early 1890 was caused by an oil lamp, the same source of lighting used in Knox College. It was not until 1897, following a successful fund raising campaign associated with the fiftieth anniversary of the college, that the board could afford to install gas lighting and ventilation fans in the building. The latter had long been a sore point with the students from the opening of the college in 1875. James A. Macdonald wrote of the issue with characteristic bluntness:

Old students know how wretchedly the class-rooms were ventilated. … No wonder "Horne's Introduction" was dreary, systematic theology dry, and apologetics a burden. There are men now in their graves and others still in the flesh, but more dead than alive, whose ministry would have brought power to the Church had it not been for the blood-poisoning they suffered during their student years. The architects and building committees responsible for unventilated school and college class-rooms deserve a term in the penitentiary.[49]

A flu epidemic in Toronto in 1890 led the city to insist that the college replace all its plumbing the following year.[50] The most pressing need, however, was additional funding and space for the library.

In his final year as college librarian, Macdonald remarked that there was no danger "of a stranger losing his way in its labyrinths, or being overwhelmed by its endless shelves, or enticed into a cosy alcove by its rare bindings," because the Knox College library was "small, plain and cheerless." There were only 12,000 volumes, many of them "worthless, too antiquated to be of use to a student and not old enough to be relics." Most came as donations from ministers' libraries. What was needed, Macdonald claimed, was money to buy modern theological literature that contained "the treasures of truth and ... the armories of criticism and defence."[51] The alumni campaign in 1891 to raise $5,000 and James Mac-Laren's bequest of $20,000 in 1892 helped with acquisitions, but was not sufficient to meet the needs for more space. In 1894, the board noted the need for a new building for the library. Nothing further happened until the alumni association approved a campaign in 1901 to build a new library in honour of the jubilee of William Caven's ordination. The plans were for a building to house 40,000 volumes with an estimated cost of $30,000. The board, appreciative as it was of the initiative, determined that it would not begin construction until the full amount was subscribed and half of it was in the hands of the treasurer. Response, however, was poor. The year of Caven's death, donations totalled less than $8,000.[52] Eventually, plans for the Caven Library were incorporated into the design for yet another college building on a new site at the heart of the university campus.

The third debate that took place throughout the final years of the Caven era concerned the range of teaching the faculty should undertake. There was no question that their primary focus was the education of the denomination's clergy, but new needs and demands for their services emerged as the mission enterprises of the church grew and the denomination's mental culture broadened to include new interpretations of the great evangelical truths.

Alumni conferences began in February of 1894, modelled on those begun at Queen's the previous year. Queen's principal George M. Grant had seen these gatherings as an opportunity for the church to "reconcile itself to all that is best in modern thought."[53] The *Monthly* described Knox's intent in terms more closely related to the practice of ministry: "[The conference provided] a retreat where special attention could be given and help obtained for the study of new problems, critical, theological, social, which are continually presenting themselves to the minister in his active work, as well as for a fuller and deeper understanding of the sacred scriptures, and the prosecution of such other studies as will the more fully prepare and furnish the mind and heart for the great work of preaching the unsearchable riches of Christ." The program consisted of over 30 lectures by 12 different speakers, including two by Caven on higher criticism (the texts of which have not survived), and was attended by 120 ministers and most of the 79 theological students at the college that year.[54] Macdonald commented in 1899 that their value lay in the freedom of thought and speech allowed. They were useful "just in so far as an open mind is preserved and a frank expression of doubts and differences encouraged. This is the place where a man has the right to be frank without hurting another's faith or endangering his own ecclesiastical head."[55]

Initiatives were also taken in the area of lay education. In the summer of 1898, one of Macdonald's editorials in the *Westminster* urged the college to follow the example of the universities in providing broader opportunities for education to its constituency. He suggested that lecture series and classes for non-theologues would broaden the church's theological culture and increase "the circle of those intelligently interested and systematically instructed in theology." Professors should shift their attention from preaching and church administration to this new form of "large but unusual service."[56] R.G. MacBeth of Augustine Church in Winnipeg and Robert Falconer of Presbyterian College, Halifax, both responded favourably to Macdonald's suggestions and pointed to the summer sessions at Manitoba College as an example of effective seminary extension work.[57] The first series of lay education lectures sponsored by Knox were given in the fall of 1900 by Thomas B. Kilpatrick, professor of apologetics and Old Testament at Manitoba College. In them, he introduced his "miscellaneous audience of students, ministers, doctors, lawyers, merchants and ladies who by night crowded the Convocation Hall" to the Back-to-Christ movement among Scottish progressive biblical scholars and met with enthusiastic reviews.[58] In July of 1903, Knox sponsored its own summer school that drew students from across the province. Most were young people, elders, and Sunday school teachers seeking a broader grounding in the scriptures and theology, though some ministers attended as well.[59]

The most important initiatives, however, were in the education of women for professional church service. William Gregg and William MacLaren had held classes in theology for young women interested in appointment to the foreign mission field as early as 1877. Not until 1897, however, was the preparation of women for mission service regularized with the creation of the Ewart Missionary Training Home. The home had the dual purpose of assessing suitability for service and providing special training for mission service. The courses in the theological disciplines in the two year program were taught by the Knox faculty, Caven in New Testament, Robinson in Old, MacLaren in church doctrine, and Ballantyne in evidences.[60] The arrangement worked well with one notable exception. In the spring of 1899, Ewart students complained about John Edgar McFadyen's views on the authority of scripture. Ewart's superintendent, Anna Ross, widow of the resolute defender of Free Church confessional orthodoxy, John Ross of Brucefield, referred in her annual report to the fact that some of McFadyen's views had "jarred and perplexed" her and the students. The matter was dropped in the fall of 1899 because McFadyen asked to be excused from teaching Ewart students, Mrs. Ross resigned for undisclosed reasons, and the students who raised the complaints graduated.[61]

The resources of Knox College were stretched to the limit, if not beyond, in attempting to keep up with the needs of an aggressive and expanding church and with the developments in a growing and diversified university. The college remained the largest of the church's schools, as evident in the statistics published by the *Westminster* in 1902. Halifax had 4 professors, 1 lecturer, 21 students, 6 graduates, and an endowment of $133,000; Montreal had 5 professors, 4 lecturers, 53 students, 10 graduates, and an endowment of $273,000; Queen's theological faculty had 4 professors, 2 lecturers, 31 students, 11 graduates, and what was simply described as a "large" endowment; Manitoba had 5 professors, 5 lecturers, 25 students, 9 graduates, and an endowment of $95,000; and Knox had 5 professors, 3 lecturers, 69 students, 10 graduates, and an endowment of $355,000.[62] From a strictly financial point of view, with an eye to cost effectiveness, Charlton's consolidation scheme made sense. Each college, however, as evident in their endowments, had established a constituency and regional role of its own and resisted any efforts to amalgamate. They also resisted an effort to establish a Standing Committee on Colleges to coordinate needs and funding suggested to the General Assembly in 1903 by the Presbytery of Toronto. The assembly rejected the overture in 1904.[63] Each of the colleges, therefore, was left largely to its own devices in building up the base of support necessary to provide the programs deemed essential as the church struggled to keep up with the demands at home and abroad.

James A. Macdonald noted in 1902 that "the larger union of evangelical Churches is the hope of Principal Caven's mature years." The spirit of optimism and new possibilities in Canada noted by J.D. Robertson in his opening address at Knox in 1903 was pervasive in the college and throughout much of the church. J.W. Bengough, journalist, social reformer, and political cartoonist, who lectured in elocution at Knox during the late 1890s, caught something of the mood in a poem published in the *Westminster* early in Laurier's first term as prime minister:

As the tribes of old beheld it
On the wide Egyptian plain,
Bringing gracious peace and union
Out of long-borne strife and pain;

Banishing old feuds and hatreds,
Giving hope and courage new;
Lighting up the broad horizon
Of a future great and true.[64]

The final lines might well have been in the mind of the illustrator who drew the picture of a young man with arms outstretched welcoming the dawn of a new era on the first cover of the official magazine of the United Church of Canada in 1925.

Caven himself had speculated on what church union might mean for theological education at the banquet held in conjunction with the alumni conference in 1900. He noted that Presbyterians, Anglicans, and Methodists took the key foundational disciplines for theological study together at the university – Greek and Hebrew for Biblical study and philosophy for apologetics. Why, he wondered, could such common teaching not continue into the theological program in those subjects that did not involve denominational essentials? He had in mind exegetics, apologetics, homiletics, elocution, and Biblical introduction, theology, and history. The subjects that should remain in the hands of denominational faculty were dogmatics, church history, and church government. There was little public response to Caven's musings at the time, but the scheme did reveal one of the most important changes brought about by the new philosophical framework and the new methods of study, especially in the Biblical field. No longer was the identity of Presbyterianism as it had been understood by the proponents of confessional orthodoxy the priority. Instead, the search for a more unified expression of the essence of Christianity, both in intellectual formulation and organizational structure, took precedence. The practical needs of the church in mission, the evolutionary worldview of British Idealism that saw diversity gradually being overcome by unity, and the critique and revision of dogmatic theology promised by Biblical theology, all played influential roles in establishing church union as a priority. The new generation of progressive faculty appointed during Caven's final years carried the vision of a united Protestantism much further than Caven. Knox College was poised to play a leading role in the creation of the United Church of Canada.

5 Promoting the United Church of Canada, 1905–1925

The church union movement in Canada was not launched by the cautious and tactful leadership of William Caven, but by the visionary thinking and passionate oratory of William Patrick and C.W. Gordon. Patrick was the principal of Manitoba College and Gordon was the minister of St. Stephen's Presbyterian Church in Winnipeg and a writer of popular novels under the pen name Ralph Connor. In the course of bringing fraternal greetings to the Methodist General Council, which met in Winnipeg in 1902, they sketched out what proved to be a convincing picture of the benefits of an organic union among Canada's leading Protestant churches. The Methodists extended an invitation to the Presbyterians and the Congregationalists to enter into talks.[1] By 1906, a Basis of Union was drafted. By 1909, it was revised and approved by all the negotiating denominations.

Church union dominated the next twenty years in the life of the Presbyterian Church in Canada, causing a bitter controversy that resulted in one-third of the membership remaining out of the United Church of Canada when it finally came into being in 1925. Throughout the conflict, with two notable exceptions, the faculty and most of the students at Knox College were enthusiastic promoters of church union. William MacLaren, the aging champion of confessional orthodoxy and Caven's successor as principal, was opposed from the beginning, while church historian James Ballantyne was anxious that union, which he favoured, not split the church.[2] The prospect of church union pervaded the life of Knox College between 1905 and 1920, touching on every aspect of the college's work and informing the college's understanding of the church, its clergy, and their theological education.[3]

A PROGRESSIVE CHURCH FOR A NATION TRANSFORMED

T.B. Kilpatrick was the most prolific and passionate proponent of progressive orthodoxy and church union among the Knox faculty. Kilpatrick was already a confirmed church unionist when he arrived in Toronto in 1905 to take up his duties as the new professor of systematic theology. His convictions had been formed by the most prominent teachers of Scottish progressive orthodoxy and his theology expressed the key elements of that orthodoxy – an evangelistic piety, an idealist world view, and a devout higher criticism. His evangelistic piety came from his father, a leader in the Revival of 1859 in Glasgow, and was strengthened by the influence of Dwight L. Moody and Henry Drummond. As a university student, he discovered in the Idealism of Edward Caird and T.H. Green a worldview that provided a respectable intellectual foundation for his spiritual and moral commitments. In the teaching of the Scottish progressives, especially George Adam Smith, A.B. Bruce, and T.M. Lindsay in Glasgow, he found an approach to biblical history and interpretation that focused on the character and conscience of God's chosen representatives whose religious experience was recorded in scripture, with great emphasis placed on the uniqueness and divinity of Jesus Christ as a revelation of the ideal divine personality.[4] Kilpatrick's convictions were further shaped by six years in Winnipeg, working closely with Patrick and Gordon while teaching Old Testament, systematic theology, apologetics, and philosophy at Manitoba College. He quickly assimilated the spirit of optimistic nationalism and aggressive Protestantism that filled the city in the first decade of the twentieth century.[5] By the time Kilpatrick moved to Toronto, his vision of a united Protestant church as a national force for spiritual and moral uplift was fully developed and he took every opportunity to promote it.

Moral and social reformers in the Presbyterian Church in Canada sought comprehensive reforms in the personal, social, economic and political realms that would Christianize civilization.[6]

They used military rhetoric to stir Canadian Christians to response. "War, as we have known it," W.R. McIntosh wrote to Presbyterian young people in 1911, "is passing, but the virtues of war – its patriotism, courage, and self-sacrifice – must continue, or civilization will become a spent force."[7] The war spirit, with its moral courage and enthusiasm, had to become enshrined in a new struggle to overthrow the social and civic evils that threatened the piety, purity, and righteousness of the nation. Few of the reformers knew how wrong they were about war being a thing of the past. Within three years, many of those young Canadians to whom McIntosh wrote were in uniform on their way to a war of unimaginable proportions.

Most of the leaders of Canada's churches experienced the First World War from a distance. They read about it in the papers, heard about it from children and parishioners in letters, glimpsed it during short visits to the front, or grappled with it in pastoral conversation and prayer with grieving families and their friends.[8] The rhetoric of moral warfare that had been developed in the campaign for moral and social reform at home continued to shape their perceptions of the conflict overseas in the early years of the war. At the opening of new Knox College buildings on the central campus of the University of Toronto in September of 1915, John Watson, the venerated professor of philosophy from Queen's, told his audience that the war was ultimately one of ideas, of the superiority of "humanity and sympathy" over "force and fraud."[9] A *Globe* editorial the day before had characterized the conflict as one between domination and mastery and self-sacrificing service,[10] and three days later expressed confidence that "the present gloom" would soon recede and seem only an episode in the advance of civilization.[11]

Patriotic sentiment ran high. George L. Robinson, former professor of Old Testament at Knox, was invited back in 1915 to receive an honorary degree and to deliver a lecture on "Palestine and the War" to the alumni conference. In an interview with the press the day before his lecture, he was blunt about his neutrality, blaming the war on the extended build up of armaments by both sides and their refusal to negotiate a resolution to their disputes. Amidst the storm of protest, Robinson cancelled his lecture and returned to Chicago. Knox issued a formal statement criticizing his views and Gandier told the *Globe* that the college would not have conferred a DD on Robinson had they known his opinions beforehand.[12]

In a statement on Christianity and the war written for the church in 1917, Kilpatrick insisted that Canadian Christians recognize the sinful complicity of both sides in starting the war, but he tempered this admonition with his acknowledgement that the war had to be fought for the values at stake.[13] Modris Eksteins has argued convincingly that the First World War was "the civil war of the European middle class," pitting the bourgeois values of the British middle class against the emerging modernist values of the German. For the British, and their British North American colonial cousins who rushed to join them on the battlefields of Europe, "the concern with utility, success, and decorum, the worship of industriousness, perseverance, and moral commitment, the veneration, above all, of socially motivated effort and service," constituted the core of their culture.[14] It was precisely this culture, in its Christian guise, that the United Church of Canada was designed to defend and propagate.

By the end of the war, the chaplains who had served overseas had a disturbing message for churches at home. T.B. Kilpatrick's own son, George, enlisted as a chaplain with the 42nd Battalion of the Royal Highlanders of Canada the week the new buildings at Knox were dedicated. Writing to his father in 1918, he admitted that the experience of horror and pain was forcing men to fall back on God, but when they did they discovered that they did not understand their faith and were "reaching and groping for ... a coherent interpretation of their inner experience." Creeds and theological statements meant little, the younger Kilpatrick reported. Men in the midst of combat sought a more personal and direct interpretation of the presence and significance of Christ in their lives.[15] After the war, George Kilpatrick was part of the team charged with preparing the official report the chaplains made in common to their churches. The questions asked of returned chaplains assumed the church had failed in its efforts to win and hold people. The responses confirmed these impressions, finding not only a widespread indifference but also a disturbing ignorance of even the most elementary tenets of Christianity. One Presbyterian chaplain wrote, "there is in some quarters an amazing ignorance of the Bible itself, and nowhere does there seem to be reliable acquaintance with the creed of the Church ... confusion is rife regarding the meaning of Conversion, the necessity of Atonement by the death of Christ. ... All kinds of vague and often ludicrous theories of eschatology abound."[16] The chaplains' final report concluded that the church had to focus its witness and mission on "the great verities of the Christian Faith" presented in a manner and language that would meet the spiritual longings of contemporary society.[17] The agenda was hardly new, having been at the heart of progressive orthodoxy for almost twenty years. Much of the determination to accomplish it more effectively was channelled into the final achievement of church union as an essential means of spiritual, moral, and social reconstruction.

The war reinforced Kilpatrick's conviction that Canada needed a national Protestant church such as that approved in the Basis of Union to guide post-war reconstruction. The church, he wrote in 1919, was "an organic whole, a living organism, a spiritual community, whose creative centre is Christ, whose vital power is the Divine spirit, whose members are held together by one faith and love." It was Christ's agency of reconstruction: "It is the task of citizenship and statesmanship to rebuild what the war has shaken to pieces. The Church possesses the key to the situation, and the dynamic which alone can set it right. It has one great function – to proclaim the sovereignty of redeeming love, and to be itself the instrument by which that love shall dominate in the lives of men. Love alone can reconstitute the shattered fabric of humanity. It is the one reconstructive principle, the one recreative energy."[18] Theology, in Kilpatrick's mind, was crucial to the task of reconstruction. It was the reflective expression of the church's experience of the divine love of Christ. It had to be reformulated by each generation, using the thought forms of its age. As long as the church acknowledged, however, that its theology was primarily a witness to its collective experience of the redemptive love of God in Christ, persuasively present in the work of the Holy Spirit, it would remain in continuity with the church which Christ founded, in which Christ dwelt, and through which Christ worked to bring about the kingdom.[19]

In drafting the Basis of Union, and especially in its doctrinal section, Kilpatrick and the others on the Joint Union Committee were convinced they had managed to "conserve all that is vital and permanent in the creeds of the past," but restated the Christian faith "in the language and terms of present-day experience and reflection."[20] They were, in effect, revising the creed for Canadian Presbyterians. They claimed that they had recaptured the high point of evangelical unity achieved by the Reformation, a unity lost in the scholasticism of the seventeenth century and the polemics and controversies that divided churches throughout the eighteenth and nineteenth centuries. Kilpatrick viewed the United Church of Canada as the answer to the pessimism and scepticism of modernity and to the scandal and inefficiencies of ecclesiastical divisions.

Kilpatrick believed that the doctrinal section of the Basis helped the church make clear to itself the contents of its Gospel message and to declare that message in a full, clear, and persuasive manner to those outside the church.[21] The twenty articles reiterated the great evangelical truths in the following order: God; Revelation; Divine Purpose; Creation and Providence; the Sin of Man; the Grace of God; the Lord Jesus Christ; the Holy Spirit; Regeneration; Faith and Repentance; Justification and Sonship; Sanctification; Prayer; the Law of God; the Church; the Sacraments; the Ministry; Church Order and Fellowship; the Resurrection, Last Things, and Future Life; and Christian Service and the Final Triumph. The ordering of the articles followed the pattern of classic Augustinian piety, moving from God, to sin, then to the means, instruments, and effects of redemption.[22] Alfred Gandier claimed that the doctrinal section offered "one of the best and richest statements to be found of evangelical Christianity, and especially of those great saving truths which lie at the heart of the gospel." Theologians, he argued, had outgrown the old controversies between Calvinism and Arminianism and recognized that God's truth was "too big ... to find exhaustive expression in finite categories." What Christians of all ages held in common was their love of and loyalty to Jesus Christ. This bond of unity had the power to raise Christians above their "lesser loyalties" to denominations into "the higher unity and larger fellowship" of the transconfessional church being created in the United Church of Canada.[23]

The Joint Union Committee took the same attitude to differences in polity that they had to differences in doctrine, i.e., that they were diminishing and, in the end, insignificant. The founding denominations, they claimed, were "engaged in the same work, with the same object in view, and earnestly endeavouring to meet the conditions confronting the churches in Canada." Forms of church government and methods of administration were becoming more and more similar in the face of the practical problems of mission at home and abroad.

The older Presbyterian boards of home and foreign mission grew in the early years of the twentieth century and new boards were established for moral and social reform, evangelism, religious education, and publications. The new boards and agencies were designed to strengthen and supplement the home, the school, and the church, all the social agencies that progressives thought essential to the creation of a unified religious and moral sentiment among the Canadian people. The basic strategy for mobilizing a Christian nation was to educate, legislate, and enforce. The primary focus of the new agencies was education. The purpose of the wide variety of educational resources produced was to inform, motivate, and mobilize the membership of the church for evangelism and moral and social reform.[24] A subtle, but significant, shift took place in the dynamics of church government, however, as a result of the development of a larger bureaucracy. The initiative in setting policy, once clearly in the hands of the courts of the church, was gradually assumed by the agencies and their staffs. By 1912, national staff and agencies were suggesting changes in policy and strategies for implementation to the General Assembly and seeking approval to proceed. In church politics, as in secular politics, resistance to reform became frustrating for its proponents and a new strategy of legislating first, then educating people in the process of implementing the policies, emerged.[25] At the same time, funds for the agencies of the church, including the colleges, were being raised through national campaigns and channeled through national structures. Direct contact between the college and the local congregation diminished and more time was devoted to diplomacy and politics in the agencies and meetings of the General Assembly.

The threats to the church's power, influence, and to its very identity posed by urbanization, industrialization, and secularization strengthened the determination of many progressive leaders to provide resources for public worship that would bind the church together and forge a common Christianity. These efforts were first evident in the publication of the hymn books. In 1880, under the leadership of William Gregg and D.J. Macdonnell, Canadian Presbyterians produced their first hymnal. By 1896, it had sold over 500,000 copies.[26] The Rev. Alexander MacMillan, lecturer in church music at Knox from 1914–1925 and full-time secretary of the Presbyterian Hymnal Committee, guided the production of a revision of the hymn book that was published in 1918. It included a much broader range of the church's tradition in hymns and church music than had the earlier books.[27] Richard Davidson and Robert

Law from the Knox faculty served with MacMillan on the revision committee.

Though early efforts to produce a collection of texts for common worship met with stiff opposition, the work continued and a *Book of Common Order* was finally issued in 1922.[28] Kilpatrick, along with his Knox colleagues J.D. Robertson and James Ballantyne, were appointed to the executive of the committee to compile a book of common order established by the Canadian General Assembly in 1908, and were later joined by Davidson. Kilpatrick had been instrumental in the publication of the *New Directory for the Public Worship of God* in the Free Church of Scotland just prior to his move to Manitoba.[29] The purpose of the volume was "to promote the ends of edification, order, and reverence in the public services of the Church, in accordance with Scripture principles, and in the light especially of the experience and practice of the Reformed Churches holding the Presbyterian system." Young ministers especially were warned of the dangers of "obtruding [their] own personal moods and experiences upon the people in prayer, of varying the accustomed Order of Service without special and intelligible reasons, [and] of partial and capricious choice of topics in prayer." In historical continuity with the whole of the Presbyterian tradition, they were urged "to meet and give expression to the spiritual wants and cravings of the earnest and living members of the Church."[30] When the Canadian *Book of Common Order* appeared in 1922, the editors hoped it would "promote Christian unity through the cultivation of a community of soul and spiritual expression in Divine Worship."

The national Protestant church the Presbyterian unionists envisioned did not come to be. The Baptists and the Anglicans declined the invitation to join the union negotiations. As early as 1906, as Keith Clifford has documented, a resistance movement began to coalesce within the Presbyterian Church in Canada, led by lay people and designed "to preserve and maintain ... an institution rather than a particular theological position."[31] They sought to defend the historic integrity of a church that they thought had proven effective over the centuries in ministry and mission. In the end, they succeeded in convincing one-third of Canadian Presbyterians to remain out of the United Church of Canada.

The entire Knox faculty and all but five of the forty-three students enrolled in 1925 did enter the United Church. The faculty all shared a strong commitment to prepare the church's leadership to present the great evangelical truths of the Christian gospel in a clear, persuasive, and practical manner. Changes in the curriculum, new programs for lay leaders, and new facilities at the centre of the country's largest university were all designed to meet the challenges that confronted a united church in twentieth-century Canada.

EDUCATING PROGRESSIVE PASTORS
FOR A UNITED CHURCH

In October of 1905, on the occasion of the installation of T.B. Kilpatrick and H.A.A. Kennedy to the chairs of systematic theology and New Testament respectively, the *Presbyterian* noted that "Old Knox has a very great part to play in the moulding of our national future, and that she was never in a better position to be a genuine vitalizing force in the public life than she is at the beginning of her sixty-second year of service."[32] W.D. Armstrong, moderator of the General Assembly that year, reminded the new professors that education for ministry "in an age of intense intellectual activity when the spirit of questioning and unrest is in the air" was most difficult. He then went on to take a stance familiar to Canadian Presbyterians with respect to progressive orthodoxy and the practical focus of theological education:

The old and tested truths must be firmly held, but they must be cast into the moulds of the new thought and made to live. [The professors'] important work was the training of preachers, and their standpoint must be practical rather than academic, keeping steadily in view the preacher, the pastor and the people. Young men are being sent out into a work in which they are faced by destiny-determining problems, and into an atmosphere that is saturated with the spirit of inquiry, and it was their privilege as teachers to equip them for that work.[33]

The *Presbyterian* concluded its report by stating that the church expected its colleges to be "not merely schools of training in theological knowledge, but spiritual dynamos, sending forth men who, breathing the atmosphere of a higher life, and yet knowing men in their sins, their sorrows and their burdens, will go to them with the word that redeems and in whose souls the Christ-like love and the Christ-like passion burns."[34]

While Kilpatrick became the most prolific of the Knox faculty in writing for the church,[35] the men the church chose as his colleagues shared his convictions on the church, its clergy, and their theological education. Harry Angus Alexander Kennedy had studied at New College, Edinburgh, and been a classmate of Robert Falconer's in Berlin. In 1904, the year before he came to Canada, his Cunningham Lectures, *St. Paul's Conceptions of the Last Things*, were published. He emphasized two things in the book. First, he treated Paul as "an Hebrew of the Hebrews, [who] carries forward in a larger atmosphere the most splendid traditions of the prophets." Second, he found the roots of Paul's eschatological hope "not in any vague speculations concerning human personality in the abstract, but in the relation of the individual soul to the risen Lord, Jesus Christ."[36] Kennedy insisted that Paul held together both the individual and the collective dimensions of redemption and that his eschatology provided the confidence for Christian service in the world.

The next appointment made to Knox was that of principal. William McLaren finally retired in 1908 at the age of eighty-two. His successor was Alfred Gandier. Gandier came to the principal's office at Knox College well-known, well-respected, and well-connected. Born in eastern Ontario and raised in the Ottawa Valley, Gandier studied arts and theology at Queen's, where John Watson and George Grant were the dominant influences. Of Watson, he later wrote that he provided "a spiritual conception of the universe" and an intellectual basis for religious faith much needed among young theological students facing the questioning of Christianity in the late nineteenth century.[37] Grant's energetic recruiting, fundraising, and building at Queen's provided an example Gandier was to follow not once, but twice, as he oversaw the funding and construction of the new Knox buildings prior to union and of Emmanuel College after union.[38] Following graduation from Queen's in 1888, Gandier went to Edinburgh for a year of postgraduate study to complete his BD. Gandier returned to minister first in Brampton, Ontario, then in Halifax, Nova Scotia. While in Halifax, he was an enthusiastic promoter of foreign missions, especially in Korea, and part of a group of clergy and theological professors who called themselves the "Round Table." Among their number were several men who would assume prominent leadership in university and theological education during the early years of the twentieth century.[39]

In 1900, Gandier accepted a call to Toronto, where he succeeded Louis H. Jordon at St. James Square Presbyterian Church. St. James Square was still the congregation of Caven and Macdonald and many of the Knox students. In addition, many of the Presbyterian political and business elite of Toronto attended. From 1902–1908, Gandier lectured regularly at Knox in apologetics, served on its board, and acted as convener of the General Assembly's Committee on Young People's Societies. His brother-in-law and close friend from the Halifax "Round Table," Robert Falconer, was appointed President of the University of Toronto in 1906.[40] Gandier continued to be an enthusiastic promoter of missions, convincing the St. James Square congregation to sponsor a missionary of their own and playing a leading role in the growth of the Laymen's Missionary Movement.[41] The respect and connections he had acquired during his relatively short career prepared Gandier to recruit students, raise the funds necessary to build the new college, and guide the college through the stormy controversies surrounding church union.

By the time Gandier was installed as principal in 1908, earlier plans to build a new library had mushroomed into plans for a new college. The building on Spadina Crescent was in need of major repairs and was too small, especially if it were to house the Toronto theological college for the United Church of Canada. A site had been acquired that was at the heart of the university campus, right next to University College. Knox did not consider its mission confined to theological education. As Gandier put it in his inaugural address, "Knox must come into touch with the Presbyterian students of the University, must perfect her optional courses for undergraduates, and have a more direct influence in the educational, social and religious life of the student body." Gandier did make it clear, however, that the central purpose of the college remained the training of people for the ministry of the church. As such, it was not only "a centre of sacred learning and of practical training," but also "a warm vitalizing centre of spiritual life and missionary effort."[42] Much of Gandier's time during his tenure was spent raising money, first for the college buildings, then for the Peace Thankoffering following the war. He preached almost every weekend somewhere in the province and often spent Monday and Tuesday in the area calling on potential donors.[43]

Raising funds for the new Knox, Gandier was selling not simply a building, but a vision of the church that the building symbolized.

The United Church of Canada, into which Gandier was determined to lead the Presbyterian Church in Canada, was called to be the central moral and religious dynamic of the nation. The new college embodied this conviction, located as it was at the centre of the country's largest university and close enough to co-operate with the other church colleges federated with the university.[44] A competition for the design of the college was held. The seven sets of drawings submitted by various Canadian architectural firms were featured in the February 1911 issue of *Construction,* the professional journal of Canadian architects, engineers, and contractors. The winning design was by Chapman and McGiffin for a Gothic structure in the tradition of Oxford and Cambridge. It combined a library, an academic wing, a chapel seating 550, and a residential wing with 100 dormitory rooms, a large dining hall, and accommodation for staff. The estimated cost, without furnishings, was $373,000. In the end, construction, furnishing, and financing costs rose to over $700,000. The architects' explanation of their design for the academic wing and chapel facing the campus revealed their bias against the design of neighbouring University College. The style for Knox was chosen, they claimed, "because it lends itself to modern academic lighting requirements and has far more of the academic and ecclesiastical character than the style of University College, which is more suggestive of a museum than an academic building." The architects, made well aware of the inadequacies of the building on Spadina Crescent by Macdonald and others, described the ventilation system for the college in great detail.[45]

Within a year of each other, in 1909 and 1910, Kennedy and Mc-Fadyen returned to Scotland to succeed their mentors, Marcus Dods and George Adam Smith respectively. For Kennedy's replacement in New Testament, Knox looked again to Scotland. Efforts were made to convince James Denney to accept the chair, but he refused, noting to a correspondent that he had no desire to teach in a colonial backwater like Toronto.[46] He did, however, recommend one of his students, Robert Law, who gladly agreed. Law had spent 24 years in various congregations in Scotland prior to coming to Knox in 1909. Richard Davidson replaced McFadyen. He was one of J.F. McCurdy's top students in the Department of Orientals at University College. Born near Ayr, Ontario, he graduated from Knox, took advantage of the travelling scholarship he won to study in Berlin for two years, received his PhD from the University of

Toronto, and taught in Toronto and Montreal until his appointment to Knox in 1910.[47] He was the first Canadian with a Canadian doctorate to teach at Knox.

Law's inaugural lecture dealt with Albert Schweitzer's recently translated *The Quest of the Historical Jesus*, a seminal study of the eschatological element in the teaching of Jesus. He used the opportunity to analyze the German and British schools of biblical criticism. The Germans often theorized prematurely and without sufficient evidence, while the British were meticulous in their research and cautious in their conclusions. Law clearly preferred the latter, warning his future students "not to grovel at the feet of German criticism" and not to "put their legs in the yoke of its dogmatism, or be intimidated by its claim to exclusive possession of the scientific spirit and method."[48] In an article in W.R. McIntosh's collection of essays, *Social Service*, a call to arms to the church's young people to promote moral and social reform, Law claimed that "the history of Christianity in the world is nothing else than the development of the manifold significances that are contained in the divine whole of truth given in Christ." The responsibility of the present age, he told the youth of the church, was "to bring out with new fullness and urgency the social significance of Christianity" as embodied in the ideal of self-sacrificing service seen in Christ.[49] In addition to teaching at the college, he ministered to Old St. Andrew's Presbyterian Church in Toronto. His writing and teaching throughout his career were closely tied to the life and experience of the parish.[50]

Davidson and Law began their teaching careers at Knox just as more skirmishes in the battle over biblical criticism were breaking out in Toronto. Renewed protests against higher criticism at McMaster, University College, and Victoria College surfaced in 1909.[51] The *Presbyterian*, speaking for the progressive majority in the church, noted that such controversy was unpleasant and inconvenient, but would not last long. "Our Canadian Churches," the editorial continued, "have too much urgent and important work to do to waste time and strength on bootless wrangling. ... The Bible is a great religious literature, and invites every generation to approach it with closest scrutiny and freest mental detachment. Otherwise it were not the living Word."[52]

The next round of appointments took place following World War One. William Manson succeeded Law in New Testament. He remained for 5 years and was replaced by John Dow in 1924. When

Ballantyne died in 1921, the Assembly appointed Canadian John T. McNeill to the chair of church history. The history of the Presbyterian Church in Canada, he wrote in 1925, was "a story of the progressive expression of great principles":

Reinterpretation, reorganization, readjustment to environment, enter into every phase of her history. But through all variation there are heard the overtones of that immortal and divine Gospel which for nineteen centuries has rapt men's souls away from the pursuit of what is base and transient to the quest of Life Eternal. ... It is the history of the loftiest fellowship humanity has known, of the pledged communion of those who seek first the Kingdom of God and His righteousness.[53]

The education of the clergy at Knox during the twenty years prior to union aimed at preparing progressive pastors for the United Church of Canada.

Article XVII of the Basis of Union dealt with the clergy. As Kilpatrick pointed out in response to an Anglo-Catholic critique of the Basis, the whole document assumed that the priesthood belonged to all believers and that sacerdotal power belonged to the whole community rather than to "a mediating priesthood." Christ desired order in his church, however, and therefore instituted a ministry "to care for the spiritual life of the brotherhood, employing mainly the instrumentality of the Word and the Sacraments."[54] These ministers were Christ's gift to the church and their call and authority came from Him. The church's role was to receive and ordain those whom Christ designated and follow their leadership.

In his moderatorial sermon in 1921, James Ballantyne reminded the Assembly that the church's testimony had always been Jesus Christ, "His incarnation, His teaching, His life, His love, His death and resurrection and coming again." Each age and each race had the responsibility to find the means of witness appropriate to their time and place. The spirit of the present age was efficiency and effectiveness. Church union, Ballantyne claimed, was "surely the way of wisdom to make a better disposition of the forces at our command" for the task of witnessing to Christ.[55]

Kilpatrick claimed that ministers faced three crises in the twentieth century. Firstly, there had been a breakdown of external authority in religion. The prevailing tendency of the age, in Kilpatrick's analysis, was not infidelity, "but rather doubt and uncertainty as to religious truth, with consequent restlessness, intellectual and spiritual disquietude." Secondly, civilization had become increasingly complex, raising perplexing questions about moral and social leadership and how to create the conditions necessary for righteousness, peace, and joy. Thirdly, a materialistic attitude to life had denigrated the spiritual consciousness and the value accorded to religious experience. These problems caused "inner fears and misgivings," even in the souls of the clergy, for they could not avoid being to some extent children of their generation. For progressive Presbyterians, the external authority of the Westminster Standards had been replaced by the internal witness of the Holy Spirit in the religious experience of communion with God in the person of Christ. God's grace, the constant prayer, love, and sympathy of devout and believing people, and a thorough theological education were the essential supports needed by those called to this highest form of service in Christ's church.[56]

Ballantyne had suggested as early as 1908 that social conditions and intellectual uncertainties had created a noticeable drop in the number of people choosing to study for the ministry. The spirit of the age was dominated by materialism and economic expansion. Even higher education had shifted its focus from the humanities to the physical and practical sciences. The student population at the University of Toronto was still largely Christian, Ballantyne claimed, noting that the YMCA had over 950 in small Bible study groups at a time when the student body numbered 4000, but many of the most promising young Presbyterians "accepted the extravagant views of the value of material wealth" and sought careers in commercial enterprises. The conception of the ministerial office was changing, Ballantyne warned, causing confusion and uncertainty among those who might consider it. Biblical criticism had shifted attention from the question of whether a person should preach the Gospel to whether there was a Gospel to preach. Students decided to study for the ministry during their arts course, before the church's teachers of Biblical theology and apologetics had an opportunity to assure them that the Gospel indeed was secure and that preaching it did not involve intellectual fettering. In addition, other callings in journalism, business, and politics seemed equally "high and honourable." For some, the ministry was seen as "soft work," rather than a "full-blooded, robust, intellectual" calling that confronted evil and degradation with the righteous and uplifting power of the

Gospel. Ballantyne's remedy for the crisis in recruitment was to emphasize the heroic and the difficult, challenging candidates to sacrifice for the sake of the Redeemer. Further, he urged the church to emphasize the prophetic qualities of ministry rather than the priestly.

In progressive minds, the prophetic literature brought the tenets and ideals of the evangelical faith to their highest expression in the Old Testament. They were then embodied and brought to fulfilment in the person of Jesus Christ. The main themes of the prophetic literature were God's righteousness, mercy, and omnipotence, humanity's sin, and God's triumphant and irresistible redemption.[57] The prophet was seen to be first and foremost "a man of God ... who believed in God, lived near God, who listened for the voice of God, who waited on the Spirit's prompting, who, to use an expressive phrase of one of the greatest of the teachers of Israel, was one of those admitted to the 'council chamber' of the Almighty." As a result of their closeness to God, they were passionate for righteousness and convinced that God's purposes would in the end triumph.[58] Richard Davidson found the truth of Christianity rooted in the prophetic personality. "It is men," he wrote, "not books, that are inspired. God has long been revealing Himself to His own; and their lives have been filled with such a fullness of Himself that whoever comes near them is aware of a presence and a power." The real authority of the bible was found in the people whose living made the bible possible. It was not the words alone of Isaiah or Jeremiah that inspired obedient lives, but the characters of the prophets who voiced them. The purpose of a devout criticism was to bring their characters alive in the imaginations of believers.[59]

Kilpatrick was convinced that self-sacrifice was the most important quality of character that the church nurtured and the noblest contribution that the church made to the welfare of humanity. Preaching and administering the sacraments were God-given means by which ministers helped to develop this discipline in the church. In everything, the source and the end of their activities was the reconciliation with God achieved by Christ's own sacrifice on Calvary. Preaching and celebrating the sacraments, he wrote, "were great acts of faith, apprehending, proclaiming, commemorating, pleading, the one Sacrifice, once offered on Calvary, and now standing in the Presence for ever, the ground of Salvation, and the means of access into communion with the Holy God, as well for believers who sojourn in this world, as for those who have passed into the heavenly region. ... The one thing requisite in worship is the attitude of souls which answers in humility and surrender to the Divine Sacrifice which has won the world's redemption."[60] Throughout his career, in both Scotland and Canada, Kilpatrick took an active part in the promotion of evangelistic campaigns that stressed the virtue of self-sacrifice in Christianizing civilization. Programs of evangelism sponsored by the Presbyterian Church in Canada were modelled on those of American Presbyterian Wilbur Chapman.[61]

In the exercise of pastoral leadership, Kilpatrick and his faculty colleagues at Knox emphasized the importance of the practical application of the values and ideals of Christianity in everyday life. The primary work of the minister was the day to day work "among the people whom he knows and loves and whom he counts it his chief joy to lead to Christ and train for Christian service."[62] Its prophetic and progressive qualities came, not simply from the public advocacy of moral and social reform, but from the confidence in and reliance upon Christ's presence and guidance in the midst of a world disrupted by moral and social problems, torn apart by war, beset by intellectual confusion, and seduced by materialism.

PROVIDING PROGRESSIVE EDUCATION

In absolute terms, the Presbyterian Church in Canada grew steadily between 1905 and 1925. Progress was especially impressive in Western Canada. In 1905, the church claimed 1692 congregations and missions in Canada and 1345 ministers in charges or appointments. The communicant membership was 241,511. In 1924, 1708 ministers were on the constituent rolls of presbyteries serving 4516 congregations and missions. Membership stood at 379,762. Enrolments in Canadian Presbyterian theological colleges did not keep pace with the rapid expansion of the denomination. In 1905, a total of 191 were studying theology at the five Presbyterian colleges in Canada, 31 in Halifax, 39 in Montreal, 38 in Kingston, 53 in Toronto, and 30 in Winnipeg. The church opened three new colleges in western Canada to serve its growing membership there. Westminster Hall opened in Vancouver in 1909, Robertson College in Edmonton in 1911, and Saskatoon College in Saskatoon in 1914. By 1925, the number of students had dropped to 144 and a significant number were studying in the new western colleges. Only 20 were studying in Halifax, 12 in Montreal, 13 in Kingston, 43 in Toronto, and 16 in Winnipeg, while 22 were enrolled in Saskatoon, 9 in Edmonton, and 9 in Vancouver. The sense of constantly falling behind in the campaign to Christianize the nation pervaded the discussions of the clergy and their theological education in the period leading up to church union.

Concern with efficiency and effectiveness led the church to attempt again to create a national body to coordinate its educational work. In 1912, over objections that the move compromised the authority of the colleges, the General Assembly established a Board of Education to deal with "the general educational policy of the Church." The Assembly insisted that their intent was not to interfere with "the autonomy or individuality" of any of the colleges, but simply to exercise its legitimate oversight over the work of its agencies. The new board screened applications for the reception of clergy from other churches, coordinated recruitment efforts, provided for the religious needs of students attending any Presbyterian educational institution in Canada, visited all the church's educational institutions, including boys' colleges, young ladies' colleges, and the Missionary and Deaconess Training Home, and reviewed all requests regarding policy or funding from the colleges. In recommending the board, C.W. Gordon argued that it would provide much needed unity and coordination in the church's educational activities and provide a forum for the discussion of matters of common interest among the colleges.[63]

In setting up the Board of Education, the Assembly adopted principles of progressive education to be implemented at all its colleges. The standard of education was to be raised to "a higher plane alike of culture and efficiency." The main purpose of theological education was to fit the majority for "practical efficiency." While some should be prepared for the work of advanced scholarly investigation, "the great majority should be made trained speakers, teachers, pastors, and moral and religious leaders." The normal course would include both Greek and Hebrew, though some exceptions were granted. Psychology, sociology, and English were prescribed arts courses in preparation for theological study. A course in the Bible in English translation was considered essential to give the student "a broad comprehensive knowledge of the outlines of Scripture history and doctrine from Genesis to Revelation."

In addition, Biblical theology and Biblical sociology were to be mastered. The relation of the church to present-day moral and social problems and the principles of social service was to have a larger place in the curriculum, either through a department of practical theology or special lecturers. Students should study "local religions, social and industrial conditions, … the relief of poverty, the prevention of crime, and other forms of social service." The students should be carefully trained, both physically and mentally, "to deliver the message of the Gospel with freedom and power." A system of options or honours courses was recommended, to allow for specialization and stimulate higher scholarship, and "an adequate course in the principles and methods of Sabbath school work and missions" was declared mandatory.[64]

Knox had already anticipated most of the changes requested. Gandier and Kilpatrick visited American cities and colleges in 1908 to review what was being done there and presented their recommendations to the senate in 1909.[65] Two concerns motivated the revision. Firstly, the faculty were determined to provide a much broader range of practical subjects to prepare the students for exercising moral and social leadership in contemporary society. Secondly, the faculty wanted to change the program so that students could earn their BD during their initial three years of study, rather than through additional study following their theological course. Of all the colleges Kilpatrick and Gandier visited to gather ideas for the curriculum revision, Kilpatrick judged Union Theological Seminary in New York the best example of a school that combined "a high intellectual standard, with an intensely practical aim."[66]

Kilpatrick insisted that the classical disciplines in theological education, properly understood in relation to one another, still constituted the essential grounding for the clergy. The Bible, studied in a spirit of reverent scholarship that discovered the records of religious experience contained in its pages, was the foundation for all preaching and personal work. The Christian verities revealed in the Bible were defended in apologetics, stated in their significance and interrelation in systematics, and traced in their historic manifestations in church history. Homiletics dealt with the construction and presentation of the sermons by which Christian truths were commended to humanity. The primary task of the clergy was to plant the Christian faith in individuals and society as "a regenerative uplifting force." To accomplish this more effectively, Kilpatrick was convinced that the classical disciplines had to be supplemented by studies in religious education, missions, sociology, church polity and organization, evangelism, and pastoral work.[67] All these subjects, classical and practical, should be presented in their Biblical origin, their historical development, and their constructive statement and application. The changes, implemented in 1911, were based on the assumption that theological education was "not merely intellectual, but above all personal and practical, the deepening of experience and the strengthening of conviction, together with an increase of power to proclaim the message of Salvation clearly, fully, and persuasively."[68]

Throughout the early years of the twentieth century, Knox continued to work closely with the Missionary and Deaconess Training Home, offering classes in all the disciplines taught at Knox to women. In his moderatorial sermon in 1921, James Ballantyne drew special attention to the place of women in the ministry of the church. Though not ready to advocate ordination to the ruling eldership or ministry of word and sacraments, as other branches of Presbyterianism had done, he urged the church to provide "wider opportunities" for women. It was the conservatism of women that particularly attracted Ballantyne. The "great creative movements" in the history of the church had been under the direction of men, according to Ballantyne's reading of church history, but it was women who had done the most to conserve the "real value in the Christian inheritance, as transmitted from age to age." Ballantyne wanted to see the theological education offered to women become the equivalent of that offered to men, but it was attitudes such as his that prevented women from serving the church more fully. Nevertheless, Caroline E. McLaren not only graduated from Knox with her BD in 1925, but also won the post-graduate fellowship as the top student in her graduating class. She returned to teaching high school following graduation.[69]

In 1913, Knox began to offer evening classes for Sunday school teachers and volunteer Christian workers. Gandier saw Knox first and foremost as "a professional school, a technical College, just as our Medical Colleges, etc.," but he recognized that the church was not able to carry out its mission "through professional agency alone." It needed "a membership who work and witness for Christ as the opportunity offers, [and] an army of helpers who give a part of their time to teaching and social service."[70] The Knox lay school was designed to train that army. Eighty-seven people registered for the first year of classes and Knox went on to develop a three-year program of lay education.[71] Following the war, the pattern changed to a two-week intensive program in the winter term.[72]

In 1920, Knox asked the assembly to create two new chairs, one in religious education and the other in homiletics. The funds for the appointment in religious education were to come, in large part, from a grant from the Missionary and Deaconess Training Home. Both institutions were anxious to extend their work in teacher training and short courses for volunteer Christian workers. The professor of religious education would coordinate and further develop the work of both colleges in lay education. The Assembly refused.

The reluctance of the Assembly to create new chairs resulted from renewed concerns about the cost of the colleges and the size of their staffs in relation to the number of students. The Presbytery of Toronto had overtured the Assembly in 1919 to bring the teaching staffs of the colleges "into due proportion" with the number of students and reduce the cost to the church by forcing them to work more within the income from their endowments. Though the motion was tabled, more presbyteries forwarded similar overtures in subsequent years. The colleges, and especially Knox, were justifiably upset by these initiatives. Their share of funds raised for the schemes of the church had actually dropped from 6.4% to 5.6% between 1905 and 1919. To suggest that the colleges become less dependent on the annual givings from congregations and rely more on their income from investments was simply not realistic. Investment income for Knox rose by a mere $3230 between 1905 and 1919, while operating expenses increased by $24,790.[73] The overtures indicated that the Board of Education was not seen to be providing efficient coordination of the church's educational institutions. At the same time, it was faced with colleges constantly complaining about it having too much power.

The Knox College report to the 1922 General Assembly contained a polite but pointed attack on the Board of Education. The college asked that it report directly to the General Assembly, that matters of appointments be brought directly to the assembly, that recommendations from the Board of Education to the assembly be referred first to the affected colleges, and that negotiations with the colleges of other churches be done by the local colleges. The

Assembly turned down the requests and left the powers of the Board of Education in place.[74]

In 1922, in response to the overtures seeking more efficiency and effectiveness, the Board of Education encouraged the greatest possible cooperation, not only among Presbyterian colleges but also with neighbouring colleges of the denominations negotiating church union. Knox was given permission to appoint either a professor of church history or of religious education, but not both. John T. NcNeill was appointed to the former chair. All other appointments were postponed until a committee to explore "the most systematic and complete cooperation" among the colleges reported to the General Board of the church before the next Assembly.[75] The colleges were able to frustrate any serious effort to consolidate or rationalize the church's resources in theological education, but their demands for further resources fell on unsympathetic ears in the Assembly.

Knox had considered asking for yet another chair in sociology in 1920, but rightly read the mood of the church and refrained. It decided to take advantage of the appointment of one of their own graduates, J.W. MacMillan, to the chair of sociology at Victoria College in 1921 and sent its students to his classes. MacMillan graduated from Knox in 1891, did post-graduate work at Union Seminary in New York, and served Presbyterian churches in Vancouver, Lindsay, Winnipeg, and Halifax. Prior to coming to Victoria, he had been professor of social ethics at Manitoba College in Winnipeg for three years.[76] This was the first concrete step in a much more ambitious plan of cooperation between Knox and Victoria in anticipation of union approved by the General Assembly in 1922.

The aims of the plan were in keeping with the desire in the church for efficiency through cooperation. They included the prevention of duplication in lectures, the differentiation of "better equipped" and "less well-equipped" students, the provision of a wider range of courses for advanced students, and the extension of the training given by the colleges to religious workers other than clergy. In the Biblical courses, cooperation took place in the first and third years and in elective courses; in philosophy of religion and systematic theology, in one term of the first year and throughout the second and thirds years and elective courses; in church history, homiletics, and pastoral theology, in all elective courses; and in public speaking, religious education, and sociology in all courses.

Church polity continued to be taught separately and the requirements for the BD were to be set independently by each college.[77]
Part of Knox's anxiety over the chair of religious education was an
agreement with Victoria that Knox would supply faculty in that area
in the cooperative arrangement. In the end, Victoria's faculty covered sociology, public speaking, and religious education.[78] Knox
was not in the vanguard of such arrangements. That honour belonged to Presbyterian College, Montreal, where a Joint Board of
Theological Colleges Affiliated with McGill University was incorporated by the Quebec legislature in 1913.[79]

The era between 1905 and 1925 had been one of growth in progressive educational programs for clergy and laity alike, stability in
the size and perspective of the faculty, decline in the number of students at Knox, and, in the end, bitter disappointment in the realization of hopes for a united Protestantism in Canada. Gandier and
Kilpatrick wrote impassioned defences of the Basis of Union that
reiterated all of the arguments for the wisdom of the progressive
strategy of church union.[80] Those who opposed church union were
pictured as resisting the leadership of the Holy Spirit in the evolution of the effectiveness of the church. The truth was much more
complex and that complexity confronted those given the task of reconstructing Knox College for the continuing Presbyterian Church
in Canada.

The hope that the Toronto college of the United Church would be
housed in the Knox College buildings was dashed by the Ontario
legislature in April 1924. The opponents of organic union presented an alternative bill which included a provision for Knox College to "stay with the Presbyterians." Consultations led to the
realization that the house sympathized with the desire of the continuing Presbyterians to retain the college.

The strength of the resistance movement to church union and its
ability to convince the Ontario legislature to give Knox to those
Presbyterians who stayed out of the United Church came as no sur-
prise to the unionists. Since 1904, a significant number of Canadian Presbyterians had organized to resist church union. By the
time the first vote was taken in 1912, they had gained the backing
of one-third of the church and held that level of support throughout the controversy. The resistance was concentrated in the urban

centres of Ontario and led by prominent laymen with deep pockets and strong political connections. Their goal was to preserve an ecclesiastical institution that had proven effective in ministry and mission in the past and seemed to them to be well-designed to meet the challenges of the twentieth century. They were unwilling to risk what they considered to be a utopian dream of interdenominational union at the price of destroying their church. The success of the resistance in retaining Knox College became a symbol of the continuing church's legitimacy in the face of repeated United Church claims that the Presbyterian Church in Canada had entered union. The reasons for resistance were complex and provided the basis for various conflicts in the continuing church that will be examined in greater depth in the next chapter.[81]

As Gandier reported to the General Assembly in 1924, the question the college and its unionist alumni faced was, "Is it not in the interests of the Kingdom that Knox should submit to an immediate injustice and make a supreme sacrifice in order the sooner to bring peace, and allow the United Church to proceed undisturbed to its great task?" He continued with the rhetoric of sacrifice to express his grief at the loss of "the splendid pile" he had worked so hard to build and his determination to carry on:

the renunciation is not easy; and it is all the harder to bear because it is unjust and ought not to be necessary. But sacrifice is the very essence of our religion and the experiences of this hour have only served to intensify our loyalty to the great principle of Union and to give a new sacredness to the bonds which unite Knox men. Knox has had many homes, from the one room in an old James Street house, with a table, a few chairs and a small book-case in the corner, to the ample and stately gothic structure on the University campus; but Knox has always been more than a building, and again today with professors, students, alumni and friends, Knox fares forth to find larger expression for her life and spirit in the United Church, and under new conditions serve a wider constituency in that spirit of unconquerable love bequeathed to us from the fathers.[82]

The bill that finally passed gave the property to the continuing Presbyterians, but left the question of the charter and the endowments to be resolved by the Dominion Property Commission. Its final report was presented in April 1927 and awarded the charter and $230,000 of the endowments of Knox to the continuing Presbyterians.[83] The library and its endowments remained under joint administration and arrangements were made to share the buildings for three years while the facilities at Victoria were expanded.

The crises of the period leading up to church union, especially the war and the loss of the college in the final resolution of the church union controversy, did not, on the surface, dampen the progressive optimism of the Knox faculty. Gandier, Kilpatrick, Davidson, McNeill, and John Dow all joined the United Church and became the faculty of Union Theological College. Kilpatrick soon retired due to ill health and McNeill went to teach in Chicago in 1927. In 1928, Union and the Faculty of Theology of Victoria amalgamated to form Emmanuel College. Gandier became principal of the new college and launched into another campaign to build a college fit for the United Church of Canada.[84]

6 Reconstructing the Continuing Church, 1925–1945

The seventy-nine commissioners who gathered in the northwest corner of College Avenue Presbyterian Church in Toronto shortly after 6:00 p.m. on 9 June 1925 were a determined group. Straining to hear each other over the thundering notes of the Hallelujah Chorus being played on the church organ, they agreed to reconvene the Assembly at Knox Presbyterian Church on Spadina Avenue at 11:45 p.m. that evening so that they would be in session when the United Church of Canada officially came into being at 12:01 a.m. on 10 June 1925. The most important piece of business at that midnight sederunt was the reading of the Protest and Claim of Right that had been declared out of order in the afternoon. Pointing out that the Basis of Union contained many features that were inconsistent with the standards the church agreed to in 1875, the signatories claimed that they could not acquiesce with the decision to merge the Presbyterian Church in Canada into another church. Their statement of the purposes that guided their efforts to reconstruct the continuing church was theological in its focus. They pledged themselves to the "advancement of God's glory, the extension of the gospel of our Lord and Saviour throughout the world, and the orderly administration of Christ's house according to His holy word."[1] The two theological colleges that the continuing church retained, Knox in Toronto and The Presbyterian College in Montreal, were key institutions in its reconstruction. Knox was the largest and its stormy history over the next two decades revealed many of the crosscurrents that swirled through the continuing church.

As Keith Clifford pointed out in his study of the resistance to church union, the Presbyterians who entered the United Church of Canada made their claims in defiance of the common law and the Presbyterians who stayed out made their claims in defiance of an act of Parliament. The parting of the ways "resolved nothing" and "set the stage for continuing the conflict."[2] Were this the only conflict that the continuing Presbyterians had to face, matters might have been simpler, but the continuing church was made up of a number of competing factions and disagreements were common. The clues to the sources of the internal conflicts were to be found in the attitudes of those seventy-nine non-concurring commissioners and the others who joined them on 11 June 1925 to continue the business of the General Assembly of the Presbyterian Church in Canada.

A MIXED BAG OF CONTINUING PRESBYTERIANS

What united the commissioners of the continuing assembly was their opposition to the organic model of church union, by which denominations gave up their previous identity and blended into a new corporate body. Beneath this unified determination to preserve the Presbyterian Church in Canada, however, there were serious differences that would complicate the work of rebuilding the denomination. Their reasons for opposing church union were different. Their visions of the church and its mission were different. Their understanding of the standards of the church and of the authority of those standards was different. This diversity was not new to the Presbyterian Church in Canada. As we have seen, previous generations consciously adopted policies and created structures that allowed a broad latitude of opinion to exist within the denomination, and those who differed found unity in the practical work the church was called to do in Canada. The acrimony and alienation of the disruption of church union, however, allowed those still committed to an older confessional orthodoxy to emerge as the most vocal and public of the leaders of the continuing church in the periods immediately before and after union. In the bitter polemics of the controversy, the strict confessionalism of their arguments was portrayed by the unionists as narrow and sectarian, bordering on fundamentalism.

To add to the complexity of the task of reconstruction and to the strength of the conservatives, a severe shortage of ministers forced the denomination to accept a large number of ministers from other countries, especially from the United States and Ireland, where Presbyterians were much more polarized over the issues of church, ministry, and theological standards, than in Canada.[3] Many of those attracted to the Presbyterian Church in Canada from other countries were convinced that the best way to deal with the challenges posed by modernity was to stand fast on the substance and form of the Westminster Standards. This party did not represent the majority in the church. The ecclesiastical culture that was reconstructed in the twenty years following the disruption of 1925 was confessional, but in a way that owed much more to the Reformation than to the scholasticism of the seventeenth century.

Allan Farris identified four perspectives represented in the continuing church.[4] Only one, the strict confessional orthodox stance, was antiunionist. The other three were ecumenical in spirit, but opposed to the particular model proposed or the strategies and methods employed to achieve it. The anti-unionists held an exclusivist view, considering the doctrine, polity, and worship of the Presbyterian church, set out in the Westminster Standards, to be the only true interpretation of the Scriptures. Their goal was the maintenance and preservation of the church that upheld those standards. The federalists were sympathetic with the unionist desire to reduce competition and give fuller expression to the unity of the church, but saw federation rather than organic union as a more promising strategy. Federalism was seen by some as a step towards fuller union, and by others as the best means to accomplish their goals. The Federal Council of the Churches of Christ in America was the model to which they pointed. The federal option was proposed as early as 1904 and revived in the 1920s as a means of avoiding schism.[5] The ethical critics were those who objected to the methods of the aggressive unionists, charging them with being coercive, unfair, and inequitable. They accused the unionists of ignoring the agreement made early in the deliberations not to proceed without the wholehearted support of the church. This group of resisters was probably the largest in number. Theologically, they were sympathetic to the progressive orthodoxy held by those who went into union, but they were not willing to destroy one church to create another.

The fourth and final group Farris identified comprised the theological objectors. They represented an "honest fear ... that the United Church would move steadily to the left into a thinner and thinner liberalism,"[6] though the reasons for their fears varied. A number of the theological objectors identified with the anti-union-ists in their fear of liberalism and resistance to any change in the Westminster Standards. A smaller number feared the thinness rather than the liberalism in the Basis of Union. Principal Daniel Fraser of Presbyterian College, Montreal, for example, found little in the Basis that took account of recent Biblical research and the scientific orientation of the modern age.[7] Yet another group, com-posed largely of younger ministers, criticized what they saw to be the lack of theological concerns on both sides of the controversy. Walter Bryden, who would be called by the continuing church to teach at Knox College following union, thought the modernism he saw among the unionists tended "to naturalize Christianity, to com-pletely humanize it, and thus to inoculate man effectively against the distinctive challenge of the Christian gospel." The "external works of the Church" were substituted for "the necessity of a true soul culture and discipline."[8] Bryden was no less critical of those who held stubbornly to confessional orthodoxy. The modernists re-duced Christianity to a set of moral rules and obligations, while the conservatives limited it to a set of intellectual propositions. Bryden's refusal to accept what he considered "the maudlin religious senti-mentalism and platitudinism of a pampered age"[9] and his determi-nation to find a more faithful interpretation of Christian orthodoxy shaped the theological identity of continuing Presbyterianism in Canada.

The choosing of the new faculty for Knox College to replace those who had entered the United Church of Canada indicated the desire of the conservatives to control the theological ethos of the denomination but the unwillingness of the General Assembly to ac-cept a narrow interpretation of how the standards of the church were to be held. Conservative hopes were raised with the appoint-ment of Ephraim Scott as interim-principal in 1925. Scott was 80 years old, still editor of the *Presbyterian Record,* moderator of the continuing assembly, and had been a leader of the antiunionist wing of the resistance from its beginnings in 1904. He had close ties to Gresham Machen and the fundamentalist wing of American Presbyterianism. His appointment, however, had more to do with his moderatorial position than his theology and he had little influence over those appointed to permanent positions.

The lecturers for 1925–1926 included three of the four men who would be permanently appointed to chairs in 1926 and 1927. Thomas Eakin taught Old Testament, homiletics, and pastoral theology, as well as serving as vice-principal. He was one of J.F. McCurdy's most respected students in the Department of Orientals at Toronto, trained in and committed to the Biblical theology of progressive orthodoxy. Born in Northern Ireland in 1871, he studied and taught at University College, Toronto, was minister at St. Andrew's Presbyterian Church, King Street, in Toronto during the war, and had been appointed professor of practical theology at Presbyterian College, Montreal, in 1920. Walter Bryden, born in Galt, Ontario in 1883 and at the time minister in Woodbridge, Ontario, taught church history. Bryden had spent a year of his theological studies in Glasgow, where he had met his wife, and earned an MA in philosophy from Toronto in 1908. He enjoyed a growing reputation as one of the church's rising young scholars, especially after the publication of *The Spirit of Jesus in St. Paul.* The introduction was by William Manson, then of New College, Edinburgh, and the foreword by John Edgar McFadyen, then at Glasgow, indicating the respect former progressive orthodox Biblical scholars who had taught at Knox had for Bryden's scholarship. New Testament classes were offered by J.D. Cunningham, minister in Welland, Ontario. He had an honours degree in classics from Toronto and used his travelling scholarship from Knox to study at United Free Church College, Edinburgh, from 1904 until 1906. Both Eakin and Cunningham had been active in the resistance movement, Eakin editing the *Message,* the official publication of the Presbyterian Church Association, and Cunningham sitting on the committee to organize the campaign for the final vote on church union in 1924. Eakin represented the continuing church on the Dominion Property Commission, the body established by the church union legislation to resolve disputes over buildings and endowments.[10] Systematic theology was taught by Stuart Parker, minister at St. Andrew's Presbyterian Church, King Street, Toronto, and F. Scott

Mackenzie of Paris, Ontario. Parker was educated in Glasgow and remained at St. Andrew's throughout the rest of his career. Mackenzie had done graduate work at Harvard, went on to teach at Presbyterian College, Montreal, in 1926, and became principal in 1929.[11]

In 1926, the college nominated Eakin, then 56 years old, as principal and professor of Old Testament, and Cunningham, then 57, to the chair of New Testament. Both were appointed, though Eakin was asked to make a public statement of his adherence to the Westminster Standards by the commissioners representing the confessional orthodox wing of the continuing church to assure them of his attachment to the standards of the church.[12] The college informed the assembly that they had been unable to find a qualified candidate for the key chair of systematic theology, in spite of the fact that E. Lloyd Morrow, author of *Church Union in Canada: Its History, Motives, Doctrine and Government,* a study of the movement sympathetic to the resistance, had been nominated by fourteen presbyteries. Born in Millbrook, Ontario in 1884 and another graduate of McCurdy's Department of Orientals, he had taken his theological training in Edinburgh and his doctorate at the University of Chicago. There was strong evidence, however, that he had lobbied for the position and the college did not consider him suitable. Nevertheless, Banks Nelson of Hamilton nominated him from the floor and the assembly appointed him. The results were disastrous for the harmony and effectiveness of the college until Morrow finally resigned in 1936, but that story will be told later. Walter Bryden was appointed professor of church history and the history and philosophy of religion in 1927, having received nominations from 24 of the church's 43 presbyteries. While it is tempting to see the appointments to the college as representing the various parties and perspectives in the continuing church, such was not the case. Eakin, Bryden, and Cunningham were grounded in the progressive orthodoxy and Biblical theology of their predecessors who entered union. Bryden, in the end, would question and challenge his roots more thoroughly than the others. Morrow is more difficult to categorize. He seems to have had considerable support in conservative circles, but described his systematic theology to Eakin in one of his letters seeking support, as "sound, modern and fresh in originality," different "from anything taught in Canada."[13] In a later letter, he expressed his concern that "a semi-educated fundamentalist should be saddled on us in the chair of systematics.[14] In the end, his sense of being persecuted and the incompetence of his teaching made his theological perspective of secondary importance. The theological issue the faculty at Knox would be called on to address immediately was the nature of the church and the perspective that should guide the reconstruction of the continuing church.

THE NATURE OF THE CHURCH

The debates that erupted among the various wings of the continuing church in the years following union tended to coalesce around two major issues, the nature of the church and its ministry in the world. When the continuing General Assembly met in St. Andrew's Presbyterian Church on King St. on 11 June 1925, a plan to reconstruct the denominational committees and agencies, developed over the previous four years, was ready for implementation. Suspicion of the power of the clergy was evident in the establishment of the Board of Administration, "not to exceed forty in number and to be composed of laymen experienced in business and finance whose duty it shall be to take the oversight of all business and financial affairs of the church." Its initial membership included all the prominent laymen who had guided and funded the resistance to union, several of whom were also appointed to the senate, board, and trustees of Knox College.[15] Thomas Eakin announced in the July *Record* that Knox was ready to offer "a complete curriculum" for the coming session in "that fine building which is not only a magnificent product of architectural art ... but a great and valuable emblem of the stability of Presbyterianism."[16]

When the college opened that fall, Ephraim Scott's memories went back to the old building on Spadina. The fact that the street had to be built around the college reminded Scott of a rock standing firm and immovable in the middle of a stream. He continued the analogy in his fervent and partisan anti-unionist rhetoric:

A great Ecclesiastical Spadina, broad enough to admit almost any religious belief, and much of unbelief, and pledged to no belief, disregarding alike its own ordination vows, its agreements and pledges, and the conscientious convictions of tens of thousands of our people – has in these latter days swept up against our Church imperiously demanding universal right of way. But that Ecclesiastical Spadina has had to follow the example of its prototype of former days, and pass around, and, as we meet to-night, we give thanks that our Church – with this our College – still stands upon the old Presbyterian foundations, – the Word of God as the only Rule of Faith and Life, and the Great Truths and Teachings of that Word as set forth in the Doctrinal Standards of our Church, the Shorter Catechism and the Confession of Faith; the Truths and Teachings, on which and for which we believe the Church of Christ was founded, Truths and Teachings centring in the Sovereign Love of God and the Deity and Atonement of Jesus Christ to which our Church is pledged![17]

As Scott had made clear in the *Record* the month before, he considered the Presbyterian Church to be a voluntary association of men and women "who accept and profess the great Scriptural Truths and Principles, the Systems of Doctrine or Religious Belief and of Polity or Church Government, which Presbyterians believe to be founded upon the Word of God."[18] The church was the people, not the clergy, and when there was a shortage of clergy, the people were capable of doing "their own housekeeping" until a suitable servant of the church could be found.[19] Scott's view that the laity constituted the core of the church and that the clergy should assume a subordinate servant role was rooted in his assessment that the clergy had abandoned the Presbyterian Church in Canada during the union controversies. It was not shared widely, especially among his fellow clergy.

Thomas Eakin's understanding of the church stood clearly in the tradition of progressive orthodoxy. In sermons preached in 1917 and 1918, he expressed his conviction that God was in control of history and that the Kingdom of God was gradually emerging. The Christianity that the war called forth was "one that cares more for duty than dogma, more for conduct [than] creed, pays more attention to orthodoxy of behaviour [than to] orthodoxy of belief." The war, in spite of its carnage and cost, convinced Eakin that a new social, economic, and political order was coming and that God was at work "in a richer and more manifold way than in any age in history."[20] The church was called to realize the ideal upon which its life and witness was based and to become "a society of men and women banded together by a common faith in God and witnessing to a moral and spiritual ideal of life based on the principles of love and sacrifice revealed in Christ and inspired by his Spirit."[21] Eakin remained convinced, however, that denominationalism was more of a blessing than a curse. Its benefits were rooted in the principles of freedom and the right of private judgement. These values, for which Canadians had sacrificed in the war, lay at the heart of Eakin's vision of Protestantism. He argued that the church must remain the church, not become a big institution or organization. If it resisted these temptations of modern culture, it would remain "a Church that will water the roots of life, a Church that will be one of devotion and worship, a Church of educated ministry."[22]

Walter Bryden was the most articulate and influential of a growing number of continuing Presbyterians who were compelled by their theological studies to rethink more radically just what the church was.[23] In the Genevan Reformation, Bryden found a renewing source of wisdom "far more profound and challenging because it is essentially theological rather than ecclesiastical." What turned Europe upside down in the sixteenth century was not a new church, but "a new vision of God," and the church in Canada needed to be open to the same radically challenging vision if it was to recover its proper sense of mission.[24] What strengthened Bryden's appeal to students was his obvious concern for and understanding of the pastor's pulpit. In a review of Bryden's first book on the Corinthian church, John Dow described Bryden as the ideal interpreter of Paul because he was "not the scholar who knows all the lore of the dictionaries, but the missionary on the field who has had fresh contact with the heathen heart, and the preacher who knows the vexations of congregational jealousies and strange teachers." Dow agreed wholeheartedly with Bryden's assessment that Paul was not "a master logician drilling all Christendom into a mechanically conceived creed, but a man on fire with Christ, pleading, exhorting, teaching a faith that saves."[25] Continuing Presbyterians found in Bryden the same spirit.

During the 1920s, Bryden was already drawing on the uncompromising critiques of contemporary liberal theology and ecclesiology coming from Swiss theologian Karl Barth and his European colleagues as they articulated their "dialectical" or "crisis" theology that formed the core of neo-orthodoxy. They stressed the contrast between the transcendent God and sinful humanity and argued that the church must maintain its distinction from the prevailing culture, challenging it with a witness to the unique Word of God in Jesus Christ.[26] In an address in Montreal in 1929, Bryden called

Barth "that stern, new prophet of Europe." He pointed to his radical understanding of how humanity came to a knowledge of God as the crucial element in the identity of the church. It could not be taught, but had to be discovered through "fierce, inner, personal conflict." Once discovered, it was to be sustained by "being steadfastly true to our highest selves at any sacrifice." All cultural, moral, and patriotic duties and all efforts in applied religion were "child's play" by comparison. Our knowledge of God was not "a corrected continuation of our own." God must first come to us and encounter us as "a wholly other" in order for us to know God truly. This assertion that the great Christian verities were not at our command, but rather, they grasped and shaped us according to God's Word, was "real Calvinism in modern dress."[27]

"Christians," Bryden wrote shortly after the outbreak of the Second World War, "should always have perceived, through their faith, that, apart from God's utterly judging, utterly saving Word, Jesus Christ, all human culture and achievements become corrupt."[28] Throughout his career, he insisted that the church was dependent on God's Word. Both Old and New Testaments, he said in his inaugural address as principal of Knox College in 1945, were unequivocal in their testimony that the church came into being "only because of the peculiar constraint which God's Word, together with the attendant Holy Spirit, had exercised on the souls of certain men. Truly the Church is the product of the Word and Spirit of God and would not have existed at all except for the power manifested by these in this world." He went on to make his characteristic connection between God's Word and the person of Jesus Christ:

To put it another way, this world would not have the remotest idea of the radical nature of God's will concerning man, were it not that this very Word had become flesh in the Person of Jesus Christ; that He thus dwelt among us – yet without sin – and that, because of this event, there had arisen a community of believers, a "fellowship of the Spirit", a "Body of Christ", charged with *one* supreme responsibility, namely, to *witness* to Him of Whom the world was ignorant.[29]

This view of the church became enshrined in the subordinate standards of the Presbyterian Church in Canada in the Declaration of Faith concerning Church and Nation, adopted in 1955. After asserting Christ's lordship over church and state, the declaration distinguished the spheres of responsibilities and the kinds of relationships that each has to Jesus Christ. The church, it stated, is ordained "to serve Him in the proclamation of His word, in the administration of His sacraments, and in the life of faith which works by love."[30]

Bryden saw in the smallness of the continuing church and the theological searching of a growing number of his students an opportunity to recover "the keen spiritual insight into and fidelity to Christ"[31] that had given power and vitality to the churches of the Genevan Reformation. Three marks of the church stood out for that movement. The church was conscious of possessing the gospel, it was missionary in spirit, and it was catholic in sympathy. Taken together, these marks produced a unique agency set apart in the world for witness and service to Christ. More often than not, these marks were obscured by human arrogance and ambition.

That the Church can contemplate with complacency conditions, in which subtle and selfish intrigue, pure ecclesiastical politics and secular ambitions, can comfortably prevail, not to say, triumph; in which the conventional moralisms and platitudinisms of a sophisticated intelligentsia, supported by the possession of wealth and so-called social prestige, are respected, is a very serious position. It is to have substituted the veneer of Christianity for the insight and knowledge of faith.[32]

Bryden readily acknowledged that his view of Presbyterianism and its theology of the church was not held by all Canadian Presbyterians, but he persisted in his prophetic role of calling the denomination back to what he called "*essential* Presbyterianism" in "its more original and universal forms" as the only kind of Presbyterianism that possessed a "particular significance and a particular challenge" for the twentieth century.[33] By the time of his death in 1952, it was the official ecclesiology of the denomination.

For Bryden, the key issues in ecclesiology were theological and the critical message the contemporary church had to hear was that its life and witness were grounded in and determined by the radical challenge to human wisdom encountered in Christ's unique life and witness. He stood in firm opposition to Ephraim Scott's confessional orthodox theology of the church as a voluntary association of the people gathered around a particular understanding of the Gospel[34] and to Thomas Eakin's progressive orthodox theology of the church as a society formed to embody and propagate moral and spiritual ideals. The church was first and foremost the Body of Christ, invested with a unique character and entrusted with a unique mission in the economy of God's salvation. In both Scott and Bryden, there was a movement back to the basics of what made the church the church, accompanied by a suspicion and mistrust of the broader culture in which they found themselves. Their strategies for reconstructing the denomination, however, were very different and those differences showed up in their theologies of ministry and the place of the clergy in the church's mission.

THE MINISTRY OF THE WORD

The second major issue faced by the continuing church focused on the theology and practice of ministry. The choice of Justice William E. Middleton of Toronto as convocation speaker at Knox in 1927 indicated the importance of the laity for the continuing church. Middleton told the graduates that their most important task was the care of those within the fold in order to build up the church of God. The primary requirement was a living faith, for "the spiritually dead cannot be the means of awakening spiritual life." The affairs of the Kingdom of God were to command the clergy's time and attention. They should have a good education and continue to read widely after graduation. The only hope of continued vitality in their vocation was the combination of prayer and meditation with reading and study. For Middleton, all of this spiritual and mental discipline contributed to preaching, the act of central importance in the minister's care of the congregation. He advised humble reverence in the pulpit, avoiding shows of intense emotion, or academic brilliance, or strong political opinion. "The great topics," he said, "Righteousness, Holiness, Mercy, Truth and Justice and the score of other exalted themes, and the practical expositions and illustrations of the Holy Book afford ample to build up the character and ennoble the lives of your parishioners." People came to church with sore and aching hearts seeking for healing and comfort and they should be able to find it. While the vine dressers did not establish the relationship between the vine and the branches, they were responsible for the yield. In the same way, the clergy were responsible for meeting the spiritual needs of their flocks, teaching and training them, feeding their hungry souls, giving medicine to their sick souls, and providing "courage to the fearful and strength to the weak and comfort to the sad."[35]

Middleton struck on several themes that ran through the thinking of the Knox faculty on ministry during the reconstruction of the continuing church. First, the focus of the clergy's attention was on the care of those within the congregation, rather than on the broader mission of the church in the world. They were to edify and equip Christians for their ministry in the world. Second, there was a continuation of the insistence on a devout and learned ministry in which the spirit and the intellect complemented one another. Third, the Gospel in its simplicity and purity was seen as the answer to the multitude of problems and the depth of pain experienced by the human race. In pleading for a strong pulpit ministry, Middleton consciously avoided taking sides in the theological disputes of the continuing church. Representatives of the differing perspectives read their own convictions into the broad framework that Middleton offered for the ministry of the Word.

Speaking for the confessional orthodox group among the continuing Presbyterians, Ephraim Scott used his moderatorial year and position as acting principal of Knox College to press the importance of the message for the clergy. The service they rendered to the people of God who constituted the church was to deliver the message that humanity was reconciled to God in Jesus Christ and urge people to be reconciled with God by accepting it. The message, in Scott's words, was "the story of God's love, and what that love has done for men, to open the way for their reconciliation to God." Clergy who sought to adapt the message to changing times, or worked to improve the physical conditions of life were abandoning their calling, which must remain true to the task of pleading with people to be reconciled with God by accepting the message unaltered: "A Ministry which makes the Scriptures its storehouse of Truth, and digs deep in that storehouse, which studies and prepares carefully its sermons, which is faithful in pastoral work, watchful above all for the young, and seeks, with God's help, to live the Gospel that it preaches, will not wear out, but will wear in, ever deeper, into the religious life of the congregation."[36] For Scott and his confessional orthodox colleagues, the truths of Scripture were "summed up in the Westminster Confession and Catechisms,"[37] while the relationship of the clergy to these standards was clearly set out in the ordination vow which required them to accept them as "founded upon and agreeable to the Word of God" and adhere faithfully to them in their teaching. For them, theological education provided the time and tools to master these truths and grounded future clergy firmly in this worldview and ethos.

Thomas Eakin, in classic progressive orthodox fashion, understood the work of the clergy to be the development of the spiritual culture of the members of their congregations by teaching, devotional leadership, and evangelical outreach.[38] The clergy nurtured the classical virtues of beauty, truth, and goodness in their Christian form. In 1929, he urged the students at Presbyterian College, Montreal, to introduce a new spiritual aesthetic into Protestant devotion and worship to satisfy the profoundest needs of the religious consciousness. They should make worship "a reverent concentration of the whole being upon the highest ideals." Eakin went on to assert that anyone who believed in a living God had to believe in an expanding truth. God adapted truth to the expanding needs of humanity and the preacher had to follow by treating the great themes of the Christian faith in a vital and positive manner. It was easy for a speaker to gather a crowd by being "fantastic, extravagant, or smart," but to turn the crowd into a church, a preacher had to exegete the religious truths of the text of Scripture. Christianity also had to be effective in practical life and its principles applied in every phase of life. The Christian life was a "strenuous and compelling adventure." Eakin was concerned, however, with the imbalance of these virtues in the modern church. The danger was that the church would lose sight of its real source of power and purpose in Jesus Christ as it became caught up in a "bewildering, kaleidoscopic" round of "conventions and resolutions and committees and talk and programs." Attention to spiritual beauty and divine truth, in Eakin's mind, was the only means of preventing this.[39]

Walter Bryden's theology of ministry was shaped by the same sense of uniqueness that had formed his theology of the church. He warned against the "modern easy habit of equating civic virtues and intellectual, cultural qualities" with true Christian spiritual life and modern humanity's failure to distinguish between world orders as such and the church, "the only realm of God's redemptive activity." The ministry of the clergy was not a professional service to civic and cultural ideals, but a vocation that came to those who had been seized by "the humbling and condemning power of the Lord, the Judge and Saviour of all the earth."[40] That vocation came from

God through a congregation and entailed a responsibility to both. It led to a personal obedience to Jesus Christ exercised primarily in the congregation. The burden of its work was to deal with "the anxieties, insecurities, fears and sins of every individual under [the clergy's] care."[41]

In a pamphlet issued by the General Assembly in 1927, Bryden described the theology of ministry he found at the heart of Presbyterianism. It affirmed that the clergy were Christ's gift to the church, given along with the "oracles and ordinances," and that their effectiveness depended on Christ's presence. This office of ministry was not the creation of men nor of the church, but "the gift of Christ Himself." In direct opposition to Scott's populist ecclesiology and theology of ministry, Bryden argued that the clergy's power in governing and guiding the church came not from the people, but from Christ. He found no warrant in Scripture for any "meticulous ecclesiastical claims for Church government or ministerial orders." The early church was not planned or programmed. The community discovered its leaders in those in whom the gift to declare the will of God was obvious. Throughout the history of the church, its vital branches had held to a high doctrine of the ministry of the clergy as Christ's supreme gift to the church.[42]

Bryden was realistic about the motivations for entering this ministry. The promise of adventure, the desire to serve, the opportunities of a reflective life, and the privileges of leadership all led people into the ministry of Word and Sacraments, but they were not sufficient to sustain the calling. Poor and selfish motives often inaugurated things, but God had a strange way of leading people into their deeper selves as the tests and trials of ministry unfolded. The clergy encountered "troubles, perplexity and opposition" in ways few others did, but if they remained just and fair to all the circumstances of human life they would "know and share the love of men and ... become a power to awaken their souls."[43]

From the beginning of his teaching career, Bryden knew that those things which made this form of ministry "the most fruitful and most satisfying of all vocations" could not be told or taught by another person or a book. They had to be discovered as an "inner quality of conviction" along the road of life.[44] What the continuing Presbyterian church did provide, however, were the opportunities to exercise such a ministry and discover these qualities. It maintained the Reformation tradition of seeking out "Godly and learned" people for the office and placed the responsibility for discerning and encouraging people of "sound scholarship and culture, moral earnestness and true spirituality" on the local congregations and their clergy. Bryden was suspicious of special efforts to recruit candidates, likening them to a special campaign to recruit "poets and artists." The church must wait on Christ to raise up those he called, but, at the same time, be constantly watchful for the signs of their giftedness.[45] As had always been the case in the history of the church, the chief agencies in the supply of clergy were "faithful, godly ministers … together with God-fearing homes."[46]

For Bryden, the primary task for the clergy was preaching. Its purpose was "preaching Christ and what that means." In the course of preaching, one's soul was unveiled as being touched by God and one's thinking was revealed as having "passed through the fires" of one's own experience of being encountered by the otherness of God. Preachers had to have a gospel and own it. Bryden warned his students that they would find people in their congregations who knew far more about the Christian faith than they did, "especially in its inwardness, its strange wisdom, and its power." As they struggled to preach the Word faithfully, however, God would unveil and use this wisdom to bless their ministry.

Using the example of Mary Slessor's missionary work among the Africans in Calabar, Bryden advised future clergy that the real test of ministry was what they would do and inwardly be "in the face of deepest disappointment and baffling frustration, in the face of those people you are sure to meet who never seem to get the real and greater meaning of the thing you believe and try to teach." What marked the response of those who responded to Mary Slessor's proclamation of the gospel was awe. Bryden considered that attitude the first thing in religion and worship and the key to sympathy and fellowship: "To see in the life around us, in the men and women we have known and in whose presence we have stood, humbled, and to see in this Christian religion, and in that unsearchable and indefinable person, Christ Jesus himself, *something* which eludes our grasp altogether and yet which haunts us as the ultimately real, which we cannot ever give up, to see this is to possess the soul of a preacher who will be able to help his fellow men." Bryden's conviction that the church could no longer impose its authority on an enlightened people led him to the conclusion that the church "like her great Head will be obliged to learn to command men's souls by her own inherent and self-evidencing power of character and by her obvious witness to the truth and by nothing else." The triumph of Christ's reality would come when preachers sounded "the authentic note of that something *'Other'* in the soul" and people heard in the preacher one who had surrendered truly and fully to God.[47]

While Bryden was suspicious of inflated trust in the abilities of humanity to find and express true Christianity, he was very confident in the positive power of the gospel to accomplish what the world needed. Speaking at the centennial celebrations of the founding of the congregation at Old Kildonan, Manitoba, he traced the sense of call that led John Black and his successors to face the challenges of missions in western Canada. "No negative, apologetic Gospel … nor any prosy Gospel," he concluded, could meet the "stupendous difficulties" that faced the church then and now. "They demand an absolute, positive, convinced Gospel, eager, joyous and triumphant, believing in itself because it knows that Christ is actually in the world, and is the strength and stay of the Church."[48] During his first twenty years of teaching at Knox, Bryden saw increasing evidence of the damage caused throughout the world by the presumptions and pretensions of humanity manifest in the Depression and the Second World War. He challenged Canadian Presbyterians to demand a tough clergy for a tough calling, but constantly reminded them that the promised presence of Christ was their sole but sufficient source of power.

Speaking to the graduating class in 1947, he warned that honest and true preaching would meet with stern opposition and require unusual courage, patience and humility, but preachers who dug deep, who were faithful, and demanded much in God's name, could not fail. He concluded with some verses from "an obscure pastor of Hessen to his fellow-ministers:"

God needs men, not creatures
Full of noisy, catchy phrases.
Dogs He asks for, who their noses
Deeply thrust into – Today,
And there scent Eternity.

Should it lie too deeply buried,
Then go on, and fiercely burrow,
Excavate until – Tomorrow.[49]

It was characteristic of Bryden to remind his listeners and readers of the presence of the extraordinary in the midst of the ordinary, whether it be the unsung missionary efforts of the Women's Missionary Society, or the week-by-week ministry of his mentors and colleagues in the clergy, or the profound and vital faith of members of congregations across the country and around the world. His high sense of the origin and authority of the ministry of the clergy never blinded him to the fact that it was a service to Christ within the church for the sake of the redemption of the world.

Bryden's theology of the church and its clergy challenged too many people at too many levels to make it truly popular. Bryden himself would have been suspicious if it had been. To an increasing number of clergy and theological students in the continuing church, however, it did ring true as the political, social, and cultural institutions around them failed to deliver what they promised in the midst of economic depression, nationalist rivalries, and world war. For those attracted to Bryden's recovery of the evangelical orthodoxy of the Reformation, the confessional orthodoxy proposed by the conservative wing of the continuing church represented an escapist retreat, while the progressive orthodoxy that spawned the United Church of Canada proved increasingly incapable of addressing the crises experienced by the human race in the twentieth century. Had the theological debates over the church and its ministry been the primary focus for the Knox faculty between 1925 and 1945, the history of the institution could be told in a more positive manner. Such was not the case.

TRIALS AND TRIBULATIONS

With the imposition of E.Lloyd Morrow on the college by the 1926 General Assembly, a decade of bitter controversy began among Eakin, Morrow, a number of the students, the board, and the church. Bryden and Cunningham managed, for the most part, to stay out of the disputes, but the college suffered severely. Bryden carried a double load in the disciplines he taught, covering both church history and the history and philosophy of religions, since pleas for funding to add to the faculty fell on deaf ears. Students of this era recall Bryden as the sole source of intellectual stimulation in the college, making him an unusually powerful influence on the generations of students that passed through his classes in the two decade following the disruption of 1925.[50] He formed close personal and pastoral ties to the students. He was the inspiration for the formation of the Trinitarian Theological Society in 1944, a fellowship of those "who share the conviction that all the practical problems facing the Church are basically theological in nature."[51] He was fondly remembered also as a keen soccer and baseball fan, coaching the Knox soccer team and taking students with him to the Maple Leaf stadium on the waterfront, where the team had given him a life-time pass.[52]

The rhetoric that accompanied the opening of the continuing Knox College in September 1925 was inflated enough to indicate that the interim administrators and faculty were concerned about their credibility. In announcing the beginning of the college year, acting vice-principal Thomas Eakin assured the church that Knox would offer a curriculum that would meet "the highest standard of theological education" and be taught by the "most competent scholars." He urged the clergy to press the vocation of ordained ministry on young men of "consecrated personality and talent."[53] When the students arrived at Knox in 1925, they found an institution very different from the one that existed the year before. Instead of 5 permanent faculty members, 2 lecturers, and 43 students, they were met by 5 lecturers and 12 students, 2 fewer than had been in the first student body in 1844. Eakin claimed that the curriculum emphasized the Bible more than ever before and that all the other subjects taught were intended to shed light on the core subjects of Old and New Testament.[54] The pre-union thrust towards a progressive emphasis on practical education had almost entirely disappeared. A budget of over $40,000 in 1924–1925 has been reduced to a little less than $13,000 in 1925–1926. Despite these drastic reductions, the continuing college showed a determination to survive in the years immediately after the disruption of 1925. That determination would be sorely tested over the next decade as the Morrow case was prosecuted through the boards, courts, and commissions of the church and drained time, energy, and focus from the faculty and student body alike.

E. Lloyd Morrow, as has been noted, was not the nominee of the college, but was appointed by the assembly in 1926 by a close vote. The problems began in his first year of teaching.[55] Students complained about the quality of his teaching, first to Eakin, who dismissed it as first-year jitters, then to the board, who appointed a small committee to investigate. The students claimed that 80% of the student body found Morrow ineffective as a teacher and untrustworthy as a person. The board took no action and the protests continued. James D. Smart, later to become a distinguished professor of Old Testament at Union Seminary, New York, complained to Eakin that Morrow simply gave them "gobs of undigested material." Eakin claimed to remember the phrase vividly because he had never heard the word "gobs" before. In 1928 and again in 1929, the complaints focused on Morrow's method of examining and charges that he had students spying on other students. Morrow gave students the examination questions in class and, in some cases, dictated the answers. His marking was unfairly weighted in favour of those few students he knew supported him. As a result of these charges, the papers were sent to Montreal and Scotland to be re-marked. The recommended marks of the outside examiners were very different from those given by Morrow.

By the spring of 1930, the circumstances led to another official protest from the students to the board, this one signed by Louis Fowler, Maurice Burch, Fred Goforth, Ross Cameron, and James Burgess. The board appointed a larger committee this time, spent over a year investigating the charges, and finally asked the General Assembly of 1931 to appoint a commission to deal with the "grave condition in the College, which seriously affects its life, influence and usefulness, and which calls for further investigation and action." The Assembly's commission, convened by Frank Baird of Pictou, interviewed all the parties concerned and gathered a record of proceedings that ran to 167,000 words. In the end, the commission concluded that conditions detrimental to the effectiveness of the college did exist and recommended that the Assembly take the steps necessary to bring the situation to an end.[56]

The Assembly tried to take firm action. It relieved Eakin of his responsibilities as principal, but left him in his teaching position, and it terminated Morrow. At the same time, it appointed a special committee to define the "duties, powers, and functions" of the faculty, senate, and board at the college.[57] Appeals and further committees and commissions dragged the matter out until 1934, when the actions of the 1932 Assembly were reversed and Eakin and Morrow were reinstated. An unsuccessful attempt was made in 1935 to send Eakin to Presbyterian College, Montreal, as principal and bring F. Scott Mackenzie to Knox.[58] Morrow finally resigned in 1936, bringing the controversy itself to an end, but leaving behind a bitter legacy of suspicion and lack of confidence in the college.

The controversies at Knox were too tempting for the public press to ignore when they surfaced at the General Assembly in 1932. The issues raised in this forum went well beyond the competence and character of the persons involved and led to charges of heretical teaching at Knox and Presbyterian College, Montreal. The most direct challenge came from the confessional orthodox wing through the Presbytery of Prince Albert. Its 1935 overture stated that the Presbyterian Church in Canada had always been "a Calvinistic Church standing without compromise upon the inspiration of the Scriptures and the great reformed doctrines as set forth in the Westminster Confession of Faith." The adherence of the church to these standards rested "almost entirely with our two theological colleges." The Presbytery was convinced, however, that the theological world in general was dominated by an approach to Biblical studies that destroyed belief in the divine inspiration of the Bible and resulted in preaching "a Gospel of good works without the atoning death of Jesus Christ." They concluded that "our colleges have been caught up in this modern theological whirlpool which would make them disloyal to the standards of our Church" and asked the Assembly to "re-establish the Colleges on a sound foundation of Presbyterian doctrine without regard to sentiment or personal consideration."[59]

The Board of Education, to which the Assembly referred the overtures, was direct in its response. "There is no reason for complaint or anxiety touching the teaching in the Colleges, but, on the contrary, the teaching in both Colleges is in conformity with the standards of our Church."[60] The Board went on to reprimand those in the church who had circulated documents and stories "injurious to the reputation of Teachers in the Colleges of the Church" and reminded them of the proper procedures for raising complaints and allegations about the doctrine of people under the jurisdiction of the church courts. The Board reminded the Presbytery of Pictou, which called for a new committee to coordinate and oversee the work of the colleges, that those responsibilities were already exercised by the Board.[61]

The controversies over administration, teaching, and doctrine at Knox College in the 1920s and 1930s drained a tremendous amount of energy from the task of educating clergy for the continuing church. Eakin characterized Morrow as puerile, vague, capricious, vindictive, unprofessional and unethical.[62] Morrow was convinced, rightly, that Eakin had mounted a determined campaign to remove him from the college. Eakin was constantly accused of teaching a view of Scripture than ran counter to the standards of the church. Several of the accusations were initiated by John Wilkie, a missionary in Tamsui and one of the students who admitted spying for Morrow. Eakin and his supporters often commented on the American origins and fundamentalist attitudes of those attacking him.[63] Board and senate members at the college were divided and often confused, as were successive Assemblies.[64] The effectiveness and reputation of the college suffered greatly from both the indecisiveness and the precipitous actions that characterized the handling of these crises.

Despite the turmoil the college survived and managed to sustain its day-to-day activities. The curriculum was greatly reduced in range because of the shortage of faculty and funds for adjunct lecturers, but the core subjects of Old Testament, New Testament, church history, systematic theology, and practical theology were taught. Enrolments rose rapidly from the 12 who gathered in the first year after union. By 1930, 25 students were studying theology at Knox and numbers remained in the mid-twenties throughout the 1930s. The Missionary Society was revived in 1926 and promised to raise $3400 to help "a needy minority group secure a church and manse." Plans were devised to supply summer fields and vacant congregations in the winter as in the past.[65] Summer schools for Sunday school and young people's leaders were begun again in 1928.[66] The Alumni Association was revived in 1927 and held its first conference in 1934, with Donald Mackenzie of Princeton as the speaker. The conference featured lectures by five graduates of the college as well, who discussed the Bible, Barth, the state of the church, and the importance of the "saving doctrines" of evangelical faith.[67] In 1933, the Assembly approved the addition of three alumni representatives to the board of Knox College. For the first ten years following church union, the faculty at Knox continued to provide classes for women students at the Presbyterian Missionary and Deaconess Training Home, but found themselves unable to do so after 1936.[68]

The Second World War disrupted the college less than had the First. Still, four students died in action. The reality of the war was brought home by letters from graduates overseas. One, read at the convocation in 1942, reflected the influence of Bryden's emphasis on the uniqueness of Christianity: "I feel our watchword, as someone else has said, must simply be, "There shall be no blackout for the Cross." Thousands of serious minded young men are ready to die to keep the Light burning. In their name I ask that the students and graduates of Knox to live for the same Light, to preach the things for which we fight, to help us so that any sacrifice we may be called upon to make shall not be made in vain."[69] The sacrificial language was similar to that used in the First World War, but the focus of the sacrifice was different. Rather than the social order and cultural values of Anglo-Saxon civilization, the focus was the unique perspective on human nature and destiny found in the the Christian Gospel, symbolized most powerfully in the cross of Christ and entrusted in a unique way to the church.

Arthur C. Cochrane was another of Bryden's students who went to study with Barth in the 1930s. In 1940, he wrote a book on the church and the war that was published with an introduction by Barth. In Bryden's review in the *Record*, he agreed with both Cochrane and Barth that the war posed a theological challenge. In the midst of war, the church was called to return again for strength and wisdom to its unique source of repentance and prayer in "an expectant waiting upon the Word and Spirit of God." There alone it would find its unique Christian conscience, different from the moral, cultural, national, patriotic, and even ecclesiastical consciences that were currently clamouring for loyalty.[70]

Ongoing concerns with Eakin's administrative abilities continued after Morrow resigned and ultimately led to a special investigative committee in 1942. The committee found much room for improvement. They acknowledged the truth of what the colleges had complained of for fifteen years, that it was understaffed and unable to offer the range of courses appropriate for a modern theological institution. Overwork induced a number of problems, including "a certain nervous strain on the part of the Faculty, and serious disappointment and discontent, amounting to unrest, on the part of the best type of student ... usually accompanied by harsh criticism of the Faculty, leading to disharmony and the undermining of discipline."[71] The committee concluded that the firmness and discipline needed to remove the causes of unrest and bring about reform were lacking and took special note of the "persistent and deep-rooted suspicion" at Knox that the principal was out of sympathy with both the students and his faculty colleagues.

The committee recommended that the church ask some of its best legal minds to clarify the relations and powers of the board, senate, and trustees of Knox, since conflicts over this matter had caused much confusion. In the interim, the principal, assisted by a joint committee of members of senate and board, would exercise necessary discipline. They further recommended that Eakin and Cunningham from Knox and W. Harvey-Jellie and F. Scott Mackenzie from Presbyterian College be retired in 1944. As a cost-saving measure for the duration of the war, the two colleges were to operate together at Knox and a new principal of Knox was to be appointed from outside the current members of the joint faculty. The committee also discovered that both colleges had scholarship funds far in excess of their needs and recommended that a scholarship for two years of post-graduate study be established to encourage "students of special brilliance" to prepare to serve the church as a professor.[72]

In passing these recommendations, with minor amendments, the Assembly laid the foundation for a major changing of the guard at Knox College immediately after the war. David Hay, appointed to succeed Morrow in systematic theology in 1940, arrived in 1944 after serving as a chaplain in the war. Bryden became principal in 1945, though not without controversy. D. Keith Andrews was appointed to the chair of Old Testament and J. Stanley Glen to that of New Testament in 1945. Donald V. Wade was appointed to the new chair of history and philosophy of religions in 1947. All had been students at Knox and had been shaped in significant ways by Bryden's vision of the church and its ministry. In Bryden's address to the graduating class in 1947, his insistence on the uniqueness of Christian experience and the understanding of reality that arose from it was clear: "Mere shibboleths are no longer serviceable; nor can Demos now be accounted the fountain of all wisdom and truth. The optimistic myth of Progress has taken on more sombre hues these days. The fiction of the essential goodness of man has lost much of its former glamour. Apart from the humble acknowledgement of God's Grace, man's virtue adds up to little more than zero."[73] The new generation of faculty that was appointed to the college chairs in the late 1940s and early 1950s shared Bryden's mistrust of human nature and culture and carried on his legacy of exploring the uniqueness of the gospel and the challenge it posed to modern civilization.

If judged by the criteria for maintaining the Presbyterian Church in Canada laid out in the Protest and Claim of Right on 10 June 1925, the college would receive mixed reviews for its work in the two decades after union. It did maintain the confession of faith and standards of the church "as previously understood," that is, with a breadth of interpretation that allowed for new insight and comprehension. In the 1920s and 1930s, the newness that came to dominate in the denomination was in fact a return to old sources, not the scholastic confessionalism of the seventeenth century, but the theological and ecclesiastical reform and renewal of the sixteenth century. It was not simply a renewed interest in the Reformation as an historical event or movement, but a genuine attempt to recover the spirit of the Reformation and be seized by "a new vision of God." The college and its faculty did advance the glory of God in its sacrificial efforts to provide adequate theological education for the clergy of the continuing church. The enthusiasm for missions at home and overseas continued without great fanfare, but with the quiet confidence that the best way to extend the gospel was through spiritually sensitive and theologically sound preachers in congregations gathered around the ordinary means of grace. Where the college failed miserably was in "the orderly administration of Christ's house according to His holy word." Clashing personalities, incompetent teaching and adminstration, continual underfunding, and the machinations of theological parties, all combined to prevent Knox from achieving the effectiveness and prestige it might have. Beneath the crises and controversies, however, a foundation was laid for the next generation of faculty to build a credible and effective theological college, complete with a graduate program.

7 Diverging Views, 1945–1977

By the end of the Second World War, the Presbyterian Church in Canada had completed what James D. Smart called its "painful inner reconstruction"[1] and was ready to move out of the garrison mentality that had developed in the aftermath of church union. An increasing number of Canadian Presbyterians were convinced that they had some unique and valuable approaches to the Gospel to offer to the Canadian church and nation, the most important of which was the neo-Reformation theological orientation shaped by Walter Bryden. The continuing church, according to Smart, had had to face the question of "the true nature, function, and destiny of the Church" and did so by returning to the Bible and the Reformation to regain its theological bearings. Smart remembered that he and his classmates at Knox who formed the Trinitarian Theological Society "began in the early thirties to see their Church's destiny as that of being the instrument through which Canadian Protestantism might be recalled to its heritage as a Church reformed and ever anew reforming according to the word of God in Scripture."[2] The catalyst for this renewal of the church's life and witness was Walter Bryden.

Smart distinguished between the minority of fundamentalists in the continuing church who sought to reform the church by following the Westminster Standards in a "slavish fashion" and the majority for whom renewed interest in the formative documents of the Reformation raised the question of what the church's witness ought to be in their contemporary context. Smart and the other Canadian Presbyterian clergy whom Bryden shaped in the 1930s and 1940s were particularly concerned with how that witness took place week by week in and through the local congregation. Bryden's teaching challenged them, Smart recalled, "to wrestle with the problems of a Biblical preaching which, while accepting the results of critical scholarship, would deal with the Scriptures in earnest as the revelation of God for today."[3]

In the seven years from 1945 until 1952 when Bryden served as principal of Knox College, he put his stamp on the institution as well as its graduates. All but one of the new generation of faculty who came to Knox between 1944 and 1952 were former students who acknowledged Bryden's formative influence. They were rooted in and committed to the core affirmations of the neo-orthodox culture that had come to be the dominant perspective among the leadership of Canadian Presbyterians. The next two successors to Bryden as principal, J. Stanley Glen from 1952 to 1975 and Allan Farris from 1976 to 1977, were drawn from this group of faculty. To add to the strength of this position at the college, all but one of the new appointments and replacements made in the 1960s were Knox graduates influenced by Bryden as well. All built on the theological foundations laid by their mentor, though they interpreted and applied Bryden's neo-orthodoxy in their own unique ways. The dominance of Bryden's students on the faculty and the fact that Knox continued to provide the majority of the clergy for the church ensured that his legacy in theology and his agenda for the reconstruction of the denomination continued to shape the church's understanding of itself, its clergy and their theological education.

So deep was the mark of Bryden's influence that when in the 1960s self-questioning and self-doubt began to ferment within the church, it was Bryden's legacy around which, and often against which, the questions arose. Diverging views became increasingly apparent among the faculty as the neo-Reformation heritage was developed and applied in different ways and eventually challenged as being too parochial. Diverging views developed outside the college as well and contributed to growing tensions between the college and various groups within the church. What Smart dismissed as fundamentalism within the denomination was in fact a much broader and more complex continuation of confessional orthodoxy.[4] Though never strong enough in numbers to win acceptance for its

views in the official documents and stances of the church, it represented a significant and vocal minority. It gained strength during
the ferment of the 1960s and 1970s by providing a clear alternative
in the midst of the questioning, by drawing on the resources of neo-
evangelicalism in the United States, and by eventually organizing itself into the Renewal Fellowship.[5] For others with growing concerns
about the effective practice of ministry in the contemporary
church, what Smart prized as the theological focus of the college increasingly seemed to be narrowly academic and remote from the
real problems facing the church. They argued for more attention to
the practical disciplines of preaching, evangelism, church administration, pastoral care, and Christian education in the curriculum.
Throughout the later 1960s and the 1970s, attacks from without
and controversies from within weakened the confidence that the
denomination felt in its ecclesiastical culture. The culture was fraying. No longer dominant as strong warps for the culture were the
clarity of creed that drove the founders of Knox, nor the passion for
progressive reform that inspired the promoters of church union,
nor the convictions about the uniqueness of the church and its witness to Jesus Christ that heartened continuing Presbyterians with a
sense of identity and purpose in the post-union era.

BRYDEN'S LEGACY AND
A NEW GENERATION OF FACULTY

Between 1945 and 1975, no less than seven of Bryden's students
were appointed to the faculty. In 1945, the same year Bryden was
inducted as principal, J. Stanley Glen became professor of New Testament and D. Keith Andrews of Old Testament. Glen was born and
raised in Saskatchewan, earned doctorates in psychology and New
Testament in Toronto, and was minister at Glenview Presbyterian
Church in Toronto when appointed to Knox. Andrews grew up in
Alberta and did graduate work in Edinburgh and Chicago. In
1947, Donald V. Wade was inducted into the newly-created chair of
Philosophy of Religion and Christian Ethics, with additional responsibilities in homiletics and pastoral theology. Raised in Inger-
soll, he completed his doctoral studies at Toronto in 1944 and
served for three years at First Presbyterian Church, Verdun, Quebec. In 1952, Bryden died and W.H. Sandham, the college librarian since 1936, retired. Allan Farris was appointed to Bryden's

chair in church history and Neil Gregor Smith became librarian. Farris was another Saskatchewan native who had served churches in Trail, British Columbia, and Bolton and Nashville in Ontario. Smith grew up in Lindsay, Ontario, and was editor of Presbyterian Publications when called to Knox. The only person in the first round of faculty appointments who was not a student of Bryden's was David Hay, a Scot who succeeded Morrow in 1944. He had been born to Scottish Salvation Army officers in South Africa, but found the individualistic piety of that tradition wanting. During his studies and ministry in Scotland and as a chaplain during the Second World War, he was drawn to the liturgical renewal movement and the recovery of the more corporate and catholic ecclesiology being developed by the Faith and Order movement. Hay shared many of the concerns central to the neo-Reformation agenda, but suggested different strategies for achieving these ends than his faculty colleagues. [6]

In 1963, a second round of appointments began. J. Charles Hay was inducted into the new chair of homiletics, evangelism, and church administration. Hay was born in Northern Ireland and raised in Cooke's Presbyterian Church, Toronto. His first ten years in ministry were spent at Leaside Presbyterian Church, Toronto, after which he was called to MacVicar Memorial Presbyterian Church in Montreal, and then to lecture in New Testament at The Presbyterian College there. W. James S. Farris replaced Don Wade in 1967, after the latter moved to Victoria University. Farris was born in south-western Ontario and taught at Laurentian University and in Jamaica prior to coming to Knox. Keith Andrews died in 1967 and was replaced in 1969 by Robert Lennox, formerly principal of the Presbyterian College, Montreal. Lennox was the first non-Knox graduate appointed to the faculty in since David Hay in 1944. All seven previous appointees had studied with Bryden, been encouraged by him to pursue graduate studies, and developed different dimensions of the Bryden legacy in their teaching and writing. The number of Knox graduates appointed led later to charges of the faculty being ingrown, though it did ensure that the ecclesiastical culture Bryden tried so hard to establish continued to shape most of Knox's graduates.

In New Testament and pastoral theology, which was later added to his teaching responsibilities, Glen picked up on Bryden's emphasis on the church's unique position in the battle of ideas raging at mid-century. Over his years of teaching, the focus of Glen's concern shifted from communism to psychology, then to capitalism and the gospel of success, but he challenged all of these ideologies with the gospel's unique distrust of human ability and accomplishment and its ultimate reliance on what God did in Christ on the cross. Andrews concentrated on teaching, emphasizing the importance of the biblical languages in exegesis and preaching. His own biblical theology focused on the theme of the unique covenant God made with Israel and the impact it had on the church's sense of identity. Kierkegaard's challenge to Western Christendom was the focus of Wade's graduate work. Ten years after he began his teaching career, a tour of mission fields in the Far East rekindled the spark that Bryden's interest in the unique mission of the church's witness had ignited. The historical substance of that witness, especially in the confessions inspired by the Genevan Reformation, fascinated both Allan Farris and Neil Smith. The recovery of the centrality of the Word revealed in Scripture and its defining power for the preaching of the church shaped the way they taught homiletics and guided their students' research in church history. Farris also promoted the re-engagement of the Presbyterian Church in Canada with the social action initiatives being taken by the ecumenical churches in the 1950s, convinced that the Reformation's recovery of the doctrine of the sovereignty of God and the lordship of Christ compelled the church to engage the social problems of its time and place with the gospel's unique witness.

Charlie Hay's doctoral studies in Gottingen and Edinburgh focused on New Testament apocalyptic and eschatology. From the beginning, he stressed that the sermon itself was a form of the unique Word of God, made effective in its witness by the Holy Spirit no matter how stumbling, mediocre, or inept its human practitioners might be. Jim Farris studied in Edinburgh as well and taught in Jamaica prior to coming to Knox to succeed Wade in 1967. His teaching in hermeneutics and Christian ethics emphasized the uniqueness of the church's mission and the necessity that theological education serve its witness. Robert Lennox approached the Old Testament convinced that its abiding significance for the witness of the church lay in the fact that God was its author, Christ was its message, and the Holy Spirit provided the final interpretation of its meaning in human hearts. Each one of this generation of Knox faculty, including David Hay and Robert Lennox, had been inspired in a significant, though different, way by Bryden's efforts to convince Canadian Presbyterians that the only true basis for the reform and reconstruction of the church's witness was to be seized by a new vision of God, just as the Reformers in the sixteenth century had been.

Each contributed in his own way to the new confidence evident within the Presbyterian Church in Canada following the Second World War. It was fuelled by the prospects of growth and reinforced by renewed acceptance and respect among other Canadian churches, including the United Church of Canada. New national structures were created and an expanded national staff developed. The church found new ways to express its commitment to ecumenism through the Canadian Council of Churches (founded in 1944) and the World Council of Churches (established in 1948).[7] The majority of Canadian Presbyterians became convinced that Smart was right and that Bryden's evangelical catholicism, rooted in the theological heritage of the sixteenth-century Reformation, promised to make an unique contribution to the church in Canada.[8]

Barely had this confidence taken hold, however, when the 1960s erupted in ferment and turmoil, calling into question many of the assumptions upon which Presbyterian confidence was based, especially the centrality of the ordinary means of grace found in the local congregation. The pressing question being asked by an increasing number of people inside and outside of the church was that of relevance. What did the church have to do to reestablish its relevance and influence in Canadian society? The faculty at Knox did not shy away from these challenges, but their engagement in the questioning that shook the church in the 1960s and 1970s was guided by Bryden's vision of the unique source and role of the gospel as a challenge to the modern world. They stressed the need to know the substance of the Gospel, both experientially and intellectually, as the primary focus for theological education. Given the time and resources available to the college, they were reluctant to make changes to the curriculum or staff that would weaken the traditional core of the educational program.

Seminal to the ferment was the publication of *The Comfortable Pew*, a critique of the contemporary Canadian church written at the invitation of the Anglican Church of Canada by journalist Pierre Berton and published in 1965. The book sold 170,000 copies in the first year.[9] Charles Hay agreed with much of Berton's condemnation of the churches for their complacency, smugness, self-satisfaction, and self-righteousness and urged Canadian Presbyterians to take such criticism seriously rather than react defensively. Hay suggested that Berton had been misled, however, by his own Sunday school indoctrination that the gospel was "just a radical, ethical idealism which should be applied to practical affairs." Berton had not found the answer to the church's problems because "that faith which is witnessed to by the Bible and confessed in the creeds of the church" alone should direct the church's response to the challenges humanity faced. The key to the church's renewal, according to Hay, was a renewal of its faith in Christ as the revelation of God's loving response to humanity's longing for meaning and hope.[10] Throughout the ferment of the 1960s and 1970s, the Knox faculty remained convinced that the church must learn anew to proclaim and teach the great evangelical truths in the spirit of the Reformers of the sixteenth century and that the most effective place for this to happen was the local congregation.

As the discussions and debates proceeded, however, diverging analyses of the problems and strategies for response emerged. As the church became more focused on its cultural relevance and its institutional effectiveness, Bryden's legacy among the faculty of a theological integrity that often set the church over against the world brought the church and the college into tension. Demands from the church for revisions or additions to the curriculum called for more attention to the practical skills required by clergy to deal with the agenda being set by the world. They were met with hesitancy and even resistance, in part because of limited funding but also because the faculty was convinced that the heart of the church's education of its clergy remained preparation to preserve and propagate the great evangelical truths the world needed to hear, whether it wanted to or not. Indeed, the social analysis offered by the faculty during the 1960s and the 1970s became more and more outspoken in its criticism of modern culture and the captivity in which it held the church.

One voice that was not heard from within the faculty during this period was that of the continuing confessional orthodox wing of the church. Though representatives of this worldview were nominated regularly for chairs at Knox, none was appointed.[11] After 1976, they began to look to Ontario Theological Seminary, which had grown out of the work of the Ontario Bible College, as their centre for theological leadership and education.[12] The possibility of a genuine dialogue within Knox between creedal and catholic Presbyterianism did not materialize. Instead, what developed was a rivalry, at times bitter and divisive, between the two schools and their supporters within the denomination.

Another voice that was not heard from within the faculty during this period was that of women. The Presbyterian Church in Canada did not agree to ordain women to until 1966. Shirley Jeffrey graduated from Knox in 1968 and was the first women ordained as clergy within the denomination. The number of female faces in the composite graduation photographs that fill the walls of the first floor hall in the college grew rapidly, but they were not matched by any female face among the faculty. Not until Helen Goggin was appointed in 1991 as a result of the amalgamation with Ewart College did Knox have a women on faculty. Women professors were available through the Toronto School of Theology, but their numbers were few and the requirements of the degree at Knox limited the number of courses that could be taken with them. The core disciplines and most of the courses in the Knox program were taught by men.

A CHURCH WITNESSING TO THE WORLD

Walter Bryden once recalled that he had been ordained in Tees, Alberta, and that he had spent a lifetime trying to tease and trouble the church to be true to its confession. Donald V. Wade, appointed in 1947 to one of the two chairs Bryden had carried since 1927, recalled his mentor as "a preacher's theologian, a theologian *of, in* and *for* the Church." He was a theologian of the Word and Spirit, "a great critic, a great unmasker," who "revelled in affirming that the Word of God put everything human on the defensive, but never without depicting and delineating human destiny in terms of God's purpose in salvation."[13] Wade's debt to Bryden was evident in his inaugural lecture at Knox: "Our first duty is never to hatch plans and policies, but always to proclaim the fundamental Gospel itself, … to call men to heed that, and then to draw out its implications for the order of society. We must approach this task not as bewildered folk groping for a solution to a problem, but as the trustees of a revelation. No external readjustment of the structure of life will usher in the Kingdom of God. Discipleship alone is the answer."[14] The church, for Wade, was made up of those who had been quickened by God's Word and Spirit, members of a body of which Christ was the sovereign head.[15] Its mission was to offer "adventuresome and creative witness" to the gospel.[16]

The relevance of the gospel, and of the church it formed, was found in its content, not in its context. The gospel becomes relevant, Wade wrote on his return from Taiwan in 1958, when "intimate acquaintance with the living reality of the Word of God" made what God had done in Jesus Christ meaningful for the individual and when an "inspired understanding of the world to which the Word is addressed" gave that meaning concrete form. "It was the coming together of these two," Wade concluded, "which made the church of the Acts of the Apostles a demonstration of the Spirit and the Power of God."[17]

Wade's faculty colleagues shared, for the most part, his emphasis on how the message of the gospel in Word and Spirit determined the identity and mission of the church. Their theology of the church shaped the shorter preamble to the ordination vows for clergy in the revised *Book of Common Order* issued in 1964. "By the operation of God's Word and Spirit," the preamble read, "the Church is gathered, equipped, and sent out to participate in [the ministry of the Lord Jesus Christ]."[18] Through that ministry, humanity was confronted with the good news of the radical intervention of God in human history in the person and work of Jesus Christ. "The coming of Christ into the world," Wade wrote at Christmas in 1948, "suggests a desire on the part of God to bring things to a head, and to confront man with an alternative. When man really sees this, something happens."[19]

One of the most important things that the church did in response to God's intervention, Bryden's students agreed, was to write creeds and confessions that stated the great evangelical truths in ways that spoke to the tenor of the times. The statements arose, Allan Farris wrote in the first of a series of eight articles on the creeds for the *Record* in 1957, whenever people sought "to make known the experience of grace which has become theirs through personal encounter with Jesus Christ." They were written under the impulse of the Spirit at times when the church sought to purify and realign itself with the teachings of the apostolic faith and served as "new occasions through which Christ may come and lay claim in Reconciling grace upon all those who as yet have not acknowledged Him as Lord."[20] Half of the series dealt with the confessions of the Reformation, a movement Farris described as "the radical renewal of the church under the impulse of the Word and Spirit of God."[21]

Farris' master's thesis dealt with Calvin's doctrine of the Holy Spirit and was a direct challenge to the "rigidity" of the confessional conservatives who crystallized Calvin's thought into the logic of their own position. Calvin, Farris argued, was deeply aware of the danger that God's speech might easily be confined to a human definition and interpretation of it. What allowed God to be God in Calvin's thought, and what those who insisted on a narrow creedal definition of Christianity missed, was the role of the Holy Spirit. Nature, the Bible, church activities, and theologies could not reveal God on their own. They had to be used by "something hidden, or something beyond the means of communication, and that is the Holy Spirit."[22] This theology of the Spirit, common to the neo-Reformation movement Bryden had introduced into Canadian Presbyterianism, was enshrined in the revision of the preamble to the ordination vows approved in 1970. The church acknowledged its historic continuity with the doctrinal heritage of the ecumenical creeds and the confessions of the Reformation, but claimed its right to reformulate the faith "in obedience to Scripture and under the promised guidance of the Holy Spirit."[23]

The church's responsibility, Farris noted in a *Record* article on missions, "was to evangelize, that is, to make Christ known." He argued that the Reformers had a much broader concept of mission than those who concentrated exclusively on individual salvation. Their vision was to bring the whole of Europe under the lordship of Christ. Their sense of mission was rooted in their theology of God's sovereignty. God was sovereign in the universe, Farris wrote, and humanity's sin was rebellion against that sovereignty. "The Grace of God," he continued, was "this sovereign power acting in righteousness and love in Jesus Christ to rectify the ruin of man's rebellion and to recreate him fit and willing to live under the sovereign will."[24] The church's relevance, Farris stated in a lecture on the Confessing Church in Germany, "was to be measured by her unwillingness to conform to accepted thought patterns; and to be 'with it' in the deepest Christian sense was to refuse categorically to conform to the popular ideology of the day." For James Farris, a cousin to Allan, a true ecclesiology demanded a true theology of

mission. Mission, he wrote while teaching in Jamaica, was "the existence medium of the People of God, and in this obedience they realize and describe their own nature and the status of all mankind in
the purpose of God."[25] For both Farrises, the mission of the church
focused on its witness and its witness focused on God's challenge to
all human pretensions.

The church's witness had clear ethical implications and the Knox
faculty gave strong support to the expansion of the Board of Evangelism and Social Action in the 1950s. As Donald Wade stated in
his inaugural address, the "root-bed of true ethics is repentant acknowledgement of the rule and mercy of God," but he and his
Knox colleagues considered God's rule and mercy universal in
scope. Obedience to Christ meant taking the message of the gospel
into every sphere of life so that God might use the church to per-
meate the world with the gospel's redemptive power. The means by
which that was done were described clearly in the church's *Declaration of Faith Concerning Church and Nation*, a revision of the church's
doctrinal standards approved in 1955, on which several of the
Knox faculty worked:

[The church] owes a manifold service to the State. Her preaching, sacraments, and discipline, confront the Nation with Christ's judgement and
grace. She offers thanksgiving and supplication to God on behalf of all
men, with particular intercession for those in authority, praying that the
overruling power of the Holy Spirit may fructify what is good and uproot
what is evil in national and international life. In discharging her commission to evangelize she promotes righteousness and peace among men. As
her Lord may lay upon her, she declares and commits herself to His will by
public pronouncements of her courts or agents. In fulfilment of the law of
Christ, she engages in special works of Christian love. Her members take
full share as their Christian calling in commerce, politics, and other social
action.[26]

While serving as convener of the Department of Social Relations
of the Canadian Council of Churches in 1959, Allan Farris urged
all the churches to use each of these means to meet the problems
created by rapid social change and manifested in industrialization,
nationalism, and racial prejudice.[27] For Farris' colleague, J. Stanley Glen, these conditions posed an unprecedented theological
problem.

Glen saw complex and rapid social change at the heart of the crisis faced by the modern world. In essence, it depersonalized human life.[28] Secular power, he warned, which was achieved through bureaucracy, technology, technique, money, and the control of goods and services, was the new idol of contemporary society, whether the ideological rationale came from neo-capitalism, communism, socialism, or fascism. Justification came through success, a goal that held the church in an invisible captivity. The seductive power of secularity eroded or displaced "genuine love (*agape*), genuine community (*koinonia*), and genuine personal freedom, truth, and forgiveness as these are depicted in the Bible and the gospel."[29] Evangelism and social action belonged together because both confronted the world with the radical challenge of the gospel.

Most of the faculty shared Bryden's suspicion of "ecclesiasticism," which he defined as the "attempt to substantiate the validity of a Church upon purely ecclesiastical grounds, or by its ecclesiastical credentials." Neither a regular ministry, nor true orders, nor a legitimate administration of the sacraments, nor an unbroken apostolic succession constituted the foundation of the church. Rather, the church was grounded in "that experienced spiritual union or fellowship which exists between Christ and His people as a whole, and in which the Grace of God is evidently manifest." The Presbyterian form of church government was highly valued and had proved effective for the witness and mission of the church, but it was clearly secondary and subordinate to the spiritual principle that constituted the church.[30] Word and Spirit were the key elements in their theology of the church.

David Hay disagreed strenuously with his faculty colleagues on this matter. For him, Word and Spirit were not enough. Hay agreed with Bryden that Christianity was not something that came naturally or represented humanity's best thoughts about life. It came from the Word of God alone, and made its way into human life by the divinely-appointed means of grace. More than any other member of the Knox faculty, however, Hay stressed the historical mediation of God's redemption through Christ's church, its holy ministry, and the unity of Word and Sacrament in its liturgy.[31] He was openly critical of the contemporary tendency "to explain everything in terms of moral and spiritual principles." The church had to retain its birth-marks if it was to remain the church.[32] He found those marks named clearly in the Westminster Confession 25:3 as "the word, the sacraments, and the ministers of the means of grace."[33] Hay's concerns for the concrete, historical forms in which the unique gospel message was preserved and propagated in the Canadian context focused on worship, the ecumenical movement, and the church's doctrine of ministry.

Hay's views on the importance of form in worship were accepted by the denomination in its approval of the revised *Book of Common Order* in 1964. The Spirit, Hay wrote in the preface, operated by the means of grace, "that is to say, through the historic work of Christ for our redemption and the means by which we know Him and are united to Him." The purpose of the book was to help the church "to handle the divinely-given forms of Christian worship with reverence and comeliness, so that the forms, which are empty without the Spirit, may potently serve the Spirit in uniting us livingly with God and His Christ."[34]

Throughout his career, Hay's affirmation of the concrete catholicity of the church led to a strong commitment to ecumenism. He shared Bryden's conviction concerning the uniqueness of the church, but expressed it in language that focused on the corporate body of Christ rather than the inner encounter with Christ. "With high approval," Hay wrote in the *Record* in 1956, "Calvin quotes the saying of Cyprian: No man can have God for his Father who does not have the Church for his Mother. ... To be joined to Christ and to be joined to the Church are aspects of one event."[35] Hay dismissed the common argument among Canadian Presbyterians that church unity was "spiritual and invisible." Visible unity in the ordering of the church was essential. To agree on cooperation in mission, Hay insisted, it was first necessary to understand the mystery of the church and its proper ordering. The Canadian Council of Churches, in which Hay took a very active role, represented but a small step in that direction. The Council, Hay stated in his presidential address in 1962, pointed towards the "wonderful and sacred mystery" of the church catholic in ways the severed denominations did not. It should challenge the denominations more boldly to break out of their "proud, isolated sovereignties" and create a more faithful ordering of the concrete, historical essentials in the church's life and witness. [36]

In spite of these clear differences with his colleagues at Knox on the importance of church order and the form it should take, Hay shared with them the neo-Reformation emphasis on the sovereignty and ultimate universality of God's redeeming grace. In his inaugural address at Knox, he grounded his theological thought in the affirmation that the chief end of humanity was to glorify and enjoy God. All other activities were subordinate and flowed from that purpose and nowhere in the church's life and witness was that end more eloquently expressed than in worship. All of life was sanctified and renewed in worship. Hay's life-long concern with revitalizing the worship life of the Presbyterian Church in Canada and leading in its ecumenical re-engagement was founded on the conviction that the church should "hold grip of the truth that the only final goal for man, immediate and prospective now and in the hereafter, is the glory and joy of God in the communion of saints."[37]

QUANDARIES OVER THE CLERGY'S CALLING

Just prior to his appointment as principal of Knox College in 1945, Walter Bryden expressed four wishes for new ministers. First, he wished for them a strong, clear, and continuing sense of vocation, dependent solely on God and constantly on guard against the dangers of professionalism. Second, he wished for them a positive message given by Christ and proved in the crucible of the experiences that produced a personality "all aglow and aflame with redemptive power." Third, he wished for them a pastoral instinct so that their practical work was motivated by a passion for the souls of their fellow human beings. Finally, he wished for them "a spirituality of mind and heart" that increasingly helped them to conform to "a likeness to the head of the Church, our Lord Jesus Christ."[38] The Knox graduates who went on to become the next Knox faculty preserved this ideal of a balance between pastor and theologian not simply in what they taught but in the way they taught their respective disciplines. They sought to educate preachers and teachers who were themselves deeply rooted in Christ and who served the church by communicating the gospel with a pastoral heart transformed by its ongoing encounter with Christ.

Stanley Glen, with doctorates in both New Testament and psychology, believed that the spiritual dimension of the clergy's development was every bit as important as their intellectual and practical preparation. For Glen, the most difficult change students faced was not the many intellectual problems encountered in their long academic program or the doubts that arose, but the acceptance of the offence of the cross. Recognizing the offence of the cross as the means to joy, satisfaction, and endurance constituted the most challenging paradox for the clergy:

The true joy of the ministry is the joy which comes of seeing the light of the Gospel illumine a darkened soul, bring peace where before there was chaos, love where before there was hate. It is the joy of seeing broken homes restored, bereaved hearts comforted, estranged people reconciled, and fear and anxiety dissolved in an atmosphere of trust. It is the joy of seeing faith deepened and instructed, personal problems clarified, and men and women coming to a spiritual maturity in which their word is dependable and their love beautiful and wholesome. But this will not be realized unless the minister himself accepts the offence of his calling as the pathway to such a reward.[39]

Coming to grips with the offence of the calling to the ministry of Word and Sacraments was important for Glen because that ministry had been given a specific commission by Christ to preach and teach the gospel and offer pastoral care through prayer and conversation that pointed clearly to the unique power of the gospel. Ministers were not free to do whatever they wanted in the light of the needs of the day, but were bound to the specific tasks of the church in their time.

Throughout his teaching career, Glen warned against his students against the irresponsible simplifications of the gospel by people who subscribed to conversionism, biblicism, or moralism. All valued religious security more than a Christian knowledge of God. As an alternative, he offered what he called a "relational hermeneutic" that required the interpreter to pay attention to the real life of those who wrote and heard the Biblical text, the real life of those to whom the text was being interpreted in the present, and the relation of the interpreter with Christ. Preaching and teaching were inseparable in Glen's mind, distinguished only by the fact that preaching related more to revelation and teaching to reason. The purpose of both was to make the gospel intelligible and to combat "vacuity and vagueness."[40] Preaching involved God being made known through, and often in spite of, the preacher by the work of the Spirit, while teaching involved the interpretation of the gospel by human means, again with the help of the Spirit. Both were "inseparably united in one act, in that the Word of God is heard through the word of man."[41] For Glen, the concrete historical meaning of the great evangelical truths lay in the freedom they offered to humanity. "The primary meaning of the gospel is that God is for man," he wrote in a critique of the humanist psychology of Erich Fromm: "It announces the radical love of God for man manifested as free, unmerited goodness toward him. Such goodness is expressed in two ways, the one with respect to God as the source (Creator) of the natural order and the other with respect to God as the solution (Saviour) of the historical order."[42]

Allan Farris was concerned that clergy were becoming caught up in the busy productivity of administration and in the search for success. He urged his students instead to cultivate a costly commitment to Christ, develop an energetic discipleship of the cross-bearing type, and to engage in serious reflection on the meaning of the service of a God of Love and Righteousness. If the current generation of clergy did not come to grips with the crying needs of their time and seek to answer them with serious theological effort and agony of spirit, they would bequeath their problems to future generations "who will then be forced to answer out of the physical agony and enslavement of a world that was not served with the liberating gospel of Life."[43]

When Charles Hay took over the teaching of preaching from Allan Farris and Neil Smith in 1963, he insisted that the traditional disciplines of theological study remain at the centre of the clergy's education. In his inaugural address, he pointed out that contemporary theologians such as Karl Barth and Rudolph Bultmann had a very high view of the pulpit because they saw preaching not just as testimony to Christ's redemption of the world but as itself part of the saving action of God in Christ. By the preaching of the gospel, Hay stated, "the redemptive act of Christ becomes not just a matter of historical record but redemptive power and experience." Preachers were by their very nature and calling theologians. They had to use every possible means to keep within hearing of the gospel and search continually for the mind of Christ. They had to recognize that they were not free-lancers, but participants in the church's mission of continuing the work of Jesus Christ. It followed, therefore, that they had to place themselves in the stream of the church's consciousness of itself and be able to accept the corporate confession of the church's faith through its theological formulations, though never in an uncritical fashion. The clergy had a special degree of responsibility for the ongoing reformulation of the faith in faithfulness to the Word of God. Equally important was to know the people to whom the gospel was addressed, not just in general, but by name. Pastoral visitation and conversation provided these contacts for the preacher and were indispensable if preaching was to remain part of the activity of the judging-saving Word in the world.[44] Significantly, preaching and evangelism were treated in the lecture, while church administration was ignored. The message of the gospel, entrusted in a special way to the clergy, was of paramount importance to Charles Hay and most of his Knox colleagues.

The exception, again, was David Hay. He considered the clergy themselves as one of the means of grace given by Christ to the church. The "divine institution and the divine status" of the holy ministry of the clergy was part of the divine economy of revelation. The apostles, who offered Jesus Christ fully to the world at Pentecost by their testimony, constituted a special ministerial order in the church who were "instruments of [Christ's] saving revelation." Hay argued for a concrete, institutional apostolic succession in the church of those "ministers of the new covenant" who were entrusted with the revelatory mysteries of Word and Sacraments. Only those ordained to this office by others who held it were qualified to be stewards of the means of grace by which Christ exercised his own personal ministry in and through the church.

David Hay was very critical of the new ecumenical understanding of ministry that emerged in the 1960s, with its emphasis on the ministry of the laity and the servant role of the clergy. He considered it exegetically wrong, finding nowhere in the New Testament authority for giving the laity the responsibility to evangelize the world. It was the clergy, in Hay's analysis, who led the church into the public realm throughout its history and bore the brunt of persecution. The new ecumenical emphasis on a servant ministry produced a false humility and abdication of power on the part of the clergy. They needed to reclaim their authority as one of the "ecclesial institutions by which redemption is now proclaimed and made effectual."[45] That authority, as described in the long preamble to the ordination vows in the 1964 *Book of Common Order*, came from Christ and restricted the preaching of the gospel, the administration of the sacraments, and the exercise of pastoral rule to the clergy.[46] Hay was every bit as concerned as his colleagues about protecting the integrity of the gospel message and integrating the gifts of pastor and teacher, but he emphasized the importance of the historical continuity of Christ's ordering and ruling the church through its clergy in achieving this.

Each in their own way, the faculty at Knox affirmed the importance of the traditional expectations of the clergy in the church and insisted that the role of the theological college in their theological education was to ground them in the balance of learning and piety provided by the study of the classical disciplines. By the 1960s, however, the ministry of the clergy in the Presbyterian Church in Canada came under question as it never had before in the denomination. Until that time, there was a broad affirmation that the clergy were pastors of souls, preachers of the gospel, teachers of the tradition, partners in ruling the church with elders, and representatives of the church in the community. Sometimes the emphasis was placed on being apologists for a tradition under attack, while at other times the emphasis shifted to being missionaries for an expanding institution. Different theological perspectives brought one or the other of these dimensions to the fore, the apologist being most important in the minds of the conservative orthodox, the missionary in the minds of the progressive orthodox, and the apologist again for the neo-orthodox. All periods and perspectives emphasized the importance of teaching and thought of the local congregation as the primary arena in which the clergy's gifts were to be exercised.

The ferment that surfaced in the 1960s called both the clergy and the local congregation into serious question. There was little consistency in the reasons for such challenges, but all called for substantial change in the practice of the church and its leadership. For some, the congregations and their clergy were out of touch with the world and needed to become more relevant. For others, the congregations and their clergy were too much in touch with the world and needed to break out of their suburban cultural captivity. For still others, the rituals, concepts, and language of the local congregations and their clergy were outdated and incomprehensible in a modern context. Yet another group looked to new schemes of uniting the churches in Canada to meet the challenges of the last half of the twentieth century. Churches were advised to let the world set the agenda and to go where the action was in order to revitalize the real witness and power of the gospel.

In 1964, a questionnaire sent to Presbyterian clergy across the country clarified the kinds of questions that were emerging: "some [problems are] caused by an apparent split between what the congregation conceives as the minister's task and the minister's own concept; some by the conflict between the traditional concept and a changing concept caused by changing social conditions. Still other problems seem to be caused by new needs and newer emphases in theological thinking for which training in the classical manner has not prepared them. There would seem to be a real measure of unrest."[47] Both the way in which the clergy interpreted the gospel and the new context in which the church found itself contributed to changing perceptions of the ministry of the clergy. Clerical leadership was still considered crucial in making the required changes in the church, but its status, credibility, and confidence were being challenged from inside as well as from outside the organization.

The *Ross Report*, published in 1969, made it abundantly clear that the church perceived much of its leadership to be out of touch and out of date.[48] The headline in the Toronto *Star* when the report was issued declared, "Presbyterians told they face extinction."[49] Morale among the clergy was reported to be extremely low and ministers were not only finding it difficult to recruit, but in some cases refusing to invite young people to consider a job like theirs. Ferguson Barr of Sarnia, convener of the Assembly's Committee on Recruitment and Vocation in 1970, warned that unless the church showed "signs of opening up to the winds of the spirit" by adopting a policy of experimental reform in every dimension of its life and witness, the denomination would see further losses in members and ministers.[50]

Flexibility in staffing and experimentation with structures became the goals of the many suggestions for reform that emerged over the next several years from the Life and Mission Project (LAMP) established to address the problems identified so vividly in the Ross Report. Implied and direct criticisms of more traditional models of ministry surfaced in much of this literature. Barr claimed that people saw the minister as a black-robed figure solemnly preaching at them on Sunday morning, trained to be a sole performer, and the only one capable of doing ministry in the community.[51] The denomination, he asserted, had to recognize ministries other than the general practitioner in the parish and mobilize the resources of the laity if it were to be relevant to the contemporary world.

Unrest within the church over the nature of ministry and the shape of theological education continued to grow. In 1969, the General Assembly established a Committee on Training of Professional Church Workers, with a mandate to explore new forms of ministry and theological education and "instruct the colleges accordingly."[52] Chaired by Professor Joseph McLelland of Presbyterian College and the McGill Faculty of Religious Studies, yet another of Bryden's students, the committee announced the death of the old model of ordained ministry that "cast the clergyman in a role of preacher, teacher, and pastor to a well-defined community, with the laity playing a relatively passive role under his general leadership." The renewed appreciation for the ministry of the laity that had developed in the previous decade called for a rethinking of the role of the clergy and a greater appreciation for the corporate ministry of the whole people of God. Reforms in theological education would be judged by their appropriateness "for a vocation of sharing or co-operation." Attention had to be paid not only to the subject matter, but also to the ways in which it was taught, so that the colleges would become laboratories where theologues learned corporate ministry. The ordained minister remained, the committee argued, "the key to that wider ministry in which every Christian participates. He trains, supports, enables, guides; no longer as an authoritarian father-figure, but nevertheless in a crucial way. If we can succeed in equipping him to act as a member of a group ministry, we will be on the way to restoring the wholeness (health) of the church."[53] The committee initiated annual consultations with the colleges, in which they urged that academic training and supervised pastoral experience be more fully integrated in the process of theological education. At the same time, however, it supported the requests of the colleges for additional funds to implement the desired changes in the curriculum.[54] In 1975, the committee became the Board of Ministry, complete with a full-time staff. The colleges complained, with some justification, that money spent on the board would have been better spent on adding to their faculties so that they could make the curriculum changes required. A subtle and unwitting shift took place in the focus of the church's thinking about its clergy in the midst of this questioning. Attention shifted from the gifts necessary for the calling to the status and authority of clergy. Overtures from presbyteries concerning ministry through-out this period consistently raised the question in terms of the power and position of the different kinds of ministries within the governing structures of the church, be it the clergy themselves, dia-conal ministers, ruling elders, or the laity. The responses to these overtures, drafted largely by the Committee on Church Doctrine, tried to sort out the place and privilege of each order or office, but with little lasting success. The focus became the individual rights and privileges of the office holder within the system rather than the contribution the individual made to the ministry of the church as a whole. In this climate of concern, the positions taken by the Knox faculty were easily distorted. The stress Bryden's students placed upon thorough preparation through university courses in arts and sciences, and biblical and theological study for preaching and teaching the gospel led to the impression that only an educated elite could interpret the gospel properly. David Hay's stress on the unique place of the clergy in the ordering of the church led to the impression that they had ultimate authority in governing the church, especially in the local congregation.

Throughout this ferment, the Knox faculty insisted that the con-tent of the gospel had to be preserved in the face of the tempta-tions of cultural accommodation and relevancy. Though sensitive to the need to communicate effectively, they insisted that the gos-pel to be communicated had to shape the methods of communica-tion. They found no convincing reason in the exploding literature on ministry to shift their attention away from the ordinary means of grace in the local congregation as the key resources in preserving and propagating the gospel truths. They disagreed on which of those means were most important and how the ministry of the church should be ordered to exercise proper stewardship over them, but there was consensus on the centrality of clergy and the local congregation in communicating the gospel.

Confusion over the identity and calling of the clergy brought the traditional forms of educating them into question as well. Knox College received full accreditation in 1948 from the Association of Theological Schools, an organization that provided the forum for much of the most searching examination of reform in theological education after the Second World War. The conferences and litera-ture covered every conceivable aspect of theological education. The topics ranged from internal questions of curriculum, students, governance, financial support, library resources, facilities, location, faculty recruitment and development, and intra- and interseminary politics to contextual questions of social change, threats from contemporary secular culture to Christian identity, differing perceptions of the purpose of the church and ministry, denominational distinctiveness, the ebb and flow of ecumenism, the congregation, the global context, regional and ethnic constituencies, gender issues, the need for continuing education, and the relation of the theological seminary with the university.[55]

The Knox faculty followed these discussions with interest and responded by insisting that the real foundations for Christian relevance in the modern world were the great evangelical truths recovered by the Reformation. They acknowledged that more attention had to be paid to the formation of ministerial character and the practical disciplines that dealt with how the gospel was communicated, but not at the expense of the traditional theological disciplines. Another factor that prevented them from expanding and reforming the curriculum in a significant way was money. In spite of repeated pleas, Knox failed to convince the church to provide adequate funding for its current program, let alone an expanded one. Curriculum revision was finally made possible by using the resources made available when Knox joined the Toronto School of Theology in 1970, but the changes remained well within the traditional pattern.

ENCOUNTERING NEW FRONTIERS
IN THEOLOGICAL EDUCATION

"It is rapidly becoming evident in all parts of the world," wrote J. Stanley Glen in the *Record* in 1956, "that serious attention must be given to matters of policy in theological education if the future ministers, missionaries and church workers are to be adequately prepared for their tremendous task in modern society." Glen attributed the new interest in educational reform to a revived interest in theology itself, the recognition of new frontiers of Christian work and witness, the challenge of menacing ideologies, and the general ferment of modern life. He pointed out that Presbyterians had never considered their theological colleges as trade schools where students acquired "an assortment of techniques irrespective of faith and the content of fundamental subjects." Rather, the true vocation of theological education was to establish "the inherent relevancy of every theological subject to real life and to the task of ministry." Such integration, done in the context of teaching each of the traditional theological disciplines, was true practical theology.[56] Glen did acknowledge, however, that Knox needed a professor of practical theology to give full-time attention to homiletics, Christian education, and field work and urged the church to provide the necessary funding.[57]

In the same article, as well as in the college's report to the Assembly in 1956, Glen also raised questions about the scope of theological education and the place of research in the work of the faculty. He agreed with those who claimed that three six-month sessions were not sufficient to properly prepare people to be clergy in the modern church. He noted that many were recommending a four-year program of basic theological study, suggested that continuing education in the form of summer schools or institutes be established, and that congregations consider giving their clergy sabbaticals. In addition, he endorsed the reintroduction of extension courses for the laity, noting that over one hundred were enrolled in the classes Knox had provided in 1955. While Glen recognized that in the Canadian church tradition the theological college had been primarily a teaching institution, giving little attention or support to scholarly research and publication, he urged that this attitude change to allow for a better balance between the two functions.[58]

Voices from outside the college called for changes as well. J.W.L. McLean from St. Andrew's Presbyterian Church in Victoria, a former moderator of the General Assembly, outlined his desires for reform in theological education in the *Record* in early 1960. He quoted James Denney on the kind of preparation needed for the ministry of the clergy, identified almost exclusively with preaching. The preacher needed to know the Bible well enough to find the gospel in it, to be so familiar with the thought of the age that preaching was directed to its needs and questions, and to be thoroughly trained in literary style and mode of delivery. McLean found the training in the English Bible seriously wanting and the training in literary style and public speaking "so meagre and perfunctory as to be a farce." McLean worried that Knox was preparing theologians, but not preachers. Of particular concern for him was the lack of attention to the Christian personality of the preacher: "A

Christian preacher must possess what he seeks to communicate: faith in the grace of God; love to God supremely; hope set on God. A definite program designed to guide students in the forming of daily devotional habits and to lead them into deeper personal experience of fellowship with the living Christ – an emphasis upon necessary spiritual resources comparable to the present emphasis upon mental equipment – this has been lacking in our church's training of men for the ministry." McLean concluded his critique of theological education by calling for more attention to personal evangelism and church government as well.[59]

With limited financial and personnel resources, however, the college was severely restricted in its options regarding curriculum expansion and revision. Its primary concern was to strengthen the ability of the clergy to communicate the gospel when confronted with the complexity of modern life and thought. Thorough preparation in the traditional theological disciplines was considered essential and the first priority for Knox was the expansion of its graduate program. Bryden was a strong supporter of the development of the Toronto Graduate School of Theological Studies, established in 1942, that pooled the resources of the Toronto theological colleges to provide courses and supervision for BDs, MThs, and ThDs. Knox amended its charter in 1948 to allow it to offer the latter two and Allan Farris became the first MTh graduate in 1951. Bryden was aware of the misgivings the addition of the power to offer graduate degrees in theology raised in the church. "Do not think," he assured the church in 1948, "that in Knox we are attaching undue importance to purely academic standing and recognition. There is only one thing of paramount importance in theological education, that is, that students know Jesus Christ."[60] Nevertheless, he and his faculty colleagues remained determined that the evangelical conviction that formed the heart of theological education must be accompanied by an intellectual integrity that met the highest standards of theological scholarship. By 1956, Knox reported 77 students in its graduate programs and in 1958 changes were made in the curriculum to provide a core program for the certificate of the college and an elective program that allowed the BD degree to be taken within the three-year period of study. A regular pattern of sabbatical leaves for faculty members was instituted in the 1950s, many of them made possible by Association of Theological Schools' grants. The library resources at Knox were significantly increased in the 1960s under librarian George L. Douglas, again with the help of Association of Theological Schools' grants.[61]

As early as 1946, the college asked for the creation of a chair in practical theology, but the Assembly took no action on this request until 1963. In the meantime, the teaching of homiletics, liturgy, Christian education, missions, church music, and church administration was allocated to existing faculty members or sessional lecturers.[62] When Charles Hay was appointed in 1963, the fields included in his position were homiletics, evangelism, and church administration, precisely the areas about which McLean had been most anxious.

Just prior to coming on faculty in 1967, James Farris suggested sweeping changes in the organization of the theological curriculum. The subjects that had to do directly with the church's life and mission should be at the centre of the curriculum rather than addenda. Indeed, Farris believed that the traditional emphasis on the biblical, historical, and systematic fields gave "a faulty image of what theology is all about."[63] He saw the ideal program of study as "the conducting of a conversation with Christian sources concerning the problems and issues confronting the living church." The purpose of the curriculum was not so much to cover a certain body of material as to introduce the student to the theological resources the church had for its ongoing mission.[64] Farris' suggestions went largely unheeded in the councils of Knox College. His colleagues claimed that they paid ample attention to the practical needs of the church in the way they taught the traditional disciplines, especially now that a chair existed for practical theology.

Knox's accreditation with the Association of Theological Schools and its joining the Toronto School of Theology at once restricted its freedom to revise its curriculum and expanded its resources to provide a thorough basic degree program. Accreditation with ATS and participation in TST required that faculty hold graduate degrees, preferably PhDs, and that most of the student body hold bachelor's degrees. These requirements rendered impossible amalgamation or closer cooperation with Ewart College, explored seriously in 1968–1970 as a cost-saving measure and as a way of increasing attention to Christian education in the Knox curriculum.[65] The Toronto School of Theology, created in 1969 to extend cooperative theological education to the basic degree level from the advanced degree level, was a federation of seven theological colleges located on the University of Toronto campus: Knox (Presbyterian), Trinity (Anglican), Wycliffe (Anglican), Emmanuel (United), St. Michael's (Roman Catholic), Regis (Roman Catholic), and St. Augustine's (Roman Catholic).

The Knox faculty was divided over the wisdom of joining TST. Stanley Glen and Allan Farris were anxious about the implications of the federation for the college's accountability to the church and its control over its own program. Charles Hay and David Hay were enthusiastic in their support. In the end, Glen and Farris became convinced that the benefits outweighed the dangers and supported the move. The federation, noted Glen in the college's report to the Assembly in 1970, offered a richer variety of courses for the student, larger resources for the development of practical training, facilitation of sabbatical leaves and the possibility of greater specialization for the faculty, and broader ecumenical encounters for both faculty and students.[66] The revision of the curriculum that took place in 1971 reflected both the limitations and possibilities created by the relation with TST.

The core of the regular course remained virtually untouched, continuing to require courses in Old Testament and New Testament literature and exegesis, systematic theology, church history, history and philosophy of religion, Christian ethics, homiletics, evangelism, church administration, pastoral theology, liturgics, Christian education, church music, and missions. The practical areas continued to receive much less class time than the traditional academic subjects, four or five courses being required in each testament, systematics, and church history, three courses in the history and philosophy of religion and Christian ethics, and one or two in each of the practical areas. Students were required to take all of their first year and at least two-thirds of their second and third years at Knox College, thereby only being able to take advantage of the resources of the Toronto School of Theology for one-third of their final two years. The revisions reflected the faculty's conviction that a solid biblical and theological grounding from Presbyterian professors was essential to theological education. They were also based upon the warranted assumption that, when the traditional disciplines were taught by people who were committed to the denomination's ecclesiastical culture and active in its institutional structures, the integration of the theoretical and practical took place in all the courses. Such limited use of the resources of TST, however, did little to cut the costs of theological education at Knox.

In the final analysis, it was money that really poisoned the relationship between the college and the church, especially in the 1970s. The problem of inadequate funding from the church to do what was thought essential to do was not new, as we have seen all through this history, but the scope of the problem and the bitterness that emerged were. In 1950, Bryden made an impassioned plea to the church through the *Record* for increased funding, noting that the accumulated deficit since 1939 was $50,000. "For Knox," he warned, "it becomes, sooner or later, a matter of 'to be or not to be' financially."[67] Bryden's plea did not work and the problem increased. By 1968, the accumulated deficit was over $209,000, all of which had been drawn from the college's unspecified capital funds. The annual dance of debt became familiar to all parties. The college asked for more money, the General Assembly referred the request to the Administrative Council, and the Council granted Knox less than it wanted. National grants did increase substantially, from $15,000 in 1945 to $124,425 in 1975, but not enough to cover the inflation in the costs of Knox's staff, programs, and facilities.[68] The result was a growing distrust and animosity between the administrative staff and governing bodies of the church and the college.

The tensions erupted at the General Assembly in 1973, after the college discovered that representatives from the Committee on Educational Needs set up by the Assembly in 1972 to study "the relation of the educational needs of our church to the resources that can be made available" had approached the University of Toronto to see whether there was any interest in buying either or both of the Knox and Ewart buildings without any consultation with the colleges. The appeals of Knox and Ewart against this action were not granted by the Assembly in 1974, but the unilateral approach to the university was deemed "injudicious" and representatives from the three colleges were added to the committee.[69] Plans to sell the buildings were dropped, but tensions over adequate funding for theological education continued. Knox continued to insist that it needed the facilities it had and a larger faculty, noting in 1978 that its enrolments in the diploma and basic degree program had increased from 30 in 1967 to 83 in 1977, while graduate enrolments averaged about 30.[70] The church insisted with continued firmness that it could not afford what Knox wanted.[71] Knox realized it was not going to get the funding it wanted from its traditional sources and welcomed discussions that TST initiated with the

University of Toronto to have the member colleges grant joint degrees with the university and thus double their government grants.[72] In addition, the college announced that it intended to launch its own financial appeal to refurbish the buildings, provide adequate scholarships and bursaries, and add to the faculty.[73]

In the midst of growing tensions on the frontier of finances and lingering concerns on the frontier of curriculum design, another frontier was crossed as a new faculty was appointed. Between 1975 and 1977, David Hay, Robert Lennox, and J. Stanley Glen retired from their faculty positions. Iain Nicol from Scotland and Stanley Walters from the United States were appointed to the chairs of systematic theology and Old Testament. Charles Hay, who had spent 7 years as Assistant Director of TST, returned full-time to the college to assume the chair of New Testament and Allan Farris was appointed principal. Donald C. Smith, a Canadian Presbyterian with a doctorate in church history from Edinburgh, was appointed as registrar and director of field education. In 1978, he assumed the newly-created chair of church and ministry.[74] Farris's tenure as principal was cut short after only one year in the office by a fatal heart attack in the summer of 1977. Charles Hay was appointed principal and moved from the chair of New Testament back to his old chair, now redefined as preaching and worship. Reformation scholar Calvin Pater, born in the Netherlands and educated in the United States, was appointed to the chair of church history in 1978, while Raymond Humphries, born and educated in Ireland with a doctorate from the Graduate Theological Union in Berkeley and four years of teaching at Memorial University in Newfoundland, was appointed to the chair of New Testament in 1979. Jim Farris continued to hold the chair of history and philosophy of religion and Christian ethics throughout this period.

In 1974, five of the six faculty members were born and bred Canadian Presbyterians, and the sixth had been teaching and working in the denomination for thirty years. Five years later, four of the seven faculty members, all teaching in the core academic disciplines, were foreign born and educated, though Humphries had pastoral and teaching experience in Canada. The four new faculty from outside the denomination were all committed to using their scholarship in the service of the church and knew the particular challenges of educating men and women for the practice of ministry, but they knew little of the culture of Canadian Presbyterianism and came to the college at a time when many traditions in the denomination were being questioned.

There were those who welcomed the addition of faculty from outside the denomination to overcome what they saw as academic in-breeding and Presbyterian parochialism. Prominent church musician Alan H. Cowle spoke for this group when he reminded readers of the *Record* in 1975 that pianist Arthur Schabel once defined tradition as a collection of bad habits. Cowle expressed the hope that "the practice of merely potting a shoot from the old stem will be replaced by the policy of planting firm, strong, new strains" in choosing new faculty. Factors that led to Knox's acceptance of Cowle's advice included the low level of faculty salaries that made it difficult for Canadian candidates to leave the parish ministry or other teaching positions to come to Knox, the lack of qualified Canadian candidates for all the chairs, and the continuing polarization within the denomination between creedal and catholic Presbyterians, especially in relation to the question of women's ordination.

James D. Smart, who had expressed such enthusiastic confidence in the Presbyterian Church in Canada in the 1950s, recorded bitter disappointment in an open letter to the *Record* as the 1970s closed. He accused Knox of turning its back on the British and Canadian traditions of emphasizing general competence and experience in the church and its parishes and adopting the American model of valuing a doctoral degree above all else. Using such criteria, Smart pointed out, neither Walter Bryden nor Allan Farris would have been appointed to Knox. Theology, he argued, was "a discipline before all else *in* the church, *of* the church and *for* the church. We are letting the academic interest take precedence over the interest of the church, which could be fatal to theology in the church." What lay behind Smart's attack was his conviction that Knox had overlooked or rejected candidates for the chairs who were more rooted in and committed to preserving and propagating the ecclesiastical culture of Canadian Presbyterianism, a culture he still deeply believed had a unique contribution to make to the church catholic. Charles Hay came to the defence of Knox. He expressed appreciation for Smart's concerns, but not for "his tone, his judgements, or his arguments." Hay assured readers of the *Record* that Knox had sought and found candidates who clearly understood the relation between their disciplines and the tasks of ministry. He acknowledged that low salaries were a problem, noting that full professors at McGill made almost double what Knox was able to offer. Knox, he continued, was no longer "the academic ghetto it was in Bryden's day" and he defended the commitment the non-Canadian faculty "to harness their formidable gifts to the preparation of men and women for ministry in the *Canadian* scene."[75] Hay saw the varied backgrounds and perspectives brought by the new faculty as important sources of critique and renewal in a denomination threatened with parochialism and decline.

The ecclesiastical culture Bryden had done so much to shape no longer dominated the teaching at Knox College nor did it play a determining role in the choice of new faculty. Rather than choosing people who were known and trusted by the denomination to formulate and reformulate its distinctive culture and guide the formation of its clergy, the college chose people who promised to introduce new perspectives and were experts in their academic disciplines. Convincing arguments for both approaches were made in public and in private, but the college's decision to introduce "new strains" of Presbyterianism that did not represent a clear and consistent shift to an alternate theological paradigm marked a significant break with its traditional practice. Hay's confidence in the new faculty remained to be proved, but another frontier had been crossed.

Cultural questioning and diversity were not the only problems Knox College faced when Charles Hay assumed the principal's office in 1977. The term of his closest friend and colleague, Allan Farris, to whom many had looked to reconcile the interests of the college and the church, had been cut short by his tragic death. The appointments of the new faculty, especially Iain Nicol and Calvin Pater, had been controversial within the church. Funding from the national church remained inadequate and efforts to tap new sources of revenue through closer ties to the university led to concerns that the college's accountability to the church was being compromised. Hay's close ties with TST and ATS were cited as strengths when the Knox Board recommended his appointment as principal, but some thought these two organizations limited the church's freedom to conduct its own theological education. Others were still not satisfied with the steps Knox had taken to provide more practical training. What was new for the college in confronting these continuing challenges was the absence of a dominant ecclesiastical culture from which to establish criteria and build consensus on questions of the identity of the church, the role of the clergy, and the design of their theological education.

Epilogue

Continuing Challenges, 1978–1994

The problems that confronted Knox College when Charles Hay assumed the principal's office were not new. They included continuing tensions between the college and the church over the funding and control of theological education, confusion within the denomination over the nature of the church, its clerical leadership, and their theological education, and concern that most of the chairs in the core disciplines of the curriculum had gone to non-Canadians with little parish experience. The seeds of many of these tensions were sown generations before, but they sprouted in the 1960s and the 1970s, came to fruition in the 1980s, and continue to challenge the college and the church today. The most thorough and perceptive analysis of the problems was written by Hay himself the year after he became principal. The title of the article, "The Seminary Speaks to the Church about Trust, Freedom, and Support," conveyed the sense that the college was standing over against the church, needing to protect itself against undue influence and at the same time relying on the church for a significant portion of its funding.

The common ground once shared by church and college of preparing people for ministry, Hay began, was now the scene of increasing unrest and growing discord. The denominational college often felt

itself misunderstood, its efforts seldom fully appreciated, convinced that it lacks the financial support it is sure it deserves, and ... hampered by strictures imposed on it from denominational headquarters that are intended to maintain or even tighten control, but which from the seminary's viewpoint only hamper and hinder its efforts to fulfil its goals effectively. The church on the other hand sees the seminary slipping out from under its control, developing lines of accountability apart from the church, not always paying close attention to the demands of its constituency, especially in the more practical aspects of preparation for ministry, and, as if that were not enough, possessing a voracious appetite for funds.[1]

Hay presented a spirited defence of the college that revealed the ways in which the college understood the growing unrest within the church about its priorities and the use of its resources.

He warned that the constant pressure for a more practically-oriented curriculum threatened to turn the seminary into a trade school[2] and he insisted that the kind of leadership the church expected from its clergy could "only come from adequate exposure to the traditional disciplines." The way the traditional disciplines were taught at Knox, however, put scholarship at the service of the Gospel. The traditional disciplines addressed questions of faith and discipleship, of the church's understanding and transmission of the Gospel in their day. In so doing, they provided students with the opportunity to more fully assimilate the tradition they were called to hand on through their ministry. Given limited faculty resources and limited space in the curriculum, Hay argued that the intellectual integrity of the curriculum must be maintained because it was essential to the effective ministry of the clergy.[3]

Hay expressed some reservations about the wisdom of the demands from the church. Knox did not exist, he noted, "to give the church exactly what it demands, to respond to its whims, to cater to the trends of the moment, to react uncritically to its requests." Rather, the college had to remain true to its own sense of how its resources could be best used to prepare people for ministry and sensitive to the needs of its other constituencies, the Association of Theological Schools, the Toronto School of Theology, and the University of Toronto, Hay acknowledged that the college had moved out of the church's orbit and into the academic context, causing considerable anxiety within the church. One of the results of the shift was "the influx of bright young PhD's to the seminary faculties, fresh from academic triumphs but somewhat anemic in the area of practical experience." Hay reminded his readers, however, that the college had no choice in making the move, since the church was not willing to provide more adequate funding and the relationship with the university did.

In addition, Hay argued that the church needed Christian scholars working "at the frontiers of their disciplines" so that new doors would be opened on the sources and expressions of the Christian faith.[4] Knox's participation in the advanced degree programs of TST, the area for which Hay was responsible while Assistant Director, grew significantly in the 1980s. Several Canadian Presbyterian students completed doctoral degrees, teaching at the college while pursuing their studies. These developments contributed to the perception that the focus at Knox was shifting from preparation for ministry to theological scholarship.

In the end, Hay pleaded for mutual trust, openness, and better communication between college and church. Both institutions were united in their quest for "the mind of Christ for our day," and had to do everything in their power to overcome the misunderstandings and divisions that had emerged. Unfortunately, Hay's article was published in *Theological Education*, the journal of the Association of Theological Schools, which circulated largely among colleges and was read by very few outside the academic community.

A similar analysis of the continuing challenges faced by Knox did appear in a publication more accessible to the key decision makers in the church. In the feasibility study for the financial campaign proposed by the college in 1977, consultant Gordon Goldie identified the college's weaknesses and strengths. Some factions in the church thought Knox was "cliquish, excessively concerned with academic standards to the detriment of its primary responsibility to the Church, and constantly querulous about the lack of both funds and academic freedom."[5] Some of Knox's graduates had not found their studies beneficial to their faith or their ability to exercise their ministry. Knox had kept too low a profile for the previous 25 years and was well known neither in the church nor the Toronto community. Finally, Goldie noted that Knox's links with Ewart were tenuous and that no efforts to strengthen the complementary roles of the two institutions were under consideration.

The feasibility study began by noting that the college had an excellent academic reputation, with enrolments more than doubling between 1974 and 1978, from 38 to 83 in the basic degree program, and that 60% of all Presbyterian ministers were graduates of Knox. Although the national church contributed $188,262 in 1978, that constituted less than 30% of the college's income from other sources, including endowment income, bequests, residence and tuition fees, rentals, and government grants. Goldie noted further that the college was taking positive steps to improve its program of professional and practical preparation for ministry in response to the strongly expressed wishes of the church.[6] Pointing out that no major campaign for the college had been conducted for 65 years, he concluded that a campaign was feasible and would not only raise much-needed money, but also provide an opportunity to improve communication with the church and build a new level of trust and support.

By 1980, a campaign organization was in place, a case had been built, and a goal of $2.5 million dollars was established – $1.5 million for renovations and $1 million for academic strengthening and expansion. Renovations focused on the electrical system, the roof, the stonework, and the kitchen area. In the academic area, proposals were approved for teaching assistants in each of the core disciplines. Three additional faculty positions were proposed, one in Biblical Interpretation and Homiletics, one in Pastoral Care and Counselling, and a third in Church Music. An endowment fund of $200,000 was suggested to bring scholars to Knox for a semester to cover sabbaticals. Further funding was requested for bursaries, to expand the field education program, to add resources to the library, and to launch programs of continuing and lay education.[7] When the campaign ended in the spring of 1987, almost $4 million dollars had been raised, making the effort the most successful fund raising program in the history of the Presbyterian Church in Canada. Almost half of the amount had come from 629 congregations. The theological alumni contributed a total of $150,000, while former residents gave over $75,000.

Steps had been taken during the campaign to develop better networks of communication within the church, including the publication of a quarterly newsletter conveying the views of the faculty, describing their various activities on behalf of the church, and reporting on the life and work of the college. The Knox College Graduates' Association was revived and has proven an effective organization for generating support for the college. Though a full professorship in church music was not feasible, John Derkson was appointed as lecturer, college organist, and choir director. The choir proved to be valuable ambassadors for the college through their several concerts and tours. New talks with Ewart College were initiated and eventually led to the amalgamation of Knox and Ewart on 1 July 1991, with two of the Ewart faculty being appointed as tenured professors in the new Knox College and a revised curriculum being approved which provided several options for those preparing for diaconal ministry in the denomination.[8]

In spite of the success of the campaign, the improved networks of communication established with the church, and the successful amalgamation of Knox and Ewart, the trust between college and church that Charles Hay had pinpointed as crucial in his 1979 analysis did not develop as both parties had hoped it would. A thorough study of the reasons for the failure must await an historian with greater access to the sources and greater distance from the events. Whoever that may be will have to take account of several factors that affected the course of events, including: 1) the continuing financial difficulties of the college and the church's inability and/ or unwillingness to be the primary means of solving them; 2) the lack of continuity in the principal's office throughout this period; 3) the competing demands on faculty from the various constituencies to which the college was now related and the lack of clarity as to how the demands should be weighed; and 4) the relationship of the faculty to the denominational culture they were entrusted with teaching.

Financial difficulties posed a serious challenge to amity between the church and the college. Both were hit hard and unexpectedly by inflation. Between 1978 and 1992, the operating costs of the college increased five-fold, from $544,000 to $2,727,000. During the same period, the church's grant to the college quadrupled from $188,000 to $801,000.[9] As early as 1981, the Board warned of the impact that inflation was having on its best efforts to provide an economically viable operation.[10] By 1988, the college acknowledged that "deficits in the operating accounts were reaching crisis proportions,"[11] and the Board's report to the 1989 General Assembly stated bluntly that most of their unrestricted endowment funds were depleted and the future of Knox College was in jeopardy.[12] Throughout the growing financial crisis, the college insisted that the essential difficulty was due to the fact that the college was under-funded, especially by the church.[13] Though not stated in so many words, the opinion of many within the church was that the college was not doing enough to cut back on its spending.

The concern about the financial viability of Knox College was one of the factors, though only one, that led the General Assembly to appoint a Taskforce on Theological Education in 1989 to review and possibly recommend the restructuring of the work of its four theological colleges. The Knox Board welcomed this initiative "emphatically."[14] The Task Force reported in 1990 and the Assembly accepted its recommendations to amalgamate Knox and Ewart and to create a Committee on Theological Education to oversee the work of the colleges and coordinate other activities in theological education. The new Knox College was to be the only place diaconal education was offered for a period of five years and it received the whole of the Ewart grant and the Ewart Resource Fund to enable it to do so.[15] The new committee was given the task within a five year period of deciding on the number of colleges that the church needed and/or could afford.

Knox College was not happy with the Task Force's final report. They claimed the report had not addressed the financial crisis, that its recommendations would add to the costs of theological education, and that its powers compromised the authority of the college boards and senates.[16] Supporters of the initiative responded that giving the Ewart grant and endowments to Knox and permitting the college to charge full tuition fees added well over $500,000 a year to their revenues,[17] that the additional costs of the committee were well worth it to provide a forum for better communication and working out the competing claims of the colleges, and that the committee did not compromise the authority of the governing bodies of the colleges, but rather provided a more effective means for the General Assembly to exercise its legitimate oversight.

It remains to be seen what the Committee on Theological Education will recommend concerning the structure of theological education and the number of colleges. Knox suffered a significant reduction in its government grant in 1993 and 1994 as a result of the restraint measures introduced by the Ontario government, and agreed, with the other colleges, to reduce its dependence on national church grants if the denomination gave it permission to raise money on its own behalf within the church. Severe cuts have been made in the number of teaching assistants and lecturers at the college. An associate director of development was appointed by Knox in 1994 to establish and coordinate an on-going financial development program.

In the midst of grappling with the growing financial crisis, unforeseeable circumstances led to a lack of continuity in the principal's office that weakened the ability of the incumbents to address the problems effectively. Between 1978 and 1994, five different people held the office. Charles Hay suffered a heart attack in 1979 and was on sick leave for the better part of a year. James Farris served as principal on an interim basis. Hay reached retirement age in 1985 and was replaced by Donald Corbett. Corbett declined to accept a second term as principal in 1990, in part because of his frustration with the failure of the church to address adequately the problems faced by the college.[18] The college appointed James Farris again for 1990–1991 while it searched for a new principal. Its nomination was Professor Alan P.F. Sell, a minister of the United Reformed Church in the United Kingdom who held the Chair of Christian Thought at the University of Calgary. For a variety of reasons, among which Sell's lack of experience in and knowledge of the Canadian church were especially noted, the Committee on Theological Education withdrew the nomination at Assembly and Knox continued its search for another year, during which time James Farris remained in the principal's office. Arthur Van Seters, nominated by 18 of the 37 presbyteries that forwarded names, was recommended to the next General Assembly and appointed. He was not able to assume office until July 1993, requiring six months to complete his work as Principal of Vancouver School of Theology and requesting a six-month sabbatical. During 1992–1993, Raymond Humphries served as principal. The lack of continuity, the conflicts concerning nominations and appointments, the tensions among the faculty, senate, and board and between the college and the Committee on Theological Education, and the frustrations arising from the inability to do any real long-range planning prevented the college from addressing its administrative and financial problems more effectively.

Other kinds of inflation, in administrative duties, the demands for scholarly publication, and teaching responsibilities at the basic and advanced degree levels, affected the college and its faculty during the years following 1978. With each new partnership formed came additional governing responsibilities in the form of committees, task groups, and consultations. Considerable time had to be devoted to the negotiating, developing, and renegotiating of the relationships with the Toronto School of Theology and the University of Toronto. The links with the Toronto School of Theology and the University of Toronto, especially as they related to faculty appointments and promotion, put greater pressure on the faculty to research and write for the academic community than had been the case for previous generations of faculty. Teaching in the graduate program and supervising graduate theses consumed a considerable amount of time as well. Nevertheless, most members of the faculty maintained the practice of writing for church publications, contributing in significant ways to denominational committees, and preaching and teaching on a regular basis in the courts and congregations of the church.

From 1987 until 1989, lengthy negotiations took place with the University of Toronto as the various parties involved in the Toronto School of Theology reviewed the agreement under which joint degrees were granted with the university and full government funding was received. The university was concerned with tenure and issues of academic freedom, while Knox, under Don Corbett's leadership, was concerned to retain an appropriate degree of accountability to the church as required by the Presbyterian polity. The compromise reached and approved in 1989 provided for a lengthy process of peer-group review at the college should a professor resign or be deposed from the ministry of Word and Sacraments, rather than allowing the General Assembly to take direct action to terminate the appointment.[19] Though the church has retained ultimate control over the teaching faculty at Knox, the efforts of the university to protect the faculty from the church were significant.[20]

The relationship of the current generation of faculty with the denominational culture of Canadian Presbyterianism is complex. They took up their positions at the college at a time when the dominance of the neo-orthodoxy introduced by Bryden and enshrined in the church's key documents, such as its ordination services and *Living Faith*, was being questioned. Unlike previous shifts in perspective among Canadian Presbyterians, however, no coherent alternative gained wide acceptance. Charles Hay, for example, in his exchange with James Smart over the new faculty appointments, described as "parochial" the neo-orthodox culture in which he had been trained and he saw in the engagement with the Toronto School of Theology and the broader academic community an opportunity to prepare the leadership of the church in a more ecumenical and cosmopolitan ethos. Others, rooted in the confessional orthodox tradition in the denomination, created the Renewal Fellowship to resist what they saw to be a drift away from the Reformed standards of the faith within the Presbyterian Church in Canada.[21] Women in ministry raised questions about the method and content of the church's theology and practice of ministry that posed new challenges to what remains a male-dominated church.[22] The Presbyterian Church in Canada has not been immune to the fraying and polarization of ecclesiastical cultures that has affected all the traditional mainline denominations in North American over the last 15 years.[23]

It cannot be said, in all honesty, that any of the problems identified by Charles Hay in 1979 have been solved. They persist and challenge the current leadership at the college and in the church. Financial shortages continue to plague the college. Curriculum revisions have failed to satisfy many within the church that the college is providing an adequate preparation for the ministry of the clergy. Mutual understanding and trust between college and church remains an elusive dream. It will not be easy to break out of the habits, patterns, and attitudes that have developed over the past fifty years. Realizing the potential Knox has to serve the church effectively, however, depends on a concerted effort by all involved. The church needs to clarify what it expects of its premier college. The college needs to decide how it can best serve the church within the limits of its financial resources.

Preserving and propagating the great evangelical truths with catholic scope and sympathy through the means of grace embodied in the local congregation constitutes the core of the ecclesiastical culture of the Presbyterian Church in Canada. Today, college and church together face the challenge of recovering and reformulating the evangelical convictions, the intellectual integrities, and the governing structures that most members recognize as marks of the great Christian tradition within which they live, and in which they seek to stand with their clergy in faithful witness to the Gospel in trying times.

Notes

INTRODUCTION

1 The first name given to Knox College was the Theological Institution of the Free Church in Canada. In 1846, the Synod decided to call the institution Knox's College. That name continued until the Act of Incorporation in 1858 adopted the current name. See William Gregg, "The History of Knox College," *Knox College Monthly (KCM)*, 9 (November 1888) 1:6.

2 R.F. Burns, *The Life and Times of The Rev. Robert Burns, D.D., Toronto* (Toronto: James Campbell & Sons, 1871), 152–174.

3 T.C. Smout, *A Century of the Scottish People, 1830–1950* (London: Fontana, 1987), 185.

4 For an account of the social position and impact of the Free Church in Scotland during the nineteenth century, see Smout, *Century of the Scottish People*, 181–202.

5 David W. Bebbington, Evangelicalism in Modern Britain: A History from the 1730s to the 1980s (London: Unwin Hyman, 1989), 108. Ian C. Bradley, *The Call to Seriousness The Evangelical Impact on the Victorians* (New York: Macmillan, 1976), 22, listed the key tenets of early nineteenth-century Evangelicalism as the doctrines of the depravity of man, the conversion of the sinner, and the sanctification of the regenerate soul.

6 For analyses of the factors leading to the creation of the Free Church in Scotland, see A.L. Drummond and J. Bulloch, *The Scottish Church, 1688–1843: The Age of the Moderates* (Edinburgh: St. Andrew's Press,

1973), and *The Church in Victorian Scotland, 1843–1875* (Edinburgh: St. Andrew's Press, 1975; S.J. Brown, *Thomas Chalmers and the Godly Commonwealth in Scotland* (Oxford: Oxford University Press, 1982); and R.W. Vaudry, " 'For Christ's Kingdom and Crown': The Evangelical Party in the Church of Scotland and the Problem of Church-State Relations, 1829–1843," *Canadian Society of Presbyterian History Papers 1981*, 21–41.

7 On the various factors involved in the Free Church controversy in the Canadas, see John S. Moir, *Church and State in Canada West: Three Studies in the Relation of Denominationalism and Nationalism, 1841–1867* (Toronto: University of Toronto Press, 1959); Ian S. Rennie, "The Free Church and the Relations of Church and State in Canada, 1844–1854" (M.A. thesis, University of Toronto, 1954); and Richard W. Vaudry, *The Free Church in Victorian Canada, 1844–1861* (Waterloo: Wilfrid Laurier University Press, 1989). On the broader influence of Presbyterian evangelicalism in Canada, see Marguerite Van Die, " 'The Double Vision': Evangelical Piety as Derivative and Indigenous in Victorian English Canada," *Evangelicalism: Comparative Studies of Popular Protestantism in North America, the British Isles, and Beyond, 1700–1990*, ed. Mark A. Noll, David W. Bebbington, and George A. Rawlyk (New York: Oxford University Press, 1994), 253–272, and Barry Mack, "Of Canadian Presbyterians and Guardian Angels," *Amazing Grace: Evangelicalism in Australia, Britain, Canada, and the United States*, ed. George A. Rawlyk and Mark A. Noll (Grand Rapids: Baker, 1993), 269–292.

8 Vaudry, *Free Church*, xiv.

9 For an account of the Synod meeting, see Vaudry, *Free Church*, 34–37. On Peter Brown and his role in the development of the Free Church in Canada, see Richard W. Vaudry, "Peter Brown, the Toronto *Banner* and the Evangelical Mind in Victorian Canada," *Ontario History*, 77 (March 1985) 1:3–18.

10 For a thorough analysis of the professions during the nineteenth century in Ontario. see R.D. Gidney and W.P.J. Millar, *Professional Gentlemen: The Professions in Nineteenth-Century Ontario* (Toronto: University of Toronto Press, 1994).

11 The role that the faculty and Board of Knox College played in the development of the University of Toronto is traced in A.B. McKillop, *Matters of Mind: The University in Ontario, 1791–1951* (Toronto: University of Toronto Press, 1994), 26–51.

12 Various accounts exist of the opening. See "Reminiscences of the Origin of Two Presbyterian Colleges in Canada," *Home and Foreign*

Record of the Canada Presbyterian Church (HFR), 6 (1866) 1:24–31;
Burns, *Life and Times*, 244; John S. Moir, "Confrontation at Queen's: A
Prelude to the Disruption in Canada," *Presbyterian History*, 15 (May
1971) 1; Hilda Neatby, *Queen's University, Volume I, 1841–1917*
(Montreal: McGill-Queen's University Press, 1978), 47; and Vaudry,
Free Church, 31.

13 Neatby, *Queen's*, 47.

14 *Ecclesiastical and Missionary Record (EMR)*, January 1845.

15 Burns, *Life and Times*, 374–375.

16 John S. Moir, *Enduring Witness: A History of the Presbyterian Church in
   Canada* (Toronto: Presbyterian Publications, 1975), 144.

17 Vaudry, *Free Church*, 127.

18 Neil Gregor Smith, "By Schism Rent Asunder: A Study of the Disruption of the Presbyterian Church in Canada in 1844," *Canadian Journal
   of Theology*, 1 (1955): 182.

19 See N. Keith Clifford, "The Paradoxes of Professionalism: A Brief Look
   at the Context of Theological Education in British Columbia," *The Jour-
   ney Continues: The Diamond Jubilee Lectures celebrating Sixty Years of Theological Education, 1927–1987*, ed. R. Gerald Hobbs (Vancouver: Vancouver
   School of Theology, 1988), 25–26. The major literature on the history
   of theological education in Canada includes: J.W. Falconer and W.G.
   Watson, *A Brief History of Pine Hill Divinity Hall and the Theological Depart-
   ment of Mount Alison University* (Halifax: Pine Hill Divinity Hall, 1946);
   Dyson Hague, et. al., *The Jubilee Volume of Wycliffe College, 1877–1927*
   (Toronto: Wycliffe College, 1927); *The Enduring Word: A Centennial
   History of Wycliffe College*, ed. Arnold Edinburgh (Toronto: University of
   Toronto Press, 1978); George Rawlyk and Kevin Quinn, *The Redeemed
   of the Lord Say So: A History of Queen's Theological College, 1912–1972*
   (Kingston: Queen's Theological College, 1980); O. W. Howard, *The
   Montreal Diocesan Theological College: A History from 1873 to 1963*
   (Montreal: McGill University Press, 1963); H. Keith Markell, *The Fac-
   ulty of Religious Studies, McGill University, 1948–1978* (Montreal: Faculty
   of Religious Studies, 1979); H. Keith Markell, *History of The Presbyterian
   College, Montreal, 1865–1986* (Montreal: The Presbyterian College,
   1987); D.C. Masters, *Protestant Church Colleges in Canada: A History*
   (Toronto: University of Toronto Press, 1966); Nora L. Hughes, "A His-
   tory of the Development of Ministerial Education in Canada from Its
   Inception until 1925 in those churches which were tributary to the
   United Church of Canada," (Ph.D. thesis, Divinity School, University of
   Chicago, 1945); and Michael Gauvreau, *The Evangelical Century: College*

and Creed in English Canada from the Great Revival to the Great Depression
(Montreal and Kingston: McGill-Queen's University Press, 1991).

20 Robert W. Lynn, "Notes Toward a History: Theological Encyclopedia
and the Evolution of Protestant Seminary Curriculum, 1808–1968,"
Theological Education, 17 (Spring 1981):118–144. See also Glenn Miller
and Robert Lynn, "Christian Theological Education," *Encyclopedia of the
American Religious Experience: Studies of Traditions and Movements, Vol. III,*
ed. C.H. Lippy and P.W. Williams (New York: Charles Scribner's Sons,
1988), 1627–1652; Glenn T. Miller, *Piety and Intellect: The Aims and Purposes of Ante-Bellum Theological Education* (Atlanta: Scholars Press, 1990);
Robert T. Handy, *A History of Union Theological Seminary in New York*
(New York: Columbia University Press, 1987); and George M. Marsden,
Reforming Fundamentalism: Fuller Seminary and the New Evangelicalism
(Grand Rapids: Eerdmans, 1987). For important insights into the comparative history of theological education in Canada and the United
States, see Robert T. Handy, "Trends in Canadian and American Theological Education, 1880–1980: Some Comparisons," *Theological Educa-
tion*, 18 (Spring 1982):175–218. For impressions of theological
education in Scotland, see Stewart Mechie, "Education for the Ministry
in Scotland since the Reformation," *Records of the Scottish Church History
Society*, 14 (1963):115–133, 161–178.

21 Vaudry, *Free Church*, 80–81.

22 *Minutes of the Synod of the Canada Presbyterian Church (Minutes of Synod),*
June 1865, 37.

23 The quotations are taken from Kenneth Burke's definition of piety. See
Kenneth Burke, *Permanence and Change: An Anatomy of Purpose* (Berkeley: University of California Press, 1984), 69–79.

24 William Westfall, *Two Worlds: The Protestant Culture of Nineteenth Century
Ontario* (Montreal & Kingston: McGill-Queen's University Press, 1989),
13–15.

25 Edgar H. Schein, *Organizational Culture and Leadership: A Dynamic View*
(San Francisco: Jossey-Bass, 1991), 9.

26 Quoted in Jackson Carroll and Wade Clark Roof, "Introduction," *Be-
yond Establishment: Protestant Identity in a Post-Protestant Age*, ed. Jackson
Carroll and Wade Clark Roof (Louisville: Westminster/John Knox
Press, 1993), 16.

27 My methodological approach has been influenced by the work of the
"new cultural historians" and their recognition that mental structures
do not depend solely on their material conditions, but in themselves
often constitute an essential element in social reality. Of particular im-

portance in their work is the effort to add historical perspective to cultural anthropological analysis. See Aletta Biersack, "Local Knowledge, Local History: Geertz and Beyond," *The New Cultural History*, ed. Lynn Hunt (Berkeley: University of California Press, 1989), 72–96.

28 Cited in Joseph C. Hough, and John B. Cobb, Jr., *Christian Identity and Theological Education* (Chico: Scholars Press, 1985), 5–18. In Osborn's scheme, the Master image was dominant during the 1600s and 1700s, the Persuader during the 1800s, the Builder in the late 1800s and the early 1900s, and the Manager/Therapist character during the middle and later 1900s. Historian Martin Marty developed another suggestive model. During what he calls "the public phase," from 1607 until 1830, the clergy occupied a public office that commanded the respect of the whole community. By 1830, "the congregational-denominational style" came to dominate, in which specialized seminaries were developed to prepare ministers for the competitive pluralism of the frontier and the city. By 1920, religious institutions were being pushed to the sidelines by a "modern, free, industrial, technological, media-dominated" society and clergy began to serve private clients as specialists in religion. See Martin E. Marty, "The Clergy," *The Professions in American History*, ed. Nathan O. Hatch (Notre Dame: University of Notre Dame Press, 1988), 73–91.

29 Pastoral manuals were first explored in depth in relation to Anglican clergy in England by Brian Heeney, *A Different Kind of Gentleman: Parish Clergy as Professional Men in Early and Mid-Victorian England* (Hamden: Archon Books, 1976).

30 Alan Pollok, *Studies in Practical Theology* (Edinburgh: Wm. Blackwood and Sons, 1907), 2–6. The manuals on ministry cited by Pollok were Richard Baxter, *The Reformed Pastor* (New York: Robert Carter and Bros., 1860); Alexandre Vinet, *Pastoral Theology; or, The Theory of the Evangelical Ministry* (New York: Ivison, Blakeman, Taylor, & Co., 1874); Philip Schaff, *Theological Propaedeutic: A General Introduction to the Study of Theology – Exegetical, Historical, Systematic, and Practical, Including Encyclopedia, Methodology, and Bibliography: A Manual for Students* (New York: Charles Scribner's Sons, 1893); Patrick Fairbairn, *Pastoral Theology: A Treatise on the Offices and Duties of the Christian Pastor* (Edinburgh: T. & T. Clark, 1875); Shedd, W.G.T. Shedd, *Homiletics and Pastoral Theology* (Edinburgh: William Oliphant, 1874); and J.J. Van Oosterzee, *Practical Theology: A Manual for Theological Students* (London: Hodder and Stoughton, 1889). Contemporary studies of the history of the clergy include Anthony Russell, *The Clerical Profession* (London: SPCK, 1980); Donald

M. Scott, *From Office to Profession: The New England Ministry, 1750–1850* (Philadelphia: University of Pennsylvania Press, 1978); Alan Haig, *The Victorian Clergy* (London: Croom Helm, 1984); Brookes Holifield, *The Gentlemen Theologians: American Theology in Southern Culture, 1795–1865* (Durham: University of North Carolina Press, 1978); Brookes Holifield, *A History of Pastoral Care in America: From Salvation to Self-Realization* (Nashville: Abingdon Press, 1983); and Charles E. Hambrick-Stowe, "The Professional Ministry," *Encyclopedia of the American Religious Experience*, ed. Lippy and Williams, 1565–1581.

31 Historians mistrust obituaries to yield accurate data on the lives of the persons remembered. If, however, the information sought has to do with the expectations a particular culture has of people in particular roles, the insights gained from the material in obituaries can be most valuable. We surveyed over 1000 obituaries, taking careful notes on some 300. We recorded the activities in which the person was engaged and the language used to describe those activities. There are some regional and chronological differences, but surprisingly few. In the picture of ordained ministry that emerged from our obituary research, Presbyterians expected their ordained clergy to be, in order of priority: pastors, preachers/teachers, presbyters, and citizens. A detailed computer analysis of the data gathered revealed that the pastoral dimension was noted in over 75% of all obituaries; preaching and teaching in 68%; presbyter in 36%; and citizen in 30%.

32 Canadian religious historians have begun to pay more attention to this dimension of the church's life in recent years. See the survey of work in this area in Marguerite Van Die, "Recovering Religious Experience: Some Reflections on Methodology." *Canadian Society of Church History Papers 1982*, ed. Bruce L. Guenther, 155–169.

33 On the origins and nature of the four-fold program, see Edward Farley, *Theologia: The Fragmentation and Unity of Theological Education* (Philadelphia: Fortress Press, 1983). On the development of the four-fold program in the United States, see Lynn, "Notes Toward a History."

34 For more extensive considerations of these theological paradigms among Canadian Presbyterians, see Brian J. Fraser, "The Public Pieties of Canadian Presbyterians," *Church and Canadian Culture*, ed. R.E. Vander Vennen (New York: University Press of America, 1991), 87–104, and "Theologia in Canada: A Presbyterian Case Study," *Theological Education in Canada: A National Consultation*, ed. Lloyd Gesner (Toronto: The Churches' Council on Theological Education in Canada, 1991), 71–84. I have revised the names of these movements in order to

emphasize the element of continuity in orthodoxy that I have found in the teaching of the professors at Knox, using the adjectives to indicate the changing method of interpretation applied to the orthodox truths. John Webster Grant has characterized the shifts described here as the assertion, reinterpretation, and reformulation of the denominational traditions. Grant's fourth phase, that of questioning the inherited traditions, happened among Canadian Presbyterians in the 1970s, just as a new generation of faculty was being appointed to Knox College. See J.W. Grant, "Religious and Theological Writings to 1960," *Literary History of Canada, Vol. II*, ed. Carl F. Klink (Toronto: University of Toronto Press, 1976), 93.

35 Cited in Handy, "Trends in Theological Education," 197–198.

36 The Association of Theological Schools in the United States and Canada has recently launched a study of effectiveness in theological education that identified four categories for analysis: a) curriculum, and student formation; b) governance and administration; c) teaching, research, and scholarship; and d) institutional resources. See "The Conversation Begins on 'The Good Theological School'," *ATS Colloquy*, 2 (November/December 1993) 2:1, and the series of background papers in *Theological Education*, 30 (Spring 1994) 2.

CHAPTER ONE

1 The lengthy account of Anderson's crisis of faith and call to ministry is found in *Reminiscences and Incidents connected with the Life and Pastoral Labors of the Reverend John Anderson*, ed. J.D. Anderson (Toronto: William Briggs, 1910), 76–146.

2 Anderson, *Reminiscences*, 152.

3 *EMR*, December 1848.

4 Neatby, *Queen's*, 25.

5 Neatby, *Queen's*, 30.

6 Moir, *Enduring Witness*, 106.

7 H. Keith Markell, *History of the Presbyterian College, Montreal, 1865–1986* (Montreal: The Presbyterian College, 1987), 7–11.

8 *EMR*, January 1845.

9 *EMR*, January 1845.

10 The list of the first students is found in "Reminiscences of the Origin of Two Presbyterian Colleges in Canada," *HFR*, 6 (1866) 1:28. The biographical information is from T.G.M. Bryan, "Biographical Dictionary of Graduates and Students of Knox College, Toronto, 1845–1945,"

(typescript in the Archives of The Presbyterian Church in Canada 1982).

11 *EMR*, October 1845.

12 Vaudry, *Free Church*, 82–83, and Richard W. Vaudry, "Theology and eduction in early Victorian Canada: Knox College, Toronto, 1844–61," *Studies in Religion/Sciences Religieuse*, 16 (Fall 1987) 4:434–435.

13 J.D. Wilson, *et al.*, *Canadian Education: A History* (Toronto: Prentice-Hall of Canada, 1970), 214–226.

14 Wilson, *Canadian Education*, 226–231.

15 The dominance of this perspective in American educational institutions is examined in D.H. Meyer, *The Instructed Conscience: The Shaping of the American National Ethic* (Philadelphia: University of Pennsylvania Press, 1972).

16 Michael Gauvreau, "Protestantism Transformed: Personal Piety and the Evangelical Social Vision, 1815–1867," *The Canadian Protestant Experience, 1760–1990*, ed. George Rawlyk (Montreal and Kingston: McGill-Queen's University Press, 1990), 90–91.

17 *EMR*, October 1845.

18 *EMR*, July 1848.

19 Vaudry, *Free Church*, 81–82. For details on the considerations that went into the formation of the academy, see the reports of the college committee in *EMR*, August 1846, October 1846, December 1846, and July 1847. On Alexander Gale, see *Dictionary of Canadian Biography, Vol. VIII, 1851–1860 (DCB VIII)* (Toronto: University of Toronto Press, 1985), 310–311.

20 On the founding of New College, Edinburgh, see Brown, *Thomas Chalmers*, 342–344.

21 *EMR*, November 1844.

22 *EMR*, October 1845.

23 *EMR*, October 1845.

24 William Klempa, "History of Presbyterian Theology in Canada to 1875," *The Burning Bush and a Few Acres of Snow: The Presbyterian Contribution to Canadian Life and Culture*, ed. William Klempa (Ottawa: Carlton University Press, 1994), 207.

25 *DCB VIII*, 272–273.

26 *EMR*, January 1845.

27 *EMR*, October 1845.

28 *Canadian Dictionary of Biography, Vol. IX, 1861–1870 (DCB IX)* (Toronto: University of Toronto Press, 1976), 104–108. See also, Paul Harrison, "Robert Burns: Founder of the Free Kirk in Upper Canada," *Called to*

Witness: Profiles of Canadian Presbyterians, Vol. I, ed. W.S. Reid
(Toronto: Committee on History, The Presbyterian Church in Canada,
1975), 144–161. For Burns' own account of his connection with the
Christian Instructor, see Burns, *Life and Times,* 108–121.

29 *EMR,* October 1845.

30 This seems to have been a matter of some discussion and eventual
agreement within the college committee. See the college committee
report to the synod in June 1847 in *EMR,* July 1847.

31 *DCB IX,* 107.

32 *EMR,* January 1848.

33 *EMR,* December 1848.

34 *EMR,* May 1848.

35 *EMR,* November 1848. See also, *Dictionary of Canadian Biography, Vol.
XI, 1881–1890 (DCB XI)* (Toronto: University of Toronto Press, 1982),
534. On Lyall's philosophical thought and its evangelical tone, see his
Intellect, The Emotions, and The Moral Nature (Edinburgh: Thomas Constable, 1855) and analyses of it in A.B. McKillop, *A Disciplined Intelligence: Critical Inquiry and Canadian Thought in the Victorian Era*
(Montreal: McGill-Queen's University Press, 1979), 44–52; Leslie Armour and Elizabeth Trott, *The Faces of Reason: An Essay on Philosophy and
Culture in English Canada, 1850–1950* (Waterloo: Wilfrid Laurier University Press, 1980), 61–84; and Gauvreau, *Evangelical Century,* 34–36.

36 John Webster Grant has written of this attitude: "The light accessible to
any rational being had to be supplemented by supernatural revelation,
of course, and great emphasis was placed on the miracles and prophe-
cies of Scripture both as proofs of its reliability and as pointers to its superiority over merely human speculation. It was generally agreed,
however, that science properly understood could never be at variance
with God's direct utterances in Scripture. ... There was general agreement, too, both that Christian faith was credible only when expressed
in moral living and that moral living was possible only through the
sanctions provided by the Christian faith." See *A Profusion of Spires: Religion in Nineteenth-Century Ontario* (Toronto: University of Toronto Press,
1988), 65–66.

37 For a concise description of colonial Calvinism, see Bruce Kuklick,
Churchmen and Philosophers: From Jonathan Edwards to John Dewey (New
Haven: Yale University Press, 1985), 5–8.

38 Quoted in Vaudry, *Free Church,* 49.

39 For a description of the changes taking place in Scottish thought and
their impact on Canada, see Gauvreau, *Evangelical Century,* 16–18,

27–31. His analysis was influenced by Richard B. Sher, *Church and University in the Scottish Enlightenment: The Moderate Literati of Edinburgh* (Edinburgh: Edinburgh University Press, 1985), J. David Hoeveler, *James McCosh and the Scottish Intellectual Tradition* (Princeton: Princeton University Press, 1981), and Mark Noll, "Common Sense Traditions and American Evangelical Thought," *American Quarterly,* 37 (Summer 1987) 2:216–238.

40 *EMR,* October 1845.

41 *EMR,* November 1845.

42 *EMR,* December 1845.

43 *EMR,* January 1846.

44 *EMR,* January 1846.

45 Henry Esson, *Critique on Dr. Burns' Letter on Knox's College* (Toronto: n.p., 1848), 3.

46 Part of the controversy centred on Esson's opposition to pluralities or dual offices. Evangelicals in Scotland, including Burns in a famous case in 1824, had long opposed joint appointments to a pulpit and a teaching post because they thought both offices required the full attention of the incumbent. William Rintoul, in his annual letter soliciting financial support for the college in 1847, made the point clearly. Much of the success of a theological professor, he wrote, "depends on his personal intercouse with the students, and the oversight which he takes of them. He must not be the mere lecturer, addressing them from the chair only; he is to be the guide of their studies during the whole time they are studying theology, – directing their reading, hearing and criticizing their discourses, and, by personal conferences, cherishing in them a spirit of devotedness to the service of the Saviour. In reference to these important parts of professorial duty, the temporary professor, however highly gifted, must be inferior in usefulness to the permanent one; just as the casual occupant of a pulpit, however able a preacher, is in ordinary circumstances less useful than he who, besides preaching, is going our and in amongst the flock, in private pastoral services." See *EMR,* November 1847. In accepting the dual position, Burns had argued that special circumstances in the colonial church made such an arrangement acceptable. On appointing Burns, however, the Synod made it clear that the plurality was tenable only until they were able to find the resources to add full-time faculty.

47 *EMR,* October 1848.

48 Henry Esson, *Statement Relative to the Educational System of Knox's College, Toronto; with Suggestions for its Extension and Improvement* (Toronto: J. Cleland, 1848), 32, 50, 53.

49 Esson, *Statement*, 6.

50 Esson, *Statement*, 50.

51 *Minutes of Synod*, June 1848, 31. For an account of the university question as it developed from 1840–1849, see J.S. Moir, *Church and State in Canada West: Three Studies in the Relation of Denominationalism and Nationalism, 1841–1867* (Toronto: University of Toronto Press, 1959), 82–105.

52 Moir, *Church and State*, 101–104.

53 On the early years of University College, see *University College: A Portrait, 1853–1953*, ed. Claude T. Bissell (Toronto: University of Toronto Press, 1953). The college had few enrolments and moved often during its first decade. W.S. Wallace, in his essay in Bissell's volume, noted "that Knox College, and later Wycliffe College, kept University College alive."

54 *EMR*, September 1849.

55 *Minutes of Synod*, June 1849, 8–9.

56 *EMR*, January 1845.

57 *EMR*, November 1844.

58 On Buchanan's extensive work with the Free Church and the broader evangelical cause, see Harry J. Bridgman, "Isaac Buchanan and Religion, 1810–1883," (M.A. thesis, Queen's University, 1969).

59 *EMR*, March 1846. According to reports in *EMR*, November 1846, the association had paid £105 to the college fund and an additional £24 to the bursary fund. Most of the money came from the sale of handiwork by women, not only in Toronto, but also in Edinburgh and Glasgow. These articles were sent to the association at Knox and sold in Toronto.

60 *EMR*, September 1848.

61 *EMR*, March 1848.

62 *EMR*, December 1853.

63 *EMR*, March 1848.

64 *EMR*, September 1849.

65 *Minutes of Synod*, June 1848, 30–31.

66 The figures are drawn from both the college reports to the Synod and articles in the *Record*. Exact figures are difficult to ascertain because some students dropped out during the term or were part-time in their studies.

67 *EMR*, December 1855.

68 *EMR*, June 1847.

69 *EMR*, September 1849.

70 *EMR*, December 1855.

71 *EMR*, December 1847.

72 *EMR*, December 1847.

73 *EMR*, December 1847. For popular accounts of Black's career, see George Bryce, *John Black, the Apostle of the Red River* (Toronto: Westminster, 1898), and Olive Knox, *John Black of Old Kildonan* (Toronto: Ryerson, 1958).

74 *EMR*, May 1849.

75 *EMR*, December 1853. A similar report for the summer of 1858 is found in *EMR*, December 1858.

76 *EMR*, June 1848.

77 *EMR*, March 1849.

78 *EMR*, September 1849.

CHAPTER TWO

1 *EMR*, May 1854.

2 On Duff's approach to the spread of the Gospel and his close connection with Thomas Chalmers, see S. Piggin and J. Roxborough, *The St. Andrews Seven: The Finest Flowering of Missionary Zeal in Scottish History* (Edinburgh: Banner of Truth Trust, 1985), esp. 108–109 and 118–119. On Chalmers' theology of mission, see H.R. Sefton, "Chalmers and the Church: Theology and Mission," and J. Roxborough, "Chalmers' Theology of Mission," *The Practical and the Pious: Essays on Thomas Chalmers (1780–1847)*, ed. A.C. Cheyne (Edinburgh: The Saint Andrew Press, 1985), 166–185.

3 On the growth of sentiment in favour of Presbyterian union and the role of the laity in its support, see John A. Johnston, " 'No Slippery Undertaking' – The Presbyterian Union of 1875," *Papers of the Canadian Society of Presbyterian History 1975*, 61–65.

4 This process among American Presbyterians has been examined in Lefferts A. Loetscher, *The Broadening Church: A Study of Theological Issues in the Presbyterian Church since 1869* (Philadelphia: Westminster Press, 1954).

5 For the text of the statement of points of agreement and disagreement between the Free Church and the United Presbyterians, see William Gregg, *Short History of The Presbyterian Church in the Dominion of Canada, from the earliest to the present time* (Toronto: C. Blackett Robinson, 1892), 151–154.

6 On the voluntary controversy in Scotland and the view that the voluntaries – "Papists, Deists, Unitarians, Independents, Anabaptists,

Quakers, Jumpers, Ranters, etc. in religion; in politics, nondescripts, Radicals, republicans, democrats, and destructives" – were a threat to social and political order and stability, see Donald C. Smith, *Passive Obedience and Prophetic Protest: Social Criticism in the Scottish Church 1830–1945* (New York: Peter Lang, 1987), 62–72, and Brown, *Thomas Chalmers*, 220–22. For a more detailed account of the controversy, see Alfred B. Montgomery, "The Voluntary Controversy in the Church of Scotland: 1829–1843; with particular reference to its practical and theological roots" (Ph.D. thesis, University of Edinburgh, 1953).

7 For an overview of the voluntarist debate, the role of the Free Church in it, and its significance for Canadian political and religious life, see Grant, *Profusion of Spires*, 85–100 and 136–151.

8 Michael Willis, *A Discourse on National Establishments of Christianity* (Glasgow: Maurice Ogle, 1833), and *Lectures on the Church Establishment Controversy* (Glasgow: William Collins, 1835).

9 David R. Nicholson, "Michael Willis: Missionary Statesman, Social Activist, Christian Educator, and Reformed Theologian" (Th.M. thesis, Toronto School of Theology, 1973), 118–124.

10 *EMR*, December 1848.

11 The quotes from Burns' debates with Barrie are found in Vaudry, *Free Church*, 115.

12 Ferrier claimed to have been received by the Presbytery of Hamilton in 1845 as an open and avowed voluntary. For the details of the Ferrier case, see Vaudry, *Free Church*, 116–119.

13 *Minutes of Synod*, June 1854, 13.

14 *Minutes of Synod*, June 1854, 12.

15 Quoted in Vaudry, *Free Church*, 119–120.

16 Moir, *Enduring Witness*, 108–109, and Vaudry, *Free Church*, 118.

17 *EMR*, April 1849.

18 These quotes are taken from a statement published by Esson, Rintoul, Gale, James Harris, and Thomas Wightman on the occasion of the publication of the proposed University Act in 1847 that would have partitioned the endowment of King's College, Toronto, among the several denominational colleges. See *EMR*, July 1847 and June 1849.

19 The details of the union negotiations are described in Vaudry, *Free Church*, 119–126.

20 The dissent was signed by John Bayne, Constable Geike, Duncan McRuar, Robert Irvine, Daniel Gordon, Andrew Wilson, James Middlemiss, and Morris Lutz, as well as Willis. Only McRuar and Wilson were Knox graduates. See *EMR*, August 1859.

21 *EMR,* August 1859.

22 Thomas Wardlaw Taylor, *The Public Statutes Relating to The Presbyterian Church in Canada* (Winnipeg: Hart and Company, 1897), 286–287.

23 For a brief overview of these developments, see Wilson, *Canadian Education,* 228–231. See also Vaudry, *Free Church,* 68–70, and Neatby, *Queen's,* 104–106 and 113–115.

24 *EMR,* March 1860.

25 For a full account of this incident, see Nicholson, "Michael Willis," 103–118. Willis used his address at the closing of the college session in 1860 to press his case on the scriptural warrant for a pure establishment. See *EMR,* May 1860.

26 George Smellie, *Memoir of the Rev. John Bayne, D.D., of Galt; with Dr. Bayne's Essay on Man's Responsibility for His Belief* (Toronto: James Campbell, 1871), 29.

27 On Young, see *DCB, Vol. XI,* 942–943, McKillop, *Disciplined Intelligence,* 172–176, Armour and Trott, *Faces of Reason,* 85–104, and Gauvreau, *Evangelical Century,* 107–108. Many of the details in the brief sketch offered here were contained in research notes kindly shared with the author by Professor Jack Stevenson of University College, University of Toronto.

28 *EMR,* June 1855.

29 *EMR,* November 1854.

30 George Paxton Young, *Miscellaneous Discourses and Expositions of Scripture* (Edinburgh: Johnstone and Hunter, 1854), 25–46. The principles of the Alliance were: 1) the divine inspiration, authority, and sufficiency of Scripture; 2) the doctrine of the Trinity; 3) the utter depravity of human nature as a result of the fall; 4) the incarnation of the Son of God and his work of atonement for the sins of humankind; 5) justification by faith alone; 6) the conversion and sanctification of the sinner by the work of the Holy Spirit; 7) the right and duty of private judgment in the interpretation of Scripture; and 8) the divine institution of the Christian ministry, and the authority and perpetuity of the ordinances of Baptism and the Lord's Supper. See *EMR,* December 1845. The Evangelical Alliance in Canada was formed in 1846 by Anglican evangelicals and Free Church Presbyterians. The immediate occasion was a British government grant to a Roman Catholic college in Maynooth, Ireland, but the broader purpose was to combat "the cunning of Jesuits, the ravages of Antichrist, and the alarming defection of Tractarians." See Grant, *Profusion of Spires,* 129–130. As Grant noted, pleas for unity and recriminations against other Protestants were often found

side by side in the denominational journals of the day. For a history of
the Alliance in the United States, see Philip D. Jordon, *The Evangelical
Alliance for the United States of America, 1847–1900: Ecumenism, Identity
and the Religion of the Republic* (New York: Edwin Mellen Press, 1982).

31 *EMR*, July 1856.

32 *EMR*, January 1849.

33 *EMR*, May 1859.

34 Gregg, *Short History*, 70–71 and 146–148, and William Caven, "Historical Sketch of Knox College, Toronto," *Canada: An Encyclopaedia of the
Country, Vol. IV*, ed. J. Castell Hopkins (Toronto: Linscott Publishing,
1898), 217. On Proudfoot, see Stewart D. Gill, *The Reverend William
Proudfoot and the United Secession Mission in Canada* (Queenston: Edwin
Mellen Press, 1991) and James A. Thomson, "Proudfoot and the
United Presbyterians: Research into the Proudfoot Papers" (M.Th. the-
sis, Knox College, 1967). There are no studies of Taylor's life and
thought. His work in Canada can be traced through the pages of the
Canadian Presbyterian Magazine (CPM) from 1852 to 1861. For his inau-
gural lecture as professor of divinity, see *CPM*, September 1852 and
October 1852.

35 Bissell, *University College*, 6.

36 *EMR*, August 1855.

37 *EMR*, September 1858.

38 On the influence of Butler on Reid and Wayland, see Meyer, *Instructed
Conscience*, 35–50.

39 *Minutes of Synod*, June 1860, 52.

40 *Minutes of Synod*, June 1869, 43 and 63.

41 On Young's work as grammar school inspector, see Wilson, *Canadian
Education*, 225–226, and Susan E. Houston and Alison Prentice, *School-
ing and Scholars in Nineteenth-Century Ontario* (Toronto: Ontario Historical Studies Series, 1988), 321–333.

42 *Minutes of Synod*, June 1864, 40 and xxxix.

43 *Minutes of Synod*, June 1864, 43.

44 John T. McNeill, *The Presbyterian Church in Canada 1875–1925* (Toronto: Presbyterian Church in Canada, 1925), 33–34.

45 McNeill, *Presbyterian Church*, 37.

46 *Minutes of Synod*, June 1866. On Caven, see *DCB, Vol. XIII*, 111–112,
and Brian J. Fraser, "William Caven: Educator of The Conscience,"
Touchstone 12 (May 1994) 2:37–44.

47 *Minutes of Synod*, June 1864, 41 and 46.

48 *Minutes of Synod*, June 1868, lv.

49 *Minutes of Synod,* June 1858, lvi-lvii, and *Minutes of the Canada Presbyterian Church General Assembly (Minutes of General Assembly),* June 1870, 47.

50 On the development of Young's thought, see McKillop, *Disciplined Intelligence,* 175–176, and Armour and Trott, *Faces of Reason,* 85–104.

51 These details of Young's career were recorded in the notes provided by Professor Jack Stevenson of University College.

52 Willis, *Discourse on National Establishments,* 121.

53 Vaudry, *Free Church,* 55–56 and Richard W. Vaudry, "Canadian Presbyterians and Princeton Seminary, 1850–1900," in *Burning Bush,* ed. Klempa, 219–237.

54 Vaudry, *Free Church,* 78–79.

55 *Minutes of Synod,* June 1867, 43–44 and lviii-lx.

56 Cited in Nicholson, "Michael Willis," 147.

57 Nicholson, "Michael Willis," 147–158.

58 The means by which the property was to be held was a contentious issue throughout the process of drafting and approving the act of incorporation. Prominent laymen were reluctant to allow the clergy or clergy-dominated church courts to have control of the material assets of the church. The tensions had their roots in the controversy over the Temporalities Bill in 1843. See Ian Rennie, "The Free Church and the Relations of Church and State" (M.A. thesis, University of Toronto, 1954), 52–56, and Moir, *Enduring Witness,* 103–107.

59 In June 1859, the Synod agreed to the following resolution concerning doctrine and how it was to be determined: "That the principles and doctrines to be taught in the said college by the professors and tutors, or other persons who shall from time to time, and at all times hereafter, be employed or appointed in giving instruction in the said college, shall be such and such only as are consistent with and agreeable to the 'Confession of Faith,' the 'Larger and Shorter Catechisms,' and the 'Form of Church Government,' all of which are called 'The Westminster Standards,' and shall comprise all theological learning consistent with the said standards: Provided always that the said 'Confession of Faith' be understood and taken with the explanatory note thereto, agreed upon by the Synod of the Presbyterian Church of Canada, met at Toronto in the year of our Lord, 1854: Provided also that the said 'Westminster Standards' be taken and understood with such other, or further directions and rules as to church government, discipline, or worship, as may from time to time be prescribed or ordained by the Synod of the Presbyterian Church of Canada, with the concurrence of a majority of the Presbyteries of the said Church, to be ascertained in

such manner as the Synod shall prescribe, and that such regulations and rules be duly recorded in the minute book of the said Synod, and signed by the Moderator and the Clerk for the time being of such Synod." See *EMR*, July 1859.

60 *EMR*, October 1858.

61 *Minutes of Synod*, June 1860, 26–28.

62 McMurrich was born in Paisley, Scotland in 1804, and came to Kingston as the representative of the Glasgow firm of Playfair, Bryce and Company in 1834. He moved to Toronto in 1837 and established Bryce, McMurrich and Company, with John Bryce managing the British side of the business and McMurrich the Canadian side. They specialized in staple British textiles, for which there was a steady market in the growing province. He was an ally of George Brown in reform politics, on the founding executive of the Anti-Clergy Reserves Association in 1850, and appointed to the first Toronto Public School Board in 1847. He was a charter member of the Toronto Board of Trade and president or director of several smaller financial, insurance, and railway companies established to serve the growing needs of the city and its hinterland. He served in the provincial legislatures from 1862–1864 and 1867–1871. His public service extended to moral reform and social service as well. He was an active member of the Toronto City Mission Society, the Upper Canada Religious Tract and Book Society, and the Sabbath Observance Association. He was an elder at Knox Church for 32 years. *See DCB, Vol. XI*, 581–582.

63 *Minutes of Synod*, June 1855.

64 *EMR*, August 1854.

65 *EMR*, July 1856.

66 *EMR*, September 1858, *Minutes of Synod*, June 1861, 22, and *Minutes of Synod*, June 1862, 45–46 and xxxvii.

67 *EMR*, July 1857.

68 The annual reports of the society were printed in December of each year in *EMR* until the creation of the Canada Presbyterian Church. See also Peter Bush, "The Knox College Student Missionary Society: A History," (paper delivered at the Canadian Society of Presbyterian History, 1987).

69 On the religious side of George Brown and his work for the Free Church reform causes of abolition, temperance, and sabbath observance, see John S. Moir, "George Brown: Christian Statesman," *Called to Witness: Profiles of Canadian Presbyterians, Vol. 2*, ed. W.S. Reid (Toronto: Committee on History, The Presbyterian Church in Canada, 1980),

39–46. Anti-Catholicism and temperance came together in the character of former priest and temperance activist Charles Chiniquy. See Paul
Laverdure, "Charles Chiniquy: A Wandering Life," *Called to Witness: Profiles of Canadian Presbyterians, Vol. 3*, ed. J.S. Moir (Toronto: Committee
on History, The Presbyterian Church in Canada, 1991), 32–42.

70 Reports from the society were published in the *Record* each year in
December or January.

71 For the details of these debates, see *Minutes of Synod* for 1864–1867.
See also H. Keith Markell, *History of The Presbyterian College, Montreal
1865–1986* (Montreal: The Presbyterian College, 1987), 7–11.

72 *Minutes of Synod*, June 1863, 37.

73 *Minutes of Synod*, June 1865, xxxix-xl.

74 *Minutes of Synod*, June 1866, 30, and June 1867, 22.

75 *Minutes of Synod*, June 1869, 62, and *Minutes of General Assembly*, June
1870, 48.

CHAPTER THREE

1 Clifford, *Resistance*, 33.

2 Johnston, "No Slippery Undertaking." The new church, uniting two
branches of Presbyterianism in central Canada and two in the Mari-
times, boasted 600,000 members and 600 ministers, over half of whom
came from the Canada Presbyterian Church.

3 Moir, *Enduring Witness*, 134–142.

4 For a detailed account and theological analysis of the heresy trial, see
McLelland, "Macdonnell," 273–284.

5 The Canadian proceedings came in the wake of a sensational heresy
trial among Presbyterians in Chicago sparked by charges from a former
Knox student, Francis L. Patton. Patton, who had completed his theological education at Princeton, was minister at Jefferson Park Presbyterian Church and brought heresy charges against David Swing in 1874.
Swing was acquitted by a vote of 48 to 13 in the Presbytery of Chicago,
but left the denomination. William R. Hutchison called the Swing trial
"the first great controversy of the New Theology" in the United States,
through which the ideas of respect for contemporary culture and
God's immanent nature began to coalesce into a program.For a full account, see William R. Hutchison, *The Modernist Impulse in American
Protestantism* (Cambridge: Harvard University Press, 1976), 48–75.

6 Quoted in McLelland, "Macdonnell," 282.

7 An interesting footnote to the proceedings was the move of George
Paxton Young to Macdonnell's church in 1877. Young left Knox College to accept the chair of logic, metaphysics, and ethics at University
College in 1871, but he continued to sit on the board of Knox until
1875 and remained as a minister on the roll of the Presbytery of Toronto until 1877. Throughout his career at University College, his
classes were filled with men preparing for study at Knox College. It is
significant that the tutors engaged to continue the preparatory department at Knox College never taught philosophy, suggesting that
Young's classes were seen to provide the appropriate grounding in
mental and moral philosophy for Presbyterian ministers in Canada.
Even so resolute a warrior for the conservative cause as Francis L. Patton, who had moved from Chicago to succeed A.A. Hodge at Princeton in 1881, remembered Young as "the greatest dialectician of this or
of any age." This comment, made at the college closing in 1885, met
with "an instant and almost dynamic outburst of cheering from the
whole body of students, who venerate deeply that veteran thinker
from whom so many of them had received an intellectual inspiration
that will never cease to operate during their lifetime." See *KCM*, 3
(April 1885) 6:178. Another former student recalled the impact that
Young's classes made in the midst of the intellectual turmoil of the late
nineteenth century. "We had the feeling," wrote H.J. Cody, "that here
was a man at the very antithesis to the materialist, that here was a man
who believed in the dominance of the intellectual and the spiritual.
We always had the impression that he was *the* typical seeker after truth:
he was a man of intense convictions because he had worked his way
through to his system of philosophy himself," (quoted in John A. Irv-
ing, "The Development of Philosophy in Central Canada from 1850 to
1900," *Canadian Historical Review,* 31 (September 1950) 3:264). Such
reminiscences suggested that it was Young's dedication to intellectual
rigour and spiritual values that stayed with his students. Among many,
however, especially later in his career, Young did sow the seeds of a less
confessional and more progressive apologetic for the Christian faith
by his critique of Scottish Common Sense philosophy and his exposition of the alternative philosophical framework he had found in
T.H. Green and British Idealism.

8 The issue of creedal revision was actively discussed in North America
and Great Britain throughout the 1880s and 1890s. On the American
debates and the decision by the northern church to employ three

methods of revision – declaratory statements, textual modifications, and supplementary statements – in 1902, see Loetscher, *The Broadening Church*, 39–47 and 83–89. On the Scottish debates and the changes to the formula for subscription to the Westminster Confession that the various Presbyterian churches there adopted between 1879 and 1910, see A.C. Cheyne, *The Transforming of the Kirk: Victorian Scotland's Religious Revolution* (Edinburgh: St. Andrew Press, 1983), 60–87. On the discussion in Canada concerning the doctrinal section of the Basis of Union of the United Church of Canada, see Clifford, *Resistance*, 39–40, 46.

9 McNeill, *Presbyterian Church*, 59.

10 *Presbyterian Record (PR)*, July 1885.

11 *Minutes of General Assembly*, June 1873, 30–33.

12 *Minutes of General Assembly*, June 1872, 52.

13 *KCM*, 1 (April 1883) 3:87–89.

14 On the development and characteristics of the New Theology, see Hutchison, *Modernist Impulse*, 78–110, and Bruce Kuklick, *Churchmen and Philosophers* (New Haven: Yale University Press, 1985), 216–229. Kuklick's use of the term "progressive orthodoxy" to describe the New Theology differs substantially from the way in which I have used the term in this book. Kuklick emphasizes the progressive dimension, while I am seeking to emphasize the continuity of the orthodox doctrines through different frameworks of interpretation in the teaching of the faculty at Knox College. As the story of transition unfolds, they will speak for themselves in defining what they mean by progress in theology.

15 For MacLaren's views on these matters, see William MacLaren, *The Glorious Gospel: A Sermon* (Toronto: Presbyterian Printing and Publishing Co., 1886); *The Inspiration of Scripture: A Lecture* (Toronto: The Canada Presbyterian, 1878); and "Conditional Immortality," *Future Punishment; or Does Death End Probation*, ed. William Cochrane (Brantford: Bradley, Garretson and Co., 1886), 141–169.

16 William MacLaren, "The New Theology and its Sources," *Canada Presbyterian (CP)*, 6 October, 1886.

17 William MacLaren, "The New Theology and its Sources," *CP*, 13 October, 1886.

18 William MacLaren, "Dr. A.A. Hodge," *KCM*, 5 (December 1886) 2: 78–79.

19 William MacLaren, "Calvinism in its Relations to Other Theistic Systems," *KCM*, 2 (November 1883) 1:20.

20 William Gregg, "Dr. Thomas Chalmers," *KCM*, 17 (November 1892) 1:347–366.

21 William Gregg, *History of the Presbyterian Church in the Dominion of Canada, from the earliest times to 1834* (Toronto: Presbyterian Printing and Publishing Co., 1885), 19–26.

22 William Caven, "The Need for an Educated Ministry," *HFR*, November 1866.

23 William Caven, *Christ's Teaching Concerning the Last Things and Other Papers* (Toronto: The Westminster Co., 1905), 123.

24 Caven, *Christ's Teaching*, 101–111. On the role of Scripture in preaching, see William Caven, "Scriptural Preaching," *KCM*, 7 (November 1887) 1:3–19.

25 William Caven, "Standards of Our Church," *Canada Presbyterian Church Pulpit, Second Series*, 85–120.

26 For Caven, the burden of proof remained clearly on those wishing to change the confessional orthodoxy of the church. An article on progress in theology in 1883 in the pages of the *Catholic Presbyterian*, the journal of the Alliance of Reformed Churches, sparked an exchange of views on the subject by leading Presbyterian theologians, including A.A. Hodge, Robert Watts, Newman Smyth, and A.B. Bruce. Caven stated that the clarity with which the scriptures displayed the great evangelical truths left nothing to be discovered. The basic economy of salvation was revealed in the bible in a way the true church could never misconceive, though it might find ways to expound that economy with greater clarity. Caven wrote two articles on the subject of progress in theology, one in 1879 and the other in 1882. The series of responses that followed were published in 1883. See William Caven, "Progress in Theology – Butler or Macauley?," *Catholic Presbyterian* (June 1879) 6:401–411; William Caven, "Progress in Theology," *Catholic Presbyterian* (October 1882) 46:273–282; John Tulloch, "Progress in Theology," *Catholic Presbyterian* (January 1883) 49:37–44; A.A. Hodge, "Progress in Theology," *Catholic Presbyterian* (February 1883) 50:121–134; Newman Smyth, "Progress in Theology," *Catholic Presbyterian* (March 188) 51:195–204; Robert Watts, "Progress in Theology," *Catholic Presbyterian* (April 1883) 52:283–295; A.B. Bruce, "Progress in Theology," *Catholic Presbyterian* (May 1883) 53: 364–376; and John Cairns, "Progress in Theology," *Catholic Presbyterian* (June 1883) 54:401–413. See also William Caven, "Clerical Conservatism and Scientific Radicalism," *KCM*, 14 (October 1891) 6:285–295.

27 William Caven, "Standards," 85–120.

28 J.J.A. Proudfoot, *Systematic Homiletics* (Toronto: Westminster, 1903), 33.

29 On Blair and Campbell, see A.L. Drummond and J. Bulloch, *The Scottish Church 1688–1843* (Edinburgh: St. Andrew Press, 1973), 98–103.

30 Cheyne, *Transforming*, 218, concludes that this *via media* was the path trodden by most of Scotland's theological teachers and characterized it as either a "fairly cautious liberalism – or open-minded conservatism."

31 *KCM*, 1 (February 1883) 1:17.

32 Quoted in D. Barry Mack, "Ralph Connor and the Progressive Vision" (M.A. thesis, Carleton University, 1986), 43.

33 *Acts & Proceedings of the the General Assembly of The Presbyteriaan Church in Canada (A&P)*, June 1879, Appendix, ccxxxiv-ccxxxv.

34 *A&P,* June 1881, lxxxv and xc.

35 Shedd, *Homiletics and Pastoral Theology*, i.

36 Van Oosterzee, *Practical Theology*, 38–39.

37 *KCM*, 1 (February 1883) 1:1–2.

38 *KCM*, 5 (April 1887) 6:372.

39 *KCM*, 3 (April 1885) 6:179.

40 For a broader discussion of the role of the press in breaking down religious consensus in the nineteenth century, see Owen Chadwick, *The Secularization of the European Mind in the Nineteenth Century* (Cambridge: Cambridge University Press, 1975), 34–35 and 38–45. The Alliance of Reformed Churches established a committee to explore the advisability of defining a consensus of Reformed confessions in 1880. J.J. Van Oosterzee, chair of the committee, reported their failure in 1884. "If the formula is wide, there is a risk of its being vague and perhaps insignificant; if it lays stress on certain doctrines, even those which are common to all our ancient Confessions, we run the risk, in satisfying conservative minds, of cooling those in the Church who are not less evangelical, but of more liberal tendencies. … In short, since there exist among Christians different theological conceptions, even on important points, as for example, Christology, we shall never be able to avoid collision with one or other of two dangers – either that of disguising the differences under vague language, or of stating them sharply, which leads to separation." See "Report of Committee on the Consensus of the Reformed Confessions," *Alliance Proceedings 1884*, Appendix, 5–6.

41 Cheyne, *Transforming*, 174. On the development of Gordon's thought and the influence of the Scottish progressives on it, especially Henry Drummond, see Mack, "Ralph Connor," 22–80.

42 *KCM*, 4 (November 1885) 1:39.

43 *KCM*, 4 (February 1886) 4:182–183.

44 *KCM*, 6 (January 1886) 3:134–135.

45 The networks of personal relationships that developed in the new denomination during this period were intricate and crucial to under-
standing the spread of new perspectives. During his visit to Scotland,
for example, Macdonald roomed with Alfred Gandier, a protege of
George Grant of Queen's and later to be principal at Knox College.
Gandier had worked as a student minister with Macdonnell and shared
Grant's more progressive approach to biblical and theological interpre-
tation, one similar to that Macdonald had begun to champion in old
Free Church circles. On the Macdonald-Gandier connection, see John
Dow, *Alfred Gandier: Man of Vision and Achievement* (Toronto: United
Church Publishing House, 1951), 12–18. On Grant, see D. Barry
Mack, "George Munro Grant, Evangelical Prophet" (Ph.D. thesis,
Queen's University, 1992).

46 *KCM*, 10 (May 1889) 1:63–64.

47 *KCM*, 11 (November 1890) 1:59.

48 For a contemporary account of this movement in Scottish theology by a
Canadian Presbyterian teaching at Queen's, see William Morgan, "Back
to Christ," *A Dictionary of Christ and the Gospels*, ed. James Hastings (Edinburgh: T. & T. Clark, 1908), 161–167.

49 *KCM*, 12 (May 1890) 1:54.

50 Macdonald's views did not go unchallenged in the pages of the *Monthly*,
and it is clear that other periodicals serving the Canadian Presbyterian
constituency, such as the *Presbyterian Record* and the *Canada Presbyterian*,
were opposed to the views of progressive orthodoxy. At the meeting of
the Alumni Association in 1890, some members criticized Macdonald
for printing Marcus Dods' inaugural address and another attack on
confessional orthodoxy, John Campbell's "Scholasticism in Modern
Theology." In the end, however, the association endorsed Macdonald's
policies of encouraging "the fullest expression of opinion" within the
church and providing space for "fair discussion of important theological questions by accredited teachers in the Presbyterian Church." See
KCM, 11 (April 1890) 6:333.

51 J.C. Smith, "Two Courses," *KCM*, 5 (1886) 1:26.

52 Robert Haddow, "Lectures in Knox College," *KCM*, 9 (March 1889)
5:279–280.

53 *KCM*, 9 (March 1889) 5:288.

54 *KCM*, 3 (February 1885) 4:122.

55 *KCM*, 9 (April 1889) 6:340.

56 *KCM*, 13 (November 1890) 1:57–58.

57 R.D. Fraser, "The College Session," *KCM*, 13 (December 1890) 2:104.

58 *KCM*, 9 (December 1888) 2:109.

59 J.F. McCurdy, "The Literary Course," *KCM*, 9 (December 1888) 2:105. See also J.F. McCurdy, "Knox College and its Literary Course," *KCM*, 9 (March 1889) 5:250–257.

60 John Laing, "The Non-Theological Department in Knox College," *KCM*, 10 (May 1889) 1:52–57.

61 *KCM*, 5 (April 1887) 6:354–371.

62 *A&P,* June 1876, 192.

63 *KCM*, 10 (May 1889) 1:61–62.

64 *A&P,* June 1886, 19–20, 24, and ccxciv-ccxcv.

65 On university federation and Caven's role in it, see Robin S. Harris, *A History of Higher Education in Canada, 1663–1960* (Toronto: University of Toronto Press, 1976), 108–113, and W.S. Wallace, *A History of the University of Toronto* (Toronto: University of Toronto Press, 1927) 114–139.

66 For further discussion on the nature of higher education in Canada during the late-nineteenth century, see McKillop, *A Disciplined Intelligence*; Gauvreau, *The Evangelical Century*; and Michael Gauvreau, "Presbyterianism, Liberal Education and the Research Ideal: Sir Robert Falconer and the University of Toronto, 1907–1932," *Burning Bush*, ed. Klempa, 42–65.

67 *A&P,* June 1887, 21.

68 *A&P,* June 1880, xci.

69 *A&P,* June 1881, 43–44.

70 *A&P,* June 1882, xcv.

71 *A&P,* June 1884, cviii.

72 *A&P,* June 1885, cxxv.

73 *A&P,* June 1888, 24 and Appendix 7, i-ii.

74 *Minutes of General Assembly,* June 1871, 45 and 53.

75 *A&P,* June 1883, 29.

CHAPTER FOUR

1 Robert N. Grant, "Knox College," *Historical Sketches of the Pioneer Work and the Missionary, Educational and Benevolent Agencies of The Presbyterian Church in Canada* (Toronto: Murray Printing, 1903), 90.

2 Donaldson Grant, "Principal William Caven, D.D., LL.D.," *Westminster,* October 1902.

3 For an overview of these developments among American Presbyterians, see Craig Dykstra and James Hudnut-Beumler, "The National Organi-

zational Structures of Protestant Denominations: An Invitation to a Conversation," *The Organizational Revolution: Presbyterians and American Denominationalism,* ed. Milton J. Coalter, John M. Mulder, and Louis B. Weeks (Louisville: Westminster/John Knox Press, 1992), 307–331.

4 For fuller accounts of the growth of the Presbyterian press in Canada, see Fraser, *The Social Uplifters,* 65–66 and 109–114, and Lorne Pierce, *The Chronicle of a Century* (Toronto: Ryerson Press, 1929), 176–191.

5 William MacLaren, *Sixty Years' Retrospect* (Toronto: Armac Press, 1907), 9, 13.

6 George L. Robinson, "Leaders in Old Testament Criticism: Samuel Rolles Driver," *Westminster,* 2 April 1898, 337.

7 On Campbell, see Markell, *The Presbyterian College,* 21–28.

8 John Campbell, "Scholasticism in Modern Theology," *KCM,* 11 (December 189) 2:61–67. The article sparked an exchange between Campbell and W.T. McMullen of Woodstock, a graduate of Knox in 1856 and Moderator of the General Assembly in 1888. See W.T. McMullen, "Scholasticism in Modern Theology," *KCM,* 12 (May 1890) 1:1–4, and John Campbell, "The Pelagianism of Modern Theology," *KCM,* 13 (December 1890) 2:61–67.

9 For a thorough study of the heresy trial, see Donald N. Young, "The Destructive Professor, or Montreal Presbytery to the Rescue O' the Kirk: The Heresy Trial of Professor John Campbell 1893–4" (M.Th. paper, Knox College, 1975).

10 These discussions can be traced better in the church periodicals than in the college reports. See *KCM,* 13 (December 1890) 2:120; 13 (April 1891) 6:339–340; 20 (August-September 1896) 3:134–141; and *Westminster,* 11 February 1899, 162–163.

11 *Westminster,* 19 February 1898, 186, and 5 March 1898, 219.

12 *KCM,* 7 (March 1888) 5:308–309. Beattie graduated from Knox in 1878, served as minister at Baltimore and Cold Springs, Ontario, from 1878–1882 and at First Church, Brantford from 1882–1888. He went to the Presbyterian Theological Seminary in Columbia, South Carolina, in 1888 as professor of apologetics and moved to the Presbyterian Theological Seminary in Louisville, Kentucky as professor of systematic theology and apologetics in 1893.

13 R.Y. Thomson, "The Evolution in the Manifestation of the Supernatural," *KCM,* 12 (October 1890) 6:293–318.

14 For summaries of the views of A.B. Davidson and Marcus Dods and their place in the controversies over Scottish biblical studies, see Cheyne, *Transforming,* 37–59, and A.L. Drummond and James Bulloch,

The Church in Late Victorian Scotland 1874–1900 (Edinburgh: St. Andrew Press, 1978), 42–48, 64–66, 264–267.

15 Ronald Sawatsky, "Henry Martyn Parsons of Knox Church, Toronto (1828–1913)," *The Canadian Society of Presbyterian History Papers 1982*, 85–120.

16 H.M. Parsons, "The Present Needs of Knox College," *KCM*, 12 (October 1890) 6:323–328.

17 William MacLaren tackled the issue of premillennialism in a paper delivered to the Toronto Ministerial Association in 1882. See William MacLaren, *Premillennialism in relation to Revelations XX:1–10* (Toronto: James Bain and Son, 1882). Parsons, who was MacLaren's minister until he and his wife became founding members of Bloor St. Presbyterian Church in 1886, debated with MacLaren following the address. The *Globe*, 7 February 1882, was satisfied that "the subject was so presented that those who have adopted premillennial views must find it a difficult matter to maintain them." On the history of Ontario Bible College and Parsons' role in it, see John G. Stackhouse, Jr., *Canadian Evangelicalism in the Twentieth Century: An Introduction to Its Character* (Toronto: University of Toronto Press, 1993), 53–70, and Sawatsky, "Parsons," 104–105.

18 A brief statemement of Thomson's views on the study of the Bible, written while he was in Germany, was published in the *Monthly* in 1886. See R.Y. Thomson, "Bible Study in the College," *KCM*, 4 (April 1886) 6:250–255.

19 *PR*, May 1896.

20 *A&P*, June 1985, 57–58 and Appendix, 10.

21 *A&P*, June 1896, 22–23.

22 James Ballantyne, "The Scope and Uses of the Study of Church History," *Westminster*, 9 October 1897, 280–281.

23 *In Memory of Rev. James Ballantyne, B.A., D.D. 1857–1921* (Toronto: Ryerson Press, 1922), 7–30.

24 *Westminster*, June 1896, 40.

25 On McCurdy and the development of biblical studies at University College, see John S. Moir, *A History of Biblical Studies in Canada: A Sense of Proportion* (Chico: Scholars Press, 1982), 1–24.

26 George L. Robinson, "The Place of Deuteronomy in Hebrew Literature," *Westminster*, 1 (October 1896) 5:201

27 *Westminster*, 11 June 1898, 586.

28 *A&P*, June 1897, 232.

29 *Westminster*, 27 August 1898, 195.

30 John E. McFadyen, *Old Testament Criticism and the Christian Church* (London: Hodder and Stoughton, 1903), 363.

31 McFadyen, *Old Testament Criticism*, 121.

32 For outlines of McFadyen's courses, see the Knox College *Calendar,* 1899–1910. The devotional books were *The Divine Pursuit* (Toronto: Westminster, 1901); *In The Hour of Silence* (Toronto: Fleming H. Revell, 1902); and *The City With Foundations* (Toronto: Westminster, 1909). The guides for bible study were *The Messages of the Prophetic and Priestly Historians* (New York: Charles Scribner's Sons, 1901); *The Messages of the Psalmist* (New York: Charles Scribner's Sons, 1904); *Prayers of the Bible* (Toronto: Westminster, 1906); and *Ten Studies in the Psalms* (Toronto: YMCA Press, 1907). The textbooks were *Old Testament Criticism* and *Introduction to the Old Testament* (London: Hodder and Stoughton, 1905).

33 Forrest was firmly rooted in the Scottish progressive school. He had been a prize-winning student of Edward Caird at Glasgow, John Cairns in Edinburgh, and Franz Delitzsch in Leipzig. He was a central figure in the Back-to-Christ movement, claiming it was "not by ideas but by personalities that God illuminates and uplifts men." Forrest's thesis, T.B.Kilpatrick remarked in welcoming the appointment, was that "the historical implies the spiritual, and is unintelligible apart from the claim which the Church makes on behalf of Christ; and that the spiritual depends upon the historical, and cannot retain its power and value if it be torn away form its root in historic fact." See David W. Forrest, *The Christ of History and of Experience* (Edinburgh: T. & T. Clark, 1897), i. On Forrest, see Sell, *Declaring and Defending*, 172–194.

34 Charles Douglas, *Andrew Halliday Douglas: Five Sermons with a Biographical Introduction* (London: Hodder and Stoughton, 1903), 234–235.

35 Douglas, *Andrew Halliday Douglas*, 15–46.

36 Douglas, *Andrew Halliday Douglas*, 96–97.

37 *Presbyterian*, 10 October 1903, 410.

38 *KCM*, 17 (December 1893) 8:478–479.

39 *Westminster,* 16 October 1897, 298.

40 *A&P,* June 1898, 48, and June 1899, 62.

41 *A&P,* June 1886, Appendix, ccxciv-ccxcv.

42 *Presbyterian*, 11 July 1903, 10–11. For an account of Charlton's role in the Queen's controversy, see Neatby, *Queen's*, 249–255. Charlton was one of the leading moral reformers in the federal House of Commons, sponsoring legislation to protect girls and women from seduction through promises of marriage and to enforce better observance of the Sabbath. See Morgan, *Men and Women 1898*, 180–181.

43 For examples of the opinions expressed in the consolidation debate, see *Presbyterian*, 25 July 1903, 73–74; 15 August 1903, 153–154 and 157; 5 September 1903, 258–259; 19 September 1903, 323; and 26 September 1903, 341–343.

44 *A&P,* June 1895, Appendix 10, ii.

45 *A&P,* June 1896, Appendix 11, ii.

46 *A&P,* June 1897, 217–218.

47 *A&P,* June 1896, Appendix 11, vi.

48 *A&P,* June 1898, 231.

49 *Westminster,* February 1897, 86.

50 *A&P,* June 1892, Appendix 8, i.

51 James A. Macdonald, "In the College Library," *KCM,* 13 (February 1891) 4:209–214.

52 *Westminster,* 19 October 1901, 462, and 7 December 1901, 676; *Presbyterian*, 20 September 1902, 357–358, and 5 December 1903, 669–673; and *A&P,* June 1902, 220, and June 1904, 225.

53 Neatby, *Queen's*, 231, 233–235.

54 *KCM,* 17 (March 1894) 11:638–640.

55 *Westminster,* 28 January 1899, 76.

56 *Westminster,* 13 August 1898, 161–162, and 27 August 1898, 193–194.

57 *Westminster,* 27 August 1898, 198–199, and 3 September 1898, 251–252. For an account of the establishment of the summer school in Manitoba, see J.A.M. Edwards, *Andrew Baird of Manitoba College* (Winnipeg: University of Winnipeg Press, 1972), 73–75.

58 *Westminster,* 17 November 1900, 591–592.

59 *Presbyterian,* 18 July 1903, 39.

60 For accounts of the education of women missionaries and the founding of Ewart, see Irene Dickson and Margaret Webster, *To Keep the Memory Green: A History of Ewart College 1897–1987* (Toronto: Ewart College, 1986), 3–11; Ruth Compton Brouwer, *New Women for God: Canadian Presbyterian Women and India Missions, 1876–1914* (Toronto: University of Toronto Press, 1990), 36, 62–65; and *Westminster,* 2 October 1897, 240.

61 For accounts of the incident and the text of Mrs. Ross' letter, see Brouwer, *New Women,* 65, and Peter Bush, "John Edgar McFadyen and the Ewart Missionary Training Home," *Presbyterian History,* 37 (May 1993) 1:1–5.

62 *Westminster,* 7 June 1902, 695.

63 *A&P,* June 1903, 64, and June 1904, 31.

64 *Westminster,* October 1897, 293. On Bengough, see Ramsay Cook, *The Regenerators: Social Criticism in Late Victorian English Canada* (Toronto: University of Toronto Press, 1985), 123–151.

CHAPTER FIVE

1 For a concise rationale of organic church union in Canada, see William Patrick, "Some Reasons for Church Union," *PR,* October 1906, 327–329. On Patrick's central role in launching the church union movement in Canada, see Clifford, *Resistance,* 13–25. The arguments presented in brief by Patrick in his *Record* article and the rationale provided by the spiritual and moral evolutionism of progressive orthodoxy were expanded in A.S. Morton, *The Way to Union* (Toronto: William Briggs, 1912). For Kilpatrick's assessment of Patrick's contribution to the Canadian church, see T.B. Kilpatrick, "William Patrick: 1852–1911, An Appreciation," *Presbyterian,* 5 October 1911, 359–360.

2 On MacLaren's attitude see Clifford, *Resistance,* 15–16, and on Ballantyne's leadership of the moderate party in the midst of the controversy, see Clifford, *Resistance,* 54–57, 97–100.

3 The two classic studies of the church union movement are C.E. Silcox, *Church Union in Canada: Its Causes and Consequences* (New York: Institute of Social and Religious Research, 1933), and John W. Grant, *The Canadian Experience of Church Union* (London: Lutterworth Press, 1967). See also B. Kiesekamp, "Community and Faith: The Intellectual and Ideological Bases of the Church Union Movement in Victorian Canada," (Ph.D. thesis, University of Toronto, 1974). As Phyllis Airhart has pointed out, however, there is surprisingly little recent analysis of the founding and history of The United Church of Canada. The work that Airhart and Roger Hutchinson are doing and encouraging for the Lilly Project on United Church Issues at Emmanuel College, University of Toronto, is beginning to correct this. See Phyllis D. Airhart, " 'As Canadian as Possible Under the Circumstances' Reflections on the Study of Protestantism in North America" (paper presented at the Wingspread Conference, 21–23 October 1993), 11–18.

4 For a more detailed biography and analysis of Kilpatrick's intellectual formation, see Fraser, *Social Uplifters,* 27–43.

5 On Winnipeg during these years, see Alan F.J. Artibise, *Winnipeg: A Social History of Urban Growth 1874–1914* (Montreal: McGill-Queen's University Press, 1975), and on the religious culture of Winnipeg Pres-

byterians, see Ian M. Manson, "Serving God and Country: Evangelical Piety and the Presbyterian Church in Manitoba, 1880–1900," (M.A. thesis, University of Manitoba, 1986).

6 For an account of efforts at the national level, see Fraser, *Social Uplifters*.

7 *Social Service: A Book for Young Canadians*, ed. W.R. McIntosh (Toronto: Presbyterian Publications, 1911), 1.

8 For an account of the impact of the war on the church in Canada, see Marshall, *Secularizing the Faith*, 156–180.

9 *Globe*, 1 October 1915.

10 *Globe*, 29 September 1915.

11 *Globe*, 1 October 1915.

12 *Globe*, 1 October 1915. Robinson's views were not unusual for progressive churchmen of his age, especially from the United States. On liberal pacifism and its collapse in Canada in the early years of the war, see Thomas P. Socknat, *Witness Against War: Pacifism in Canada, 1900–1945* (Toronto: University of Toronto Press, 1987), 19–59, and Fraser, *Social Uplifters*, 155–165. James A. Macdonald voiced sentiments similar to Robinson's a month later at a peace rally in San Francisco and had to step down as managing editor of the Toronto *Globe* as a result.

13 T.B. Kilpatrick, *The War and the Christian Church* (Toronto: Presbyterian Church in Canada, 1917), 5–6.

14 Modris Eksteins, *Rites of Spring: The Great War and the Birth of the Modern Age* (Toronto: Lester & Orpen Dennys, 1989), 185.

15 Quoted in Marshall, *Secularizing the Faith*, 166–167, 172.

16 Quoted in Marshall, *Secularizing the Faith*, 177. Following the war, Knox faculty members Robert Law, Alfred Gandier, and T.W. Manson all published books on eschatology and the foundation for the church's mission provided by a proper understanding of this dimension of the Christian faith. All three had worked on the theme prior to the war, but the loss of life that touched most communities in Canada, together with the growth of spiritualism and premillennialism, convinced them to offer an alternative interpretation of the hope of personal immortality and the confidence Christians had in the life beyond. See Robert Law, *The Hope of Our Calling* (New York: George H. Doran, 1918); Alfred Gandier, *The Son of Man Coming in His Kingdom* (New York: George H. Doran, 1922); and William Manson, *The Incarnate Glory: An Expository Study of the Gospel According to St. John* (London: James Clarke, 1923).

17 Marshall, *Secularizing the Faith*, 178.

18 T.B. Kilpatrick, "The Church of the Twentieth Century," *Constructive Quarterly,* 7 (September 1919) 3:406, 420–421.

19 Kilpatrick, "Church of the Twentieth Century," 430–432.

20 Kilpatrick, *Common Faith,* 67–68.

21 Kilpatrick, *Common Faith,* 59.

22 On the Reformed character of United Church theology, see N. Keith Clifford, "The United Church of Canada and Doctrinal Confession," *Touchstone,* 2 (May 1984) 2:6–21.

23 Alfred Gandier, *The Doctrinal Basis of Union and its Relation to the Historic Creeds* (Toronto: Ryerson Press, 1926), 47–48.

24 For a detailed analysis of this strategy, see Fraser, *Social Uplifters,* 99–125.

25 I have examined this shift in much greater detail in *Social Uplifters,* 99–154.

26 For an account of the production of the first hymnal, see W. Barclay McMurrich, *Historical Sketch of the Hymnal Committee of the Presbyterian Church in Canada* (Toronto: Henry Frowde, 1905).

27 On MacMillan's contribution to hymnody in the Presbyterian and United churches, see N. Keith Clifford, "The Contribution of Alexander MacMillan to Canadian Hymnody," in *Burning Bush,* ed. Klempa, 171–195.

28 Protesting against efforts to produce common worship resources in the 1890s, J.J.A. Proudfoot wrote that they were ritualistic and taken from "prelatic churches," were not Scriptural, were "opposed and repugnant to Presbyterian principles and usage," and had "originated with a higher social circle, composed mainly of city ministers." See *Westminster,* 3 June 1899, 591–592.

29 On the liturgical movement in Scotland, see Cheyne, *Transforming,* 88–109.

30 *New Directory for the Public Worship of God* (Edinburgh: MacNiven and Wallace, 1898), v-xiv. The directory was laid out in three sections: resources for the order of service at the ordinary public worship of the Lord's Day; resources for the sacraments of baptism and communion; and resources for services on special occasions, such as admission to full communion, marriage, burial, ordinations, and building dedications.

31 Clifford, *Resistance,* 4.

32 *Presbyterian,* 5 October 1905, 452.

33 *Presbyterian,* 5 October 1905, 452.

34 *Presbyterian,* 5 October 1905, 453.

35 In addition to the several articles and books referred to in the endnotes throughout this chapter, Kilpatrick wrote nine major articles for the series of dictionaries and encyclopedia edited by James Hastings. See *Dictionary of the Bible*, s.v. "Conscience" and "Philosophy;" *Dictionary of Christ and the Gospels*, s.v. "Character of Christ" and "Incarnation;" *Encyclopedia of Religion and Ethics*, s.v. "Anger (wrath) of God," "Benevolence," "Salvation (Christian)," "Soteriology," and "Suffering." On Hastings and his role in popularizing progressive orthodoxy in the Anglo-American churches, see J.A.H. Dempster, "Incomparable Encyclopaedist: the life and work of Dr. James Hastings," *Expository Times*, 100 (1988):4–8.

36 H.A.A.Kennedy, *Paul's Conceptions of the Last Things* (London: Hodder and Stoughton, 1904), 341. Kennedy paid tribute to the influence of Marcus Dods and A.B. Davidson.

37 John Dow, *Alfred Gandier: Man of Vision and Achievement* (Toronto: United Church Publishing House, 1951), 9. The details of Gandier's life are taken largely from Dow's biography.

38 Gandier attended Queen's during Grant's first decade of leadership, during which the first major endowment campaign was conducted. See Neatby, *Queen's*, 151–167.

39 Dow, *Gandier*, 50–67, and James G. Greenlee, *Sir Robert Falconer: A Biography* (Toronto: University of Toronto Press, 1988), 71–75. Included in the group were Robert Falconer, then principal of Pine Hill, later president of the University of Toronto, and soon to marry Gandier's sister; Donald M. Gordon, George Grant's successor as principal of Queen's University; Walter Murray, first president of the University of Saskatchewan; Clarence Mackinnon, future principal of Pine Hill; and Arthur S. Morton, later professor of history at the University of Saskatchewan and first provincial archivist there.

40 Greenlee, *Falconer*, 115–118.

41 John S. Moir, "'On the King's Business': the Rise and Fall of the Laymen's Missionary Movement in Canada," *Les Mouvements de Laics dans les Eglises aux XIXe et XXe Siecles*, ed. A. Tihon (Bruxelles: Facultes universitaires Saint-Louis, 1980).

42 Dow, *Gandier*, 75–76

43 Dow, *Gandier*, 77–92.

44 Dow, *Gandier*, 87–91.

45 *Construction*, 4 (February 1911): 49–74. A pictorial on the completed building appeared in *Construction*, 8 (November 1915): 453–463.

46 On Denney, see Sell, *Defending and Declaring*, 195–220. Sell notes that Denney was anxious that the theological colleges in Scotland remain under the control of the church and that ministerial training should be more important than academic education for its own sake.

47 Moir, *Sense of Proportion*, 27.

48 *Globe*, 12 October 1910. See also Robert Law, *The Tests of Life: A Study of the First Epistle of St. John* (Edinburgh: T. & T. Clark, 1909). Greeted by the *Scotsman* as "a fresh and lucid exposition of a sane and reverent faith," the book treated the epistle as an extended and effective polemic against Gnosticism and its hellenizing of Christianity. In Law's analysis, this was a reactionary rather than a progressive movement, especially in its emphasis on dualism. Knowledge of the ultimate Reality, the Being who is Eternal Life, was the goal of both Gnosticism and Christianity. For the Gnostics, this was attained by "flights of intellectual speculation or mystical contemplation," while for John, it was reached "only by the lowlier path of obedience and brotherly love" (29–30).

49 Robert Law, "Jesus and Social Service," in *Social Service*, ed. McIntosh, 7–21.

50 See Robert Law, *The Emotions of Jesus* (New York: Charles Scribner's Sons, 1915), and *The Great Adventure and Other Sermons* (New York: George H. Doran, 1916), *The Hope of Our Calling* (New York: George H. Doran, 1918), and *Optimism and Other Sermons* (Toronto: McClelland and Stewart, 1919).

51 Moir, *Sense of Proportion*, 33–38. On the controversy at University College, see Greenlee, *Falconer*, 127–134. Thomas Eakin, later appointed principal of Knox College after church union, was a central figure. On Jackson and the course of the controversy in the Methodist church, see Phyllis Airhart, *Serving the Present Age: Revivalism, Progressivism, and the Methodist Tradition in Canada* (Montreal and Kingston: McGill-Queen's University Press, 1992), 89–93.

52 *Presbyterian*, 18 March 1909, 323.

53 McNeill, *Presbyterian Church*, 271.

54 T.B. Kilpatrick, "A Response to Father Kelly," *Constructive Quarterly*, 5 (December 1917): 632.

55 *In Memory of Rev. James Ballantyne, B.A., D.D. 1857–1921* (Toronto: Ryerson Press, 1922), 31–40.

56 T.B. Kilpatrick, "For the Work of the Ministry," *Presbyterian*, 14 May 1908, 620.

57 J.E. McFadyen, *The Messages of the Prophetic and Priestly Historians* (New York: Charles Scribner's Sons, 1901), 76–83.

58 This description of the prophet is taken from a memorial tribute to Robert Law. See T.B. McCorkindale, "The Rev. Robert Law, D.D.: An Appreciation," in Law, *Optimism*, 13–14.

59 Richard Davidson, "The Living Truth," *Canadian Journal of Religious Thought*, 1 (March-April 1924) 2:162–163.

60 Kilpatrick, "Church of the Twentieth Century," 418.

61 On Kilpatrick's promotion of evangelism in the Presbyterian Church in Canada, see Fraser, *Social Uplifters*, 33–38. For his views on the centrality of evangelism for the mission of the church and the strategies appropriate for its conduct, see T.B. Kilpatrick, *New Testament Evangelism* (Toronto: Westminster, 1911), and T.B. Kilpatrick and J.G. Shearer, *The Kootenay Campaign: Evangelism and Moral Reform* (Toronto: Committee on Evangelism, Presbyterian Church in Canada, 1909), and T.B. Kilpatrick, *Counsels to a Young Missioner* (Toronto: General Assembly's Committee on Evangelism, 1909). One of the first simultaneous evangelism campaigns Kilpatrick conducted was with William Patrick and C.W. Gordon in Winnipeg in 1902, reported in *Presbyterian*, 29 March 1902, 385. On Chapman and his work among American Presbyterians, see Dale E. Soden, "Anatomy of a Presbyterian Urban Revival: J.W. Chapman in the Pacific Northwest," *American Presbyterians* 64 (1986) 1:49–57, and Bryan D. Gilling, "Revivalism as Renewal: J. Wilbur Chapman in New Zealand, 1912–1913," *American Presbyterians*, 70 (1992) 2:83–92.

62 T.B. Kilpatrick, "Evangelism, Not Revivalism," *Presbyterian*, 7 October 1909, 356.

63 *A&P,* June 1912, Appendix, 337–338.

64 *A&P,* June 1912, Appendix, 338.

65 *Minutes*, Senate of Knox College, 25 January 1909.

66 Kilpatrick, "Work of the Ministry," 620–621. For a description of Union during this period, see Robert T. Handy, *A History of Union Theological Seminary in New York* (New York: Columbia University Press, 1987), 95–157. Interestingly, it was precisely at this point in Union's history that it shifted its focus to advanced scholarship and built up its post-graduate programs.

67 T.B. Kilpatrick, "Work of the Ministry," 620.

68 Quoted from Kilpatrick's course description for systematic theology in *Calendar of Knox College, Toronto, 1909–1910* (Toronto: Knox College, 1909), 15.

69 *A&P,* June 1925, Appendix, 163.

70 Quoted in Dow, *Gandier,* 90.

71 *A&P,* June 1913, Appendix, 171,

72 *A&P,* June 1922, Appendix, 186

73 The figures used in these calculations are drawn from the annual summaries of statistics for the assembly's theological colleges and the comparative table of statistics for the church's entire operation, both printed annually in *A&P.*

74 *A&P,* June 1922, Appendix, 183.

75 *A&P,* June 1922, 81–82.

76 For his inaugural lecture in Winnipeg, "The Preacher's Business," see the *Presbyterian,* 18 November 1915, 490.

77 *A&P,* June 1922, Appendix, 184–185.

78 *A&P,* June 1923, Appendix, 199.

79 Markell, *Presbyterian College,* 110–112.

80 See Kilpatrick, *Common Faith,* and Gandier, *Doctrinal Basis.*

81 For a thorough account of the resistance to church union, see Clifford, *Resistance.*

82 *A&P,* June 1924, Appendix, 160. Harry Lennox of Vancouver, one of the five Knox students who stayed out of union, recalls that Gandier gave his annual dinner for the graduating class the evening the bill passed and became quite bitter in his remarks about the loss of the college.

83 Clifford, *Resistance,* 198. The continuing Presbyterians were ordered to pay the United Church the sum of $145,000 as their share of the endowments.

84 On the transition from Knox to Emmanuel, see Kenneth H. Cousland, *The Founding of Emmanuel College of Victoria University in The University of Toronto* (Toronto: Victoria University, 1978), 45–75.

CHAPTER SIX

1 Quoted in Clifford, *Resistance,* 191.

2 Clifford, *Resistance,* 191.

3 The Committee on the Reception of Ministers reported to the 1931 General Assembly that 438 ministers had applied for reception since 1925, but only 187 had been approved. Still, that represented 27% of the 700 active ministers in the denomination. See *PR,* August 1931, 235. On the American Presbyterian ethos during this period, see Bradley L. Longfield, *The Presbyterian Controversy: Fundamentalists, Modernists, and Moderates* (New York: Oxford University Press, 1991).

4 Allan L. Farris, "The Fathers of 1925," *Enkindled by the Word: Essays on Presbyterianism in Canada,* ed. Neil G. Smith (Toronto: Presbyterian Publications, 1966), 59–82.

5 For a more detailed account of the federalist option, see Clifford, *Resistance,* 43–59, 137–141.

6 The quote is taken from a letter to Farris in 1963 from E.S. Lautenslager, Principal of Emmanuel College. He went on to claim that the fears had not been realized. See Farris, "Fathers," 75.

7 Fraser's views reached a broad audience in an article in the *Harvard Theological Review* in 1915, and in a sermon printed in the *Presbyterian Standard* in 1923. To use the language of the catholic creeds, he wrote, "as a modern statement of the Trinity of Christian experience, to use the language of the Westminster Divines on the fall of Adam and Eve, in order to explain the depravity of modern society, to use the language of John Wesley to express the new evangelism, is surely not in the interests of correct thinking, not to say of intellectual integrity. It is not a good omen that the United Church should enter upon its career, almost boasting of its freedom from doctrinal trammels and presenting a theological document which indicates practically the cessation of vigorous and honest thinking." See Farris, "Fathers," 78–79.

8 Quoted in Farris, "Fathers," 80.

9 Bryden, *Why,* 80.

10 Clifford, *Resistance,* 102, 170, 194.

11 Markell, *Presbyterian College,* 38.

12 During the debate over Eakin's appointment, Ephraim Scott stated, "At a previous session of this Assembly, in supporting the nomination by the Board of Knox College, of Dr. Thomas Eakin as Principal of that College, I stated that Dr. Eakin had said to me in the intimacy of private conversation – 'I have already taken, at my different inductions, the vows required by our Church of her Ministers, and when occasion requires, I am ready to take them again, without evasion, equivocation, or mental reservations.' " Scott went on to specify what Eakin believed concerning the doctrines of the inspiration of Scripture and the person and work of Christ. Eakin indicated that Scott represented him truly. A further effort was made to have another name considered by A.B. Winchester and J.G. Inkster of Knox Presbyterian Church, Toronto, but it was defeated. See *A&P,* June 1926, 36–37.

13 E.L. Morrow to T. Eakin, 1 May 1925, Eakin Papers 207/0421, Knox College Archives.

14 E.L. Morrow to T. Eakin, 28 September 1925, Thomas Eakin Papers, 207/0421, Knox College Archives.

15 They included C.S. McDonald of Brampton, John Penman of Paris, Thomas McMillan of Toronto, G. Tower Ferguson of Toronto, and F.H. Chrysler of Ottawa. McDonald was convener of the board of Ewart College as well. The extent of their contribution to the resistance to church union is chronicled throughout Clifford, *Resistance.*

16 *PR*, July 1925, 199.

17 Ephraim Scott, "The Ministry and its Message," *PR*, September 1925, 270.

18 Ephraim Scott, "What is the Presbyterian Church?," *PR*, June 1925, 164.

19 *PR*, August 1925, 231.

20 Quoted in Stuart Macdonald, "From Just War to Crusade: The War-Time Sermons of the Rev. Thomas Eakin" (M.Div. thesis, Knox College, 1985), 33.

21 Quoted in Macdonald, "War-Time Sermons," 12.

22 Quoted in R.J. Graham Kennedy, "The Question of Identity in The Presbyterian Church in Canada, 1900 to 1925" (M.Th. thesis, Knox College, 1984), 25–26.

23 The most thorough study of Bryden's career and theology is John Vissers, "The Conception of Revelation in the Theology of Walter W. Bryden" (Th.D. thesis, Toronto School of Theology, 1988). See also, Joseph C. McLelland, "Walter Bryden: By Circumstance and God," *Called to Witness, Vol. II,* ed. W. Stanford Reid (Toronto: Committee on History, Presbyterian Church in Canada, 1980), 119–126, and Donald V. Wade, "The Theological Achievement of Walter Bryden" (paper presented at the Barth Colloquium, Toronto, 22 March 1974).

24 For the most mature exposition of his theology, see Walter W. Bryden, *The Christian's Knowledge of God* (Toronto: Thorn Press, 1940). The incentive for writing the book, Bryden claimed, came from the uncertainty and ambiguity of preaching in the Protestant churches. J.G. Berry reviewed it for the *Record* and noted that it represented a revived Protestantism in the spirit of Luther and Calvin in a time "of the seeming failure of liberal theology, a time of theological perplexity, of the lost radiance of Christianity, of the dominance of secularism, of optimism about man and the world though this has faded in the face of the world crisis [and] of the decay of worship." See *PR*, February 1941, 45.

25 John Dow, review of *The Spirit of Jesus in St. Paul,* by Walter W. Bryden, *Canadian Journal of Religious Thought,* 4 (January-February 1927): 89–90.

26 On Karl Barth and his theological thought and influence, see Eberhard Jungel, *Karl Barth: A Theological Legacy* (Philadelphia: Westminster, 1986).

27 Walter W. Bryden, "The Triumph of Reality," *PR*, July 1929, 214–215,220. On Bryden's appreciation of the resistance of the Confessing Church, see "Continental Movements and the Theological Thought of Tomorrow," *United Church Observer*, 5 June 1941, 11,28. "The supreme thing that this Church is to say to other Churches," Bryden stated, "is simply this: that the Church does not actually exist except when confession actually exists: moreover, that there is no power of God, no true language of God, no true theology, which does not emanate from confession. But confession here, observe, is a deep and radical thing." Other influences, preceding and coincident with Barth and the Confessing Church, were James Denney, P.T. Forsyth, John Oman, and John Dickie. Dickie was the principal of Knox College, Dunedin, New Zealand. Bryden claimed to have found in Dickie's work the most satisfying presentation of evangelical theology he had ever read. See Walter W. Bryden, review of *The Organism of Christian Truth: A Modern Positive Dogmatic*, by John Dickie, *Canadian Journal of Religious Thought*, 9 (January-February 1932): 73.

28 Bryden, "Triumph of Reality," 28.

29 Walter W. Bryden, *Separated Unto the Gospel* (Toronto: Burns and MacEachern, 1956), 50–51.

30 For the text of the declaration and an account of its drafting, see Arthur C. Cochrane, "A Declaration of Faith Concerning Church and Nation by the Presbyterian Church in Canada," *Antwort. Karl Barth sum siebzigsten Geburtstag am 10 Mai 1956* (Zollokon-Zurich: Evangelischer Verlag AG, 1956).

31 Bryden, *Separated*, 78.

32 Bryden, *Why*, 166–169.

33 Bryden, *Why*, 7.

34 This stance invited open attacks from the more fundamentalist wing of conservative Presbyterians in Canada. See, for example, R. Allan Killen, "Canadian Ministerial Students are Taught the Bible has Discrepancies, Contradictions, Doubtful Morality and Religious Myths," *Christian Beacon*, 3 April 1947, 2.

35 W.E. Middleton, "The Pew to the Pulpit," *PR*, June 1927, 187–190.

36 Scott, "Ministry and its Message," 269–274.

37 Ephraim Scott, *"Church Union" and the Presbyterian Church in Canada* (Montreal: John Lovell and Son, 1928), 108.

38 *PR*, May 1927, 141.

39 Thomas Eakin, "The Work of the Ministry," Eakin Papers 207/0870, Knox College Archives.

40 Walter W. Bryden, "The Church and the College," *PR*, September 1945, 233.

41 Bryden, *Separated*, 118–119.

42 Bryden, *SeparatedG*, 120–124.

43 Bryden, *Separated*, 124–126.

44 Bryden, "Triumph," 215.

45 Bryden, *Separated*, 126–128.

46 Bryden, "Church and College," 233.

47 Bryden, *Separated*, 140–145.

48 Bryden, *Separated*, 165.

49 Bryden, *Separated*, 166–167.

50 James D. Smart, "Lest We Forget," *PR*, September 1975, 6–7.

51 *PR*, March 1949, 85.

52 W.J. McKeown, "Memoirs of Dr. Bryden," *PR*, October 1975, 8.

53 *PR*, July 1925, 198, 199.

54 *PR*, September 1925, 262.

55 The following account is based on the documentation found in the Committee of Investigation files 114/0001–0068, Knox College Archives, which survived the carrying out of the Assembly's order to destroy all the proceedings of the commissions and committees involved in the investigations. I have been helped in sorting this material by Andrew Fullerton, "The Knox College Affair: Post-Union Crisis in the 1930s" (M.Div. paper, Knox College, 1984).

56 *A&P*, June 1932, 28.

57 *A&P*, June 1932, 46–50. The whole situation led W.D. Reid to give notice of motion that professors be appointed for five year terms and re-engaged only if their records were satisfactory. There is no record of the motion being put.

58 *A&P*, June 1934, 55.

59 *A&P*, June 1935, 159.

60 *A&P*, June 1935, 37.

61 *A&P*, June 1935, 38.

62 See Eakin's statement to the Senate of Knox College on 21 July 1931, 21, in Committee of Investigation files 114/0002, Knox College Archives.

63 See the correspondence with H. McAllister Griffiths, David Ross, and J. Douglas Wilkie in the Eakin Papers 207/0344, 207/0406, Knox College Archives.

64 See, for example, the minority report submitted to the 1933 General Assembly. *A&P,* June 1933, 76.

65 *PR,* March 1926, 68, and December 1928, 368.

66 *PR,* June 1928, 184.

67 *PR,* December 1934, 372. The Knox graduates were Harold Reid, James D. Smart, Lewis McLean, Fred Goforth, and William MacKay. Reid pursued graduate studies in Strasbourg and Tübingen in the late 1920s and Smart did the same at Marburg and Berlin in the early 1930s.

68 Dickson and Webster, *Ewart College,* 26.

69 *PR,* May 1942, 149–150.

70 Walter W. Bryden, review of *The Church and The War, with a letter by Karl Barth,* by Arthur C. Cochrane, *PR,* January 194nm, 16.

71 *A&P,* June 1943, 38.

72 *A&P,* June 1943, 37–39.

73 Bryden, *Separated,* 166.

CHAPTER SEVEN

1 James D. Smart, "Canadian Presbyterianism Since 1925" *PR,* February 1954, 17. On Smart's career and perspective, see M. Beth McCutcheon, "The Structure of the Biblical Hermeneutic of James Dick Smart," (Th.M. thesis, Knox College, 1988).

2 Smart, "Canadian Presbyterianism," 17

3 Smart, "Canadian Presbyterianism," 19.

4 For an analysis of the varieties of evangelicalism closely associated with fundamentalism, see Ian S. Rennie, "Fundamentalism and the Varieties of North Atlantic Evangelicalism," *Evangelicalism,* ed. Noll, *et al,* 333–350.

5 On the perspectives and activities of the confessional orthodox wing of Canadian Presbyterianism, see Ian S. Rennie, "Conservatism in the Presbyterian Church in Canada in 1925 and Beyond: An Introductory Exploration," *Canadian Society of Presbyterian History Papers 1982,* 29–59, and A. Donald MacLeod, "A Twenty-fifth Anniversary: the Silver Jubilee of October 17, 1966," *Channels,* 8 (Summer 1991) 2:7–10.

6 For a biographical sketch of Hay, see *PR,* December 1944, 359.

7 The Presbyterian Church in Canada was a founding member of both councils. David Hay reported from the first meeting of the World Council that the most outstanding feature of the gathering was "the realization that the unity of the church is not a matter to be humanly en-

gineered by union and reunions but is something already given in Jesus Christ." He noted further "the weighty influence wielded on all points by Reformed continental theology." See David W. Hay, "World Churches Hold Significant Meetings in Amsterdam," *PR*, October 1948, 268–269.

8 Renewed ecumenical interest led again to tensions within the denomination between those who favoured a broader, catholic Presbyterianism and those who insisted on a narrower form of confessionalism that demanded doctrinal agreement prior to any cooperation. The key confrontation between these two parties in the post-war period was at the 1947 General Assembly. F. Scott Mackenzie, principal at the Presbyterian College, Montreal, presented the case for the Reformed catholic evangelicalism Bryden had defended in *Why I Am A Presbyterian*, a position the Assembly adopted almost unanimously. See Moir, *Enduring Witness*, 253. The Assembly statement read, "The General Assembly, while maintaining steadfastly, in harmony with the re-affirmation made by the General Assembly in 1925, its adherence to the ancient and historic standards of the Presbyterian faith, nevertheless places itself on record as interpreting these standards in harmony with the best traditions of the Church, that is to say, as not only encouraging but enjoining as a duty the fullest possible co-operation with all other Christian bodies, for the glory of God and the triumph of His purposes among men." See F. Scott Mackenzie, "Assembly Affirms True Presbyterianism," *PR*, August 1947, 173–174. W. Stanford Reid replied for those who opposed the cooperative movements. See *PR*, February 1948, 44. The tensions between the continuing defenders of confessional orthodoxy and proponents of neo-orthodoxy continued within the denomination, however, as evident in Allan Farris, "The Differences," *PR*, April 1964, 6–9.

9 Moir, *Enduring Witness*, 259.

10 J. Charles Hay, "The Restless Church," *PR*, May 1966, 2–3.

11 For example, Murdo Nicholson received several nominations for the chair of homiletics, evangelism and church administration in 1963, Ian Rennie and W. Stanford Reid for the chair of church history in 1978, and Mariano DiGangi and Ed McKinley for the chair of preaching and worship in 1978. See *A&P*, June 1963, 445, and *A&P*, June 1978, 345–346

12 For a brief history of the development of Ontario Theological Seminary and the key role played by Canadian Presbyterian Ian Rennie in its growth, see Stackhouse, *Canadian Evangelicalism*, 121–130.

13 Wade, "Bryden," 4,6.

14 Donald V. Wade, "Our Trust and Our Task," *PR*, December 1947, 280.

15 Donald V. Wade, "Some Conditions of 'The Advance'," *PR*, March 1946, 74.

16 Donald V. Wade, "Ferment in the Far East, *PR*, September 1958, 6.

17 Wade, "Ferment," 32.

18 *Book of Common Order of the Presbyterian Church in Canada* (Toronto: Presbyterian Publications, 1964), 354.

19 Donald V. Wade, "The Central Fact of Christmas," *PR*, December 1948, 320.

20 Allan L. Farris, "How the Creeds Began," *PR*, March 1957, 10–11.

21 Allan L. Farris, "Europe and The Scottish Reformation," *PR*, January 1960, 10.

22 Allan L. Farris, "Calvin's Doctrine of the Holy Spirit" (M.Th. thesis, Toronto Graduate School of Theological Studies, 1951), 5–6. Farris went on to study in Edinburgh and at the University of Chicago, completing the course work for his doctorate and much of the research for a thesis on Theodore Beza. Sadly, the thesis was never completed.

23 *The Book of Common Worship* (Toronto: The Presbyterian Church in Canada, 1991), 325.

24 Allan L. Farris, "Missions and the Reformation," *PR*, October 1950, 279–280.

25 W.J.S. Farris, *The People of God: Their Unity and Mission* (Kingston, Jamaica: Coke House, 1963), 3.

26 *Declaration of Faith Concerning Church and Nation*, Section 8.

27 Allan L. Farris, "Christian Responsibility In An Age of Change," *PR*, October 1959, 12–13, 27.

28 J. Stanley Glen, *The Individual and Contemporary Social Change* (Toronto: The Board of Stewardship and Budget, The Presbyterian Church in Canada, 1971), 13. Glen elsewhere described his view of the way the gospel affirmed "the preciousness of the personal." "The primary meaning of the gospel is that God is for man. It announces the radical love of God for man manifested as free, unmerited goodness toward him. Such goodness is expressed in two ways, the one with respect to God as the source (Creator) of the natural order and the other with respect to God as the source (Saviour) of the historical order. The latter is characterized by the participation of God in history and this by his self-movement toward men. This movement may be described as his grace or his love in action. It is expressed in the form of his forgiveness of sins through Christ (cross) with this forgiveness objectified and con-

firmed in its positive creative significance in the mystery of the resurrection (Easter). In this sense it signifies being saved from something (negative) in order to be saved to something (positive). Its purpose is to make men free. Its aim is to enable him to live the life that he was created to live with all its creative potentialities." See J. Stanley Glen, *Erich Fromm: A Protestant Critique* (Philadelphia: Westminster Press, 1966), 210.

29 J. Stanley Glen, *Justification by Success: The Invisible Captivity of the Church* (Atlanta: John Knox Press, 1979), 108.

30 Bryden, *Why,* 29–41.

31 The theology of church and ministry with which David Hay started his teaching career at Knox was laid out in his inaugural address. See David W. Hay, "The Direction of the Church's Effort, or The Orientation of the Church's Life," *PR,* June 1945, 4–8, 10. The development of these views in the Canadian context can be traced in the following *Record* articles: D.W. Hay, "Concerning The Church," *PR,* June 1956, 18–19; "Spirit, Word and Form," *PR,* May 1961, 10–11, 27; and "A Program for Presbyterians," *PR,* November 1975, 10–12.

32 David W. Hay, "The Basis of Ministry" (paper for the Committee on Church Doctrine, 1971), 1.

33 Hay, "Program for Presbyterians," 12.

34 *Book of Common Order,* iii-iv. See also, D.W. Hay, "Presbyterians and Liturgy" (Charles MacDonald Lecture, Knox College, 1979).

35 David W. Hay, "Concerning the Church," *PR,* June 1956, 18–19.

36 David W. Hay, "The Mystery of the Church: Reflections on the Existence of a Council of Churches," *Canadian Journal of Theology,* 9 (1963) 1:3–11.

37 David W. Hay, "The Direction of the Church's Effort or The Orientation of the Church's Life," *PR,* January 1945, 4–10.

38 *PR,* May 1945, 150.

39 J. Stanley Glen, "The Pastoral Responsibility of Theological Education," *Scottish Journal of Theology,* 6 (1953) 4:402. In a radio address in 1960, Glen charged that the offence of the cross had been obscured in most congregations, especially in their work with teenagers: "Our weakness has been that we have represented the Christian faith in too easy a form, both in respect to what we have taught our young people and in the requirements of church membership. Always there is the serious risk that the easier we make things for the learner the more he will despise us for it in the end. Our Lord warned us against this. He always imposed the cross upon those He would win. ... Let us have the cour-

age to confront our teenagers with the solid substance of the Bible in a language they can understand, with every opportunity to learn, to ask questions, to grasp its length and breadth and depth and above all with that dimension of its teaching which is strange, absurd, costly and provocative of wonder." See J. Stanley Glen, "Confront the Teenagers!," *PR*, May 1960, 13.

40 J. Stanley Glen, *The Recovery of the Teaching Ministry* (Philadelphia: Westminster Press, 1960), 36.

41 Glen, *Recovery*, 87.

42 Glen, *Erich Fromm*, 210. Glen was convinced that a nihilistic gnosticism combined with the proliferating power of the bureaucratic and administrative complexes of contemporary society was denying the value of the personal. For him, the identity of the individual was grounded in God's identification with us in the incarnation, death, and resurrection of Christ. This decisive event in human history was the ground of true human freedom and the basis of "the radical emphasis of the Christian faith in the preciousness of the personal, on the high particularity of the personal over the impersonal, which in nothingness reaches its deepest point." See Glen, *Individual and Contemporary Social Change*, 13.

43 Allan L. Farris, "On Being a Successful Minister," *Canadian Journal of Theology*, 5 (1959) 3:141–142.

44 J. Charles Hay, "Theological Concerns and the Preacher's Task," *Canadian Journal of Theology*, 10 (1964) 3:203–210. Hay considered the crisis in the ministry that emerged in the 1960s to be a matter of faithfulness to the Gospel as well as a matter of relevance to cultural expectations. Ministers, he said at a panel at Calvin Church in Toronto in 1967, "are not sure that the claims of the gospel are valid claims with respect to Christ and to God and in relation to people today." He insisted that there was a place for preaching in the church, but not of the old authoritarian type. There needed to be a dialogue between the pulpit and the pew. See "The Crisis in the Ministry," *PR*, February 1967, 20–21.

45 David W. Hay, "The Adventures and Misadventures of the Presbyterian Doctrine of the Holy Ministry" (typescript in Knox College Library, 1970), 2–5.

46 *Book of Common Order*, 352. Hay described the nature of the clergy as a special vocation created by Christ and distinguished it clearly from the vocation of the laity. "The fact that human history is the history of fallen men and that God in Christ has taken redemptive action in that history has introduced a new vocation into the human order. This is the apostolic vocation of those who are 'ministers of Christ and stew-

ards of the mysteries of God' (I Cor.4:1). Since the redemption took place by means of a historical event, its power can now be brought to play in the world only by the means of grace – specifically the Word and the Sacraments – through which Christ exercises his power continuously among men. Along with these means he has appointed a special ministry which has thereby a stewardship different in kind from the layman's stewardship of the gifts of creation." See David W. Hay, "For Such a Time as This," *Ambulatio Fidei: Essays in honour of Otto W. Heick,* edited by Erich R.W. Schultz (Waterloo: Waterloo Lutheran University, 1965), 49. The long preamble was dropped when the revisions to the ordination vows were approved in 1970. The revision of the shorter preamble states that Christ entrusts the standards of the church "in a special degree of responsibility" to the clergy, described primarily as pastors and teachers. See *Book of Common Worship,* 372.

47 "The Ross Report Delivers a Moment of Truth," *PR,* February 1970, 7.

48 The Ross Report was compiled by P.S. Ross and Partners, a firm of management consultants, under the direction of Howard Culp, Hugh Auld, and Sandy Aird. It cost the church $40,000 and was criticised for being too expensive and applying business principles in an inappropriate way to the to the church. Nevertheless, it did provide a provocative portrait of the Presbyterian Church in Canada at the end of the 1960s. It identified two major sources of the "illness and infirmity" of the church: the failure to update the church's organizational structures and the lack of intelligent and creative policies in the selection, training, nurture, and development of personnel. It concluded that people, clear purpose, and structure were of key importance if the church was to renew itself. See "Moment of Truth," 7–10.

49 Valerie M. Dunn, "Whatever happened to the Ross report?," *PR,* February 1971, 2–3.

50 Cited in Dunn, "Ross report," 2–3.

51 Cited in Dunn, "Ross report," 2.

52 *A&P,* June 1970, 650–652.

53 *A&P,* June 1971, 460.

54 *A&P,* June 1973, 335.

55 For a review of this literature, see James M. Gustafson and Tod D. Swanson, "Reflections on the Literature on Theological Education published between 1955 and 1985," *Theological Education, Supplement II 1988,* 9–31.

56 J. Stanley Glen, "New Frontiers in Theological Education," *PR,* January 1956, 24.

57 *PR*, January 1957, 23, and July-August 1957, 14.

58 Glen, "New Frontiers," 24–25. See also the report on Knox College at the General Assembly in 1956 in *PR*, July-August 1956, 12–13.

59 J.L.W. McLean, "Training for the Ministry," *PR*, January 1960, 4–5, 31.

60 *PR*, May 1948, 122.

61 *A&P*, June 1963, Appendices, 340.

62 In 1947, for example, Keith Andrews taught Christian education, David Hay taught homiletics and liturgy, and Stanley Glen taught pastoral theology. Carmen Milligen lectured in church music, Ted Johnson in missions, and Walter McCree in church government. See *A&P*, June 1947, Appendix, 72–73.

63 W.J.S. Farris, "Toward a Relevant Theology" (paper given at the National Consultation on Theological Education in Canada, Port Credit, 1966), 5–6.

64 W.J.S. Farris, "Hermeneutics and Ecumenical Mission" (paper given at the National Consultation on Theological Education in Canada, Port Credit, 1966), 13.

65 *A&P*, June 1970, Appendices, 426–427, and Dickson and Webster, *Ewart College*, 41.

66 *A&P*, June 1970, Appendix, 428. In 1970, Charles Hay accepted the half-time position of Assistant Director of TST, coordinating advanced degree work. His teaching at Knox was limited to homiletics alone.

67 Walter W. Bryden, "Knox College, To Be Or Not To Be," *PR*, June 1950, 182.

68 One of the most pressing issues from Knox's perspective during this period was professors' salaries. The ATS review in 1968 noted that faculty salaries were inadequate and in 1969 the Board presented data to the General Assembly that indicated that in comparable colleges in Canada professors were earning between $15,800 and $17,000, as opposed to the $10,800 paid by Knox. See *A&P*, June 1969, 623.

69 *PR*, July-August 1974, 11.

70 *A&P*, June 1978, 260.

71 Joseph C. McLelland, commenting on the 1973 Assembly, suggested that it illustrated an ominous change in the way the Canadian Presbyterian system worked. Policy initiative and executive power, which properly belonged the presbytery, had passed to the administrative council. "I suggest," he wrote, "that we suffer from ecclesiastical paternalism, with the chairman of the council cast as godfather. One could phrase our logic like this: 1) Assembly is an affair of budgetary decisions; 2) the administrative council makes all such decisions prior to Assembly;

therefore 3) Assembly is a rubber stamp for council. One saw this logic at work in the case of Knox College." See *PR*, October 1973, 6.

72 *A&P,* June 1978, 261, 486–487.

73 *A&P,* June 1977, 433.

74 In outlining the goal of creating the chair, the college claimed that its traditional approach to theological education stressed the acquisition of knowledge in the major academic theological disciplines and produced candidates with a high degree of competence in preaching, teaching, and worship. It acknowledged, however, that inadequate attention had been given to "the minister as administrator, counsellor, innovator, facilitator and leader in the life of the congregation and the Church" and "the ability to minister to the community outside the congregation – to develop a prophetic ministry that is sensitive to social issues and which can assist in the righting of injustices, the meeting of human needs and the enhancing of community life." In each of these areas, however, all ministerial practice had to be subjected "to the scrutiny of the Church's biblical and theological perspectives." See *A&P,* June 1979, 474.

75 *PR,* June 1978, 2–3.

EPILOGUE

1 J. Charles Hay, "The Seminary Speaks to the Church about Trust, Freedom, and Support," *Theological Education,* 15 (Spring 1979) 2:123.

2 The "trade school" concern was not unique to Hay. Joseph C. McLelland raised the same concern in arguing for the wisdom of the relationship between Presbyterian College and McGill in 1970. Without the university, McLelland argued, "theology tends to become subjective, parochial and pietistic – the vital link is missing, the critique of reasons for believing. Here is where university keeps church honest. Left to itself, a theological college related exclusively to its church may turn into a mere trade school, turning out apprentices trained in the skills of a clerical trade. Its bondage to the church ('he who pays the piper calls the tune') robs it of its most important task: to listen to God's word for our day and to judge all things, including its church, in the freedom of that hearing." See Joseph C. McLelland, "The Best of Both Worlds," *PR,* February 1970, 21–22. The idea that the secular university would protect the college from the church introduced a new theme into the discussion of theological education among Canadian Presbyterians.

3 Hay, "The Seminary Speaks," 124, 127.

4 Hay, "The Seminary Speaks," 125–126.

5 *A Covenant for Tomorrow, 1979–1987* (Toronto: Knox College, 1987), A4-A5.

6 *Covenant for Tomorrow,* A4

7 *Covenant for Tomorrow,* E1-E7.

8 *A&P,* June 1990, 420,423, 425–426, and *A&P,* June 1991, 496–498.

9 These figures represent the cost of the degree programs and the residence operation. Between 1978 and 1986, the residence operation lost money each year and built an accumulated deficit of $421,000.

10 *A&P,* June 1981, 260.

11 *A&P,* June 1988, 300.

12 *A&P,* June 1989, 286.

13 *A&P,* June 1988, 300.

14 *A&P,* June 1989, 287.

15 In all of the discussions leading up to the amalgamation, both Ewart and Knox argued that the amalgamation should ensure that all the assets of Ewart – its grant, its endowment funds, and the proceeds from the sale of the building – should go to the new Knox College. That recommendation was not accepted by the church. Instead, the grant and the endowment funds went to the new Knox, while the income made available through the sale of the building was designated for theological education and to be distributed by the newly-formed Committee on Theological Education. Once the committee had assured itself that the needs for diaconal education were being met, it was free to grant funds to other institutions or programs that served the theological education enterprise of the denomination. See *A&P,* June 1992, 215–216.

16 *A&P,* June 1990, 286–287.

17 It should be noted that Knox did have to assume the cost of two new tenured faculty with the Ewart amalgamation and that the charging of tuition fees increased the demands on the college's bursary funds, though Knox had argued along with the other colleges that tuition fees were a means of providing access to the bursary funds for the operating costs of the college.

18 *A&P,* June 1990, 306.

19 *A&P,* June 1989, 292–294.

20 See John S. Moir, " 'Who Pays The Piper …': Canadian Presbyterianism and Church-State Relations," *Burning Bush,* ed. Klempa, 67–81.

21 MacLeod, "A Twenty-fifth Anniversary," 7–10.

22 The nature and scope of the questioning is reflected in *Counting the*

Women, ed. Dorcas Gordon and Margaret MacNaughton (Toronto: Women in Ministry Committee, The Presbyterian Church in Canada, 1994).

23 The most insightful studies of the fraying of ecclesiastical cultures come from the United States. See especially Robert Wuthnow, *The Restructuring of American Religion:Society and Faith Since World War II* (Princeton University Press, 1988), and *Christianity in the 21st Century: Reflections on the Challenges Ahead* (New York: Oxford University Press, 1993). The published results of a massive research project on American Presbyterianism, funded by the Lilly Endowment and based at Louisville Presbyterian Theological Seminary, yield further insights and suggests intriguing parallels for Canadian Presbyterians. See *The Presbyterian Predicament: Six Perspectives*, ed. M.J. Coalter, J.M. Mulder, and L.B. Weeks (Louisville: Westminster/John Knox, 1990); *The Confessional Mosaic: Presbyterians and Twentieth-Century Theology*, ed. M.J. Coalter *et al* (Louisville: Westminster/John Knox, 1990); *The Mainstream Protestant "Decline": The Presbyterian Pattern*, ed. M.J. Coalter *et al* (Louisville: Westminster/John Knox, 1990); *The Diversity of Discipleship: Presbyterians and Twentieth-Century Christian Witness*, ed. M.J. Coalter *et al* (Louisville: Westminster/John Knox, 1991); *The Organizational Revolution: Presbyterians and American Denominationalism*, ed. M.J. Coalter *et al* (Louisville: Westminster/John Knox, 1991); *The Re-Forming Tradition: Presbyterians and Mainstream Protestantism*, ed. M.J. Coalter *et al* (Louisville: Westminster/John Knox, 1992).

Index

Aberdeen, University of, 33
Anderson, John, 18
Andrews, D. Keith, 163,
  167, 168
Armstrong, W.D., 123
Association of Theological
  Schools, 185, 188, 189,
  194, 198, 199, 213n36

Baird, Frank, 159
Ball, William S., 22
Ballantyne, James, 79, 97,
  100, 101, 103, 108, 112,
  115, 122, 128, 129–130,
  134
Barr, David, 22
Barr, Ferguson, 183
Barrie, William, 45
Barth, Karl, 15, 148, 149,
  161, 162, 180
Baxter, Richard, 54
Bayne, John, 4, 21, 25, 26,
  27, 35, 50
Beattie, F.R., 98, 231n12
Beaven, James, 34
Bebbington, David, 4
Bengough, J.W., 113
Berkeley, Bishop, 57
Berlin, University of,
  246n67

Berton, Pierre, 170
Black, Edward, 25
Black, John, 22, 40, 156
Blair, Hugh, 76
Book of Common Order, 122,
  173, 177, 181
Book of Praise, 121–122
Bradley, Ian C., 207n5
Brown, George, 62, 64,
  67
Bruce, A.B., 15, 81, 94,
  102, 116
Bryden, Walter W., 143,
  144, 148–150, 153–157,
  163, 164, 165, 166, 172–
  173, 174, 176, 178, 185,
  188, 193, 194, 205,
  243n25, 244n27
Buchanan, Isaac, 22, 36,
  51, 62
Bultmann, Rudolph, 180
Burch, Maurice, 159
Burgess, James, 159
Burke, Kenneth, 210n23
Burns, Robert, 3, 5, 7, 8,
  18, 21, 25, 26, 30–31,
  32–34, 44–50, 51–52,
  53, 55, 58, 89, 216n46
Burns, Elizabeth, 36
Butler, Joseph, 31, 54

Caird, Edward, 102, 116
Cairns, John, 104
Cambridge University,
  126
Cameron, Ross, 159
Campbell, George, 76
Campbell, John, 95–96
Campbell, Robert, 67, 68
Canada Presbyterian
  Church, 9, 10, 44,
  48–50, 53, 54, 68
Canadian Council of
  Churches, 170, 175, 177
Candlish, Robert, 26
Carlyle, Thomas, 104
Caven, William, 56, 69, 70,
  71, 74–75, 77, 82, 85,
  86, 87, 91, 93, 94, 97,
  101, 102, 105, 108, 110,
  111, 112, 113–114, 115,
  125, 227n26
Chalmers, Thomas, 4, 26,
  29, 31, 43, 71, 73
Chapman, Wilbur, 13,
  240n61
Charles Street Presbyterian
  Church, Toronto, 95
Charlton, John, 107–108,
  112
Cheyne, George, 21

Chicago, University of, 97, 139, 145, 167

China Inland Mission, 99

Clark, William Mortimer, 87, 99, 102, 107

Clifford, N. Keith, 122, 141

Cochrane, Arthur C., 162, 244n30

Confessing Church in Germany, 174, 244n27

Cooke's Presbyterian Church, Toronto, 71,

Corbett, Donald, 203, 204

Cote Street Presbyterian Church, Montreal, 35

Cowle, Alan H., 193

Cragg, Gerald, 16

Croft, Henry Holmes, 34

Cunningham, J.D., 144, 145, 157, 163

Cunningham, William, 15, 26

Davidson, A.B., 15, 80, 81, 98

Davidson, Richard, 121, 126, 127, 130, 139

Dawson, William, 64

Denney, James, 15, 126, 187, 239n46, 244n27

Derkson, John, 200

Dickie, John, 244n27

Dickson, David, 22

DiGangi, Mariano, 247n11

Dods, Marcus, 15, 80, 98, 126, 229n50

Dort, Synod of, 28, 30

Douglas, George L., 189

Douglas, W. Halliday, 97, 103, 104

Dow, John, 127, 139, 148

Drummond, Henry, 81, 97, 102, 103, 104, 116

Duff, Alexander, 24, 35, 43–44

Eakin, Thomas, 144, 145, 146, 147–148, 150–151, 153, 157, 159, 161, 162, 163, 242n12

Ecclesiastical and Missionary Record, 23, 24, 30, 36, 37, 39, 41, 47, 49

Edinburgh, University of, 26, 27, 50, 104, 124, 145

Edinburgh Christian Instructor, 26

Elmslie, W.G.

Emmanuel College, 124, 139

Esson, Elizabeth, 36

Esson, Henry, 6, 21, 23, 24, 25, 28, 30–31, 32–34, 35, 36–37, 40, 46, 47, 50, 51, 216n46

Evangelical Alliance, 51, 64, 220n

Ewart College (Ewart Missionary Training Home), 112, 132, 134, 162, 172, 189, 191, 199, 201, 202, 254n15

Falconer, Robert, 111, 124, 125, 238n39

Farris, Allan, 17, 141–143, 166, 167, 169, 173–174, 175, 180, 188, 190, 192, 193, 194, 248n22

Farris, W. James S., 168, 174–175, 189, 192, 203

Federal Council of the Churches of Christ in America, 142

Ferguson, James, 40

Ferrier, Andrew, 45, 46

First Presbyterian Church, London, 70

First Presbyterian Church, St. Mary's, 56

Forrest, D.W., 103

Forsyth, P.T., 15, 244n27

Fowler, Louis, 159

Fraser, Daniel, 143, 242n7

Fraser, R.D., 83

Free Church in Canada, 3, 4–6, 10, 14, 19, 22, 35, 44, 45, 46, 55

Gale, Alexander, 6, 7, 21, 23, 24, 25, 26, 28, 37, 46, 47

Gandier, Alfred, 117, 120, 124–126, 133, 134, 137,

138, 139, 229n45, 236n16, 241n82

Gauvreau, Michael, 22

Geertz, Clifford, 11

Germany, influences from, 14, 118

Gladden, Washington, 103

Glasgow, 4, 116

Glasgow, University of, 27, 33, 94, 102, 103, 145

Glasgow Colonial Society, 3

Glen, J. Stanley, 163, 166, 167, 168, 175, 176, 178–180, 186–187, 190, 192, 248n28, 249n39, 250n42

Glenview Presbyterian Church, Toronto, 167

Goforth, Fred, 159

Goforth, Jonathan, 85

Goggin, Helen, 172

Goldie, Gordon, 199–200

Gordon, Charles W. (Ralph Connor), 77, 132, 240n61

Gottingen, University of, 169

Grant, George M., 110, 124

Grant, John W., 16, 213n34, 215n36

Grant, Robert N. (Knoxonian), 91, 106

Gray, Patrick, 22

Green, T.H., 57, 103, 104, 116

Gregg, William, 65, 71, 73–74, 82, 86, 97, 99, 111, 121

Haddow, Robert, 82

Harris, James, 21

Harvard Divinity School, 145

Harvey-Jellie, W., 163

Hastings, James, 238n35

Hay, David W., 163, 168, 169, 176–178, 181–182, 185, 190, 192, 246n7, 250n46

Hay, J. Charles, 168, 169, 171, 180, 181, 189, 190,

192, 193, 197–199, 201, 203, 205, 250n44
Henning, T., 24
Hill, George, 15, 54
Hodge, A.A., 15, 70, 72–73, 94, 95
Hodge, Charles, 15, 54, 58, 70, 94, 95
Hogg, Hope W., 99
Horne, Thomas Hartwell, 54, 109
Hudson, Andrew, 27
Humphries, Raymond, 192, 203

Inglis, David, 65, 71
Ireland, influences from, 5, 71, 94, 142, 144, 168, 192

Jeffrey, Shirley, 172
Jordon, Louis H., 125

Kellogg, S.H., 80
Kemp, A.F., 64
Kennedy, H.H.A., 123, 124, 126
Kilpatrick, George, 118
Kilpatrick, Thomas B., 111, 116, 118, 119–120, 121, 123, 124, 128, 130, 131, 133, 137, 139, 240n61
King, Andrew, 6, 21, 25, 36
King, John Mark, 57, 65
Knox College: curriculum, 6, 8, 12, 14, 24–25, 29–32, 32–34, 52, 53–54, 72–76, 77–78, 82–83, 107, 110–111, 113–114, 132–135, 136–137, 146, 158, 161, 189, 190, 198, 200, 252n62, 253n74; financial support, 36–37, 38, 61–63, 64–66, 85–86, 88–90, 108–110, 125–126, 135, 138–139, 158, 191, 199–200, 201–203; governing structures, 20–21, 22, 24, 34, 35–38, 60–61, 86–88, 132,

135–136, 159, 161, 163, 202; preparatory program, 24, 84, 106–107; student activities, 38, 39–41, 43, 63–64, 84–85, 158, 161, 200
Knox College Monthly, 76, 79, 82, 86, 99, 110
Knox Presbyterian Church, Dundas, 84
Knox Presbyterian Church, Hamilton, 51
Knox Presbyterian Church, Ottawa, 18, 71, 100
Knox Presbyterian Church, Toronto, 7, 21, 35, 98, 140, 242n12
Kuklick, Bruce, 226n14

Laing, John, 65, 84
Law, Robert, 122, 126, 127, 236n16, 239n48
Leaside Presbyterian Church, Toronto, 168
Leipzig, University of, 99, 100
Lennox, Harry, 241n82
Lennox, Robert, 168, 169, 192
Lindsay, T.M., 15, 94, 102, 116
Lyall, William, 27–28
Lynn, Robert W., 8

MacBeth, R.G., 111
McCaul, John, 34
McColl, Angus, 22
McCorkle, Robert, 26,
McCosh, James, 29
McCurdy, J.F., 84, 101, 126, 144
Macdonald, James A., 79, 80–82, 83, 86, 92, 96, 101, 102, 109, 110, 111, 113, 125, 126, 229nn45, 50
Macdonnell, D.J., 68–69, 96, 121
McFadyen, John Edgar, 96, 97, 102–103, 104, 112, 126, 144

McGillivray, D., 85
McGregor, Malcolm, 76
Machen, Gresham, 144
McIntosh, W.R., 117, 127
McKenzie, Alexander, 53
Mackenzie, F. Scott, 145, 160, 163, 247n8
McKenzie, W.J., 22, 39
McKenzie, W.P., 85
McKinley, Ed, 247n11
McKinnon, John, 22
McLaren, Caroline E., 134
MacLaren, James, 90
MacLaren, William, 65, 70, 71, 93–94, 99, 102, 105, 110, 111, 112, 115, 124, 232n17
McLean, J.W. Lewis, 187–188
McLelland, Joseph C., 184, 252n71, 253n2
McMaster University, 127
MacMillan, Alexander, 121
MacMillan, J.W., 136
McMurrich, John, 35, 36, 62, 66, 99, 223n62
McNab Presbyterian Church, Hamilton, 71
McNeill, John T., 128, 136, 139
McPherson, Laughlin, 22
MacVicar, Donald H., 65, 106
Manitoba College, 9, 86, 112, 115, 116, 131, 136
Manson, William, 127, 144, 236n16
Marburg, University of, 102, 246n67
Marty, Martin, 211n28
Middleton, Justice William, 151–152
Moir, John S., 8
Moody, Dwight L., 97, 116
Morrin College, 86
Morris, William, 20–21, 28
Morrow, E. Lloyd, 145, 157, 159, 161, 162
Morton, A.S., 108, 235n1, 238n39
Mowat, Oliver, 85
Munger, Theodore, 72

Nelson, Banks, 145
New College, Edinburgh, 24, 26, 36, 38, 71, 98, 100, 124, 144, 167, 169, 192
Niagara Bible Conference, The, 99
Nicholson, Murdo, 247n11
Nicol, Iain, 192, 194
Nicol, Robertson, 80

Oman, John, 244n27
Ontario Bible College, 99, 172
Ontario Theological Seminary, 171, 247n12
Ormiston, William, 56, 65
Osborn, Ronald, 11, 211n28
Oxford University, 99, 126

Paley, William, 54, 57
Parker, Stewart, 144
Parsons, Henry Martyn, 98, 99
Pater, Calvin, 192, 194
Patrick, William, 115, 116, 240n61
Patton, Francis L., 79, 224n5
Pollok, A., 12, 16
Presbyterian, 108, 123, 127
Presbyterian Church in Canada, 9, 10, 12, 16, 17, 69, 77, 88, 92, 104, 105, 116, 126, 128, 131, 135–136, 137–138, 140, 141–143, 147, 164, 165, 170, 182–185, 192–193, 204–205; consolidation of colleges within, 86–87, 107–108, 112, 136; governing structures of, 22, 41, 89, 92, 120–121, 146, 159, 160, 162–163, 183–185, 191, 202–203
Presbyterian College (Pine Hill), Halifax, 12, 27, 86, 112, 131
Presbyterian College, Montreal, 9, 21, 64–65, 55,

86, 88, 95, 112, 131, 137, 140, 144, 145, 159, 160, 168
Presbyterian Record, 99–100, 143, 146, 147, 173, 193
Presbytery of Hamilton, 21, 23, 35
Presbytery of Kingston, 83
Presbytery of London, 100
Presbytery of Montreal, 64
Presbytery of Toronto, 21, 35, 68, 100, 112, 135
Princeton Theological Seminary, 58, 70, 79, 99, 100, 161
Proudfoot, J.J.A., 70, 71, 75–76, 103, 237n28
Proudfoot, William, 53
Pym, John, 26

Queen's University, 3, 6, 20, 23, 28, 83, 86, 88, 107, 112, 124

Rainy, Robert, 15
Redpath, John, 35, 62, 64, 67
Reid, Harold, 246n67
Reid, Thomas, 54, 57
Reid, W.D., 245n57
Reid, W. Stanford, 247n8
Renewal Fellowship, Presbyterian Church in Canada, 167
Rennie, Ian, 247n11
Rintoul, William, 6, 7, 20–21, 25, 27, 28, 30, 31–32, 35, 36, 41, 46, 47, 216n46
Robb, Ralph, 26, 50
Robertson, John D., 97, 104–105, 113, 121, 122
Robertson College, Edmonton, 131
Robinson, George L., 97, 99, 100, 101, 108, 109, 112, 117
Ross, Anna, 112
Ross, George W., 85
Ross, John of Brucefield, 22, 112
Ross Report, 183, 251n48

Ryerson, Egerton, 22, 49, 54

St. Andrew's Presbyterian Church, King Street, Toronto, 68, 144, 146
St. Andrew's Presbyterian Church, Victoria, 187
St. Andrew's University, 43
St. James Square Presbyterian Church, Toronto, 80, 125
St. Stephen's Presbyterian Church, Winnipeg, 115
Sandham, W.H., 167
Saskatoon College, Saskatoon, 131
Schaff, Phillip, 12
Schein, Edgar H., 10
Schweitzer, Albert, 127
Scotch Presbyterian Church, Montreal, 25, 28
Scotland, influences from, 3, 4, 5, 15, 23, 26, 27, 28, 36, 45, 67, 68, 79–80, 80–82, 94, 116, 124, 126, 168
Scott, Ephraim, 143, 146, 150, 151, 152, 154, 242n12
Scott, John, 22
Sell, Alan P.F., 203, 239n46
Shedd, W.G.T., 78
Sheraton, J.P., 101
Slessor, Mary, 155
Smart, James D., 159, 165, 166, 167, 193, 204, 246nn67, 1
Smith, Donald C., 192, 218–219n6
Smith, George Adam, 80, 94, 102, 116, 126
Smith, J.C., 82
Smith, Neil Gregor, 8, 168, 169, 180
Smyth, Newman, 72
Somerville, James, 25
Stalker, James, 81
Strasbourg, University of, 246n67
Sutherland, William R., 22

Taylor, John, 53
Taylor, William, 64, 65
Thompson. Andrew, 26
Thomson, Robert Yuile, 82,
  97–98, 99
Topp, Alexander, 62, 65,
  99
Toronto, University of, 16,
  22, 34–35, 87, 125, 129,
  167, 190, 191, 198, 204
Toronto Academy, 7, 18,
  23, 24, 28
Toronto Bible Training
  School, 99
Toronto Graduate School
  of Theological Studies,
  188
Toronto School of Theol-
  ogy, 172, 186, 189, 190,
  191, 192, 194, 198, 199,
  204, 205
Trinitarian Theological
  Society, 158, 165
Tübingen University,
  246n67

Union Theological Semi-
  nary, New York, 78, 133,
  136, 159, 240n66
United Church of Canada,
  8, 113, 115, 118, 119–
  120, 125, 126, 128, 137–
  138, 139, 140, 143, 157,
  169

United Presbyterian
  Church in Canada, 44,
  45, 53, 56, 60
United States of America,
  influences from, 58, 72,
  92, 94, 131, 142, 144,
  161, 167
University College, Tor-
  onto, 49, 54, 84, 127,
  144
Utrecht, University of, 78

Vancouver School of
  Theology, 203
Van Oosterzee, J.J., 78
Van Seters, Arthur, 203
Vaudry, Richard, 5, 8
Victoria College, 56, 127,
  136, 137

Wade, Donald V., 163, 167,
  169, 172, 175
Wallace, Robert, 22
Walters, Stanley, 192
Wardrope, Thomas, 18, 65
Watson, John, 117, 124
Watts, Robert, 94, 227n26
Wayland, Francis, 54
Webster, C.A., 85
Westfall, William, 10
Westminster, 101, 102, 107,
  111
Westminster College, Cam-
  bridge, 103

Westminster Hall, Vancou-
  ver, 131
Westminster Standards, Canadian Presbyterian attitudes towards, 14, 15, 31,
  44, 46, 47–49, 50, 54,
  68, 69, 73, 75, 94, 96,
  107, 119–120, 129, 140,
  142, 143, 145, 147, 149–
  150, 152, 160, 165, 175,
  176, 222n59, 225n8,
  242n7
Whatley, Richard, 54
Wightman, Thomas, 24
Willis, Michael, 8, 19, 26,
  27, 28, 29, 44–50, 53,
  55, 57, 58, 59–60, 65, 70
Willkie, John, 161
Women's Missionary Soci-
  ety, Presbyterian Church
  in Canada, 157
World Council of
  Churches, 170
World War I, 117–119,
  147, 162
World War II, 149, 156,
  162
Wycliffe College, Toronto,
  101

Yale Divinity School, 79
Young, George Paxton, 8,
  50, 51, 53, 54, 57–58,
  70, 95, 98, 225n7